GRAVE MATTERS

Big Lagoon postcard, 1908

GRAVE MATTERS

THE CONTROVERSY OVER EXCAVATING
CALIFORNIA'S BURIED INDIGENOUS PAST

TONY PLATT

HEYDAY, BERKELEY, CALIFORNIA

Library of Congress Cataloging-in-Publication Data

Names: Platt, Tony, 1942- author.
Title: Grave matters : the controversy over excavating California's buried
    Indigenous past / Tony Platt.
Description: New edition. | Berkeley, California : Heyday, [2021] |
    Includes bibliographical references and index.
Identifiers: LCCN 2021025728 | ISBN 9781597145596 (paperback) | ISBN
    9781597145626 (epub)
Subjects: LCSH: Yurok Indians--California--Big Lagoon--Antiquities. | Yurok
    Indians--Funeral customs and rites--California--Big Lagoon. | Yurok
    Indians--California--Big Lagoon--Government relations. | Human remains
    (Archaeology)--Moral and ethical aspects--California--Big Lagoon. |
    Grave goods--Moral and ethical aspects--California--Big Lagoon. |
    Archaeologists--Professional ethics--California--Big Lagoon. | Cultural
    property--Protection--California--Big Lagoon. | Big Lagoon
    (Calif.)--Antiquities. | Big Lagoon Rancheria, California--Antiquities.
Classification: LCC E99.Y97 P57 2021 | DDC 979.4/12--dc23
LC record available at https://lccn.loc.gov/2021025728

Cover Photo: Martin Swett
Cover Design: Ashley Ingram
Interior Design/Typesetting: Lorraine Rath

Published by Heyday
P.O. Box 9145, Berkeley, California 94709
(510) 549-3564
heydaybooks.com

Printed in East Peoria, Illinois, by Versa Press, Inc.

10 9 8 7 6 5 4 3 2 1

FSC
www.fsc.org
MIX
Paper from
responsible sources
FSC® C005010

In the summer of 2006 my forty-year-old son died. Daniel left a clear written message that he wanted a funeral at Big Lagoon, the northwestern California village on the coast where we have a vacation cabin. We honored his request, sending his ashy remains off into the lagoon. Some eighteen months later I discovered that the Yurok who lived in this area "since time immemorial" had been buried a few hundred yards away from my cabin. But unlike Daniel's, their remains were prey to looters, archaeologists, and collectors, and their lives and deaths scrupulously forgotten in the region's public history. Since this discovery I have felt compelled to remember them as well as I remember my son. This book is dedicated to their remembrance.

"We cannot conceive of a time when stabilizing the world will become an irrelevant act."

—Julian Lang, Karuk, 1991

"We tell stories of events to allude to the unspeakable."

—Kara Walker, 2006

"The meeting of sea and continent, like the meeting of whites and Indians, creates as well as destroys. Contact was not a battle of primal forces in which only one could survive. Something new could appear."

—Richard White, *The Middle Ground*

"Who does not seek to be remembered? Memory is Master of Death, the chink in his armor of conceit."

—Wole Soyinka, *Death and the King's Horseman*

"People who have learned how to care tenderly for the bodies of the dead are almost surely people who also know how to show mercy to the bodies of the living."

—Thomas G. Long, 2009

Know
that I want to sleep here amid the eyelids
of sea and earth.
I want to be swept
down in the rains that the wild
sea wind assails and shatters
and then to flow through subterranean channels,
toward the deep springtime that's reborn.

—Pablo Neruda, *Canto General*, "Dispositions"

Contents

Preface to the New Edition

More than a decade ago, a sudden personal tragedy and a gradual awareness of a social tragedy impelled me to write *Grave Matters*.

Two places, one rural and one urban, figure prominently in the story: Big Lagoon, a park and residential village in Humboldt County that abuts the fierce Pacific Ocean, a tranquil lagoon, and remnants of old-growth forests; and Berkeley, home since 1873 to the first campus of the University of California. I have shared a cabin in Big Lagoon since the mid-1970s, and I have lived and worked in Berkeley for some fifty-seven years since I came here as an immigrant from England in 1963, planning to stay for a year of study but never leaving. The Free Speech Movement and Berkeley's progressive politics changed my mind and shaped my future.

As an activist and academic, my intellectual work prior to this book focused on the history of the American carceral state, with an emphasis on race. Then, Native* and California histories were peripheral to my expertise and curiosity. My son's death in 2006 and his request to be buried in Big Lagoon triggered my interest in funerary rituals. It turned out, serendipitously, that how we memorialized our son by launching his ashy remains into the lagoon echoed how the local Yurok had imagined their ancestors traveling through a river into the underworld. This connection meant and still means a great deal to me.

A year after our personal memorial service, the Yurok Tribe passed a resolution calling for the protection, preservation, and

---

* Since the first publication of this book in 2011, it has become increasingly common for the words "Native" and "Indigenous" to be uppercase when referring to people, a convention I follow in this new preface.

cultural management of O-pyúweg (Where They Dance or Big Lagoon), a "place of ceremonial renown" that had been an important Native settlement prior to the genocidal devastation of peoples who had lived in this region since time immemorial. They were well established here long before a Spanish naval expedition planted its flag on top of a nearby hill; long before fortune-hunters passed by on their way to the gold mines; long before homesteaders tried to farm the rugged landscape and fish the turbulent coast; long before lumber companies extracted and marketed ancient redwoods for everything from construction materials to decorative doodads; and long before the northwest coast of California became a post-industrial bucolic retreat for people like me wanting relief from the metropolis.

In March 2009, I participated in the Yurok-led Coalition to Protect Yurok Cultural Legacies at O-pyúweg. Despite tensions between defenders of individual property rights and Native advocates of communal patrimony, the coalition of disparate stakeholders worked together to successfully lobby the Humboldt County Board of Supervisors to support, at least in principle, measures to acknowledge and secure Where They Dance. It was while working with the coalition that I discovered how, in the early twentieth century, amateur archaeologists, collectors, and tourists had excavated the main village site at Big Lagoon and removed skeletons, funerary offerings, and artifacts. This happened throughout the region in the wake of the Gold Rush, genocide, and land dispossession.

Yurok elders know this history in sorrowful detail. Some remember stories passed on by their grandparents. They also introduced me to the long history of Native resistance to the widespread plunder of graves and appropriation of cultural artifacts: from respectful petitions to authorities, to the rambunc-tious militancy of the Red Power movement. In northern California, the intertribal Northwest Indian Cemetery Protective Association (NICPA), founded in 1970, physically confronted amateur and professional archaeologists and put a stop to unauthorized excavations, setting a precedent for national legislation some twenty years later.

Doing the research for this book was a learning experience and a journey into new terrain. *Grave Matters* describes the work I did to overcome my unfamiliarity with what I should have known; and how I investigated the workings of a global trade in everything Indian that in the second half of the nineteenth century stocked public and university museums from Moscow to Berkeley.

It took me by surprise to find out that the University of California had played a prominent role nationally in the accumulation of Native body parts, artifacts, and what today is known as intellectual property. Such a narrative does not sit comfortably with Berkeley's global reputation as a site of post–World War II radicalism. A decade ago, when I wrote this book, the university did not make it easy to do research in its internal records or the archaeological archives of the Hearst Museum that is the official custodian of Native ancestors. Still, in *Grave Matters* I was able to document with compelling evidence how the university had pillaged hundreds of Native burial sites through either their own expeditions or local surrogates, and unilaterally removed thousands of human remains that they subjected to eugenic postmortems in the anthropological laboratory.

This was not something carried out secretly in the darkness of night, but in public in the full light of day with the enthusiastic support of university administrators. In 1948, the university proudly showed off to *Life* magazine its staff of physical archaeologists at work using craniometers to measure skeletal remains that had been sorted into boxes of chemically preserved body parts, bone by bone. By then, the university had accumulated more than ten thousand Native ancestors and excavated at least twice as many gravesites.

Given the solidity of my research, I expected the university to take my findings seriously. Minimally, I hoped that it would bolster the claims of California Indians to repatriate their ancestors via the 1990 federal Native American Graves Protection and Repatriation Act (NAGPRA), groundbreaking legislation that empowered Tribes and Native organizations to seek restoration of ancestors and sacred objects from institutions such as the University of California that are recipients of federal funds.

The university treated me the same way that it treated Native claimants: ignoring, evading, dismissing their demands. For two decades, without having to face the now defunct NICPA, or reckon with Native political clout in the legislature, or respond to a movement for reparative justice on campus, the university begrudgingly complied with the narrowest interpretation of NAGPRA while attempting to extinguish its spirit.

As I've learned from many progressive struggles for social justice, to be successful requires honing our long-range vision far beyond the here-and-now. And being ready for unexpected opportunities. So it is, a decade after I worked with the Coalition to Protect Yurok Cultural Legacies at O-pyúweg and wrote *Grave Matters*, that the University of California is beginning to accept accountability, in the words of Berkeley Chancellor Carol Christ, for "the pain our actions have caused" California Tribes.

It took a great deal of activism and stamina to get to this point. The breakthrough occurred in April 2017, when representatives of more than fifty Tribes convened the California Indian Tribal Forum at Berkeley to witness the University of California's history of heartless actions and malign neglect. Berkeley in particular, concluded the forum, "has yet to establish positive collaborative relationships with Native Americans that acknowledge and remedy the devastation wrought by early Berkeley anthropologists and researchers."

In 2018, almost thirty years after passage of NAGPRA, the university reported that it still possessed close to nine thousand remains of ancestors, of which ninety percent are housed at Berkeley. "Our history as a university is deeply flawed," observed University of California regent John Pérez. The California legislature and governor, under increased pressure from Tribes, in turn put pressure on the university to stop stonewalling claims for repatriation. In September 2018, Governor Jerry Brown signed legislation that recognizes "repatriation of human remains [as] a fundamental human right for all California Native American tribes." The following year, Governor Gavin Newsom issued an executive order that acknowledges "over a century of depredations and prejudicial policies against California Native Americans." Newsom apologized on behalf of the state for "many instances of violence, maltreatment, and neglect," including genocide. The executive order created a Truth and Healing Council to "bear witness" to the "historical relationship between the State of California and California Native Americans."

For the first time, the university responded positively to this demand for accountability. Its president and Berkeley's chancellor went on record pledging to implement the right of the "Indigenous peoples" of California "to the repatriation of their ancestral remains," and "to return ancestors as swiftly and respectfully as possible to their descendants for reburial." A campus committee called upon the university "to acknowledge its participation in a system that damaged and extracted Indigenous people's cultural heritage, to listen to those who have been harmed, and to take actions to help repair the harm." I began to sense that, in the words of Michael Yellow Bird, we had an opportunity for "truth-telling and the revision of settler history."

But history is more like a zigzag than a line of forward progress. As I write in November 2020, a legislative audit has once again blasted the university for "not adequately overseeing its return of Native American remains and artifacts." Unlike several east coast universities that are grappling with the paradox of enlightened knowledge coexisting with the trade in enslaved Africans, Berkeley has not yet reflected on how its anthropology department rose to international prominence by organizing the plunder of thousands of Native graves in the name of science and "salvage archeology."

Berkeley's stumbling first step towards dignified repatriation has us heading in the right direction. Now, promises require actions. Hopefully, they will not only happen soon, but also be followed by the university's apologies and reparations to California's Tribes and peoples, such as the Yurok of O-pyúweg, whose cemeteries were desecrated.

As for historians, writers, and storytellers, we too have our work cut out for us. It is our responsibility to make it a matter of public knowledge how the new state launched the University of California in the 1860s by profiting off land taken by the federal government from Tribes throughout California. How the university in the 1870s appropriated land for a campus in the East Bay that prior to Spanish conquest had been the homeland of the Ohlone for thousands of years. And how Berkeley erased these histories and substituted an origins myth (branded as *fiat lux*) that credits academia with bringing Civilization into the Wilderness.

The long struggle for repatriation is only one part of a larger history still to be told.

—Tony Platt, November 15, 2020

Illustrations

8.1   Hidden from history: the statue of George Washington in the National Museum of American History, Washington, D.C., March 27, 2010. Photograph by Tony Platt.

9.1   Descendants of Big Lagoon Yurok, carrying a 1928 photograph of Pete Peters, gather at O-pyúweg in April 2011 to commemorate their ancestors. Bertha Peters with (left to right) great-nephews William Peters and Damien Scott and great-niece Jesselyn Peters. Photograph by Tim Wells.

9.2   Descendants of Big Lagoon Yurok. Back row, left to right: Zack Brown, Terrance Brown, Pliny Jackson. Front, left to right: Rachel Sundberg, Joy Sundberg, Linnea Jackson, Betty Jackson, Jacqueline Winter, Troy Simon Fletcher Jr. Photograph by Tim Wells.

Acknowledgments

Working on this book I was reminded of Raphael Samuel's admonition that we need to understand history as a social form of knowledge, the work of many hands, brains, archivists, and storytellers; and that local history is indispensable to creating a national story.

I came to this project as an outsider. Though I've been visiting and staying in Humboldt County for some thirty years, I live in a metropolis and am very much a city boy. I have no formal training in anthropology and I started this project with little knowledge about archaeology. I've taught race relations for most of my academic career, but this is the first time that I've done in-depth research on issues affecting native communities. I was lucky to find many generous teachers and guides who welcomed me inside their worlds, shared their knowledge, and trusted how I would use it. I am especially grateful to:

Coleen Kelley Marks, who encouraged me to set out on the journey when I didn't know where I was heading.

Janet Eidsness, who shared with me a technical report that snagged my attention, and then gave me a cram course on socially responsible archaeology.

Elders and officials of the Yurok Tribe, especially Gene Brundin, Tom Gates, Bob McConnell, and Shaunna McCovey; Virgil Moorehead of the Big Lagoon Rancheria; Joy Sundberg of the Trinidad Rancheria; and descendants of Big Lagoon Yurok, all of whom helped me to see between the lines.

Joan Berman and Edie Butler, librarians extraordinaire who demanded that I dig into all the nooks and crannies of the Humboldt Room at Humboldt State University.

Sandra Burton, Callie Lara, Frank Lara, and Walt Lara Sr., who shared their personal knowledge of the remarkable Marks-Lara family.

Jentri Anders, Jim Benson, Walt Lara Sr., Tom Parsons, Chris Peters, Joy Sundberg, and other veterans and supporters of the Northwest Indian Cemetery Protection Association who recalled the heady days of 1970s activism.

Anthony Garcia, Bambi Kraus, Buffy McQuillen, and Hélène Rouvier, who helped me to understand the complex policies and Byzantine politics of repatriation.

Pam Service, who willingly opened up the files of the Clarke Historical Museum.

The many curators of knowledge who helped me to find my way through archives and collections—especially Larry Felton at California's Archaeological Research Facility; Joan Knudsen and Alicja Egbert at the Hearst Museum; David Kessler and Susan Snyder at the Bancroft Library; Cara Fama, Carrie Feldman, and Pat Nietfeld at the National Museum of the American Indian's Cultural Resource Center; Deborah Hull-Walski and Felicia Pickering at the National Museum of Natural History's Department of Anthropology; and Jim Hamill at the British Museum's Centre for Anthropology.

Dave Fredrickson, Victor Golla, Ira Jacknis, Kent Lightfoot, Michael Moratto, Larry Myers, Polly Quick, Jamie Roscoe, and Don Verwayen, who shared their insights about the history of anthropology and archaeology.

My fellow cabinistas at Big Lagoon—Nancy Barr, Ellen Drury, Bob Gould, John Hylton, Peter Panuthos, Jeannie Pfaelzer, Kristy Sturges, Peter Sturges, and Pat Sutton—who listened, discussed, and encouraged this project every step of the way.

My colleagues who critically read and commented on earlier drafts and chapters of this book: Jim Benson, Janet Eidsness, Tom Gates, Jeannine Gendar, Victor Golla, George Lipsitz, Ed McCaughan, Bob McConnell, Dennis Sherman, and Orin Starn; and Cecilia O'Leary, who, as always, demanded my best.

Local historians—especially Jerry Rohde, Ned Simmons, Don Tuttle, and Susie Van Kirk—who provided so many important details.

Tom Hannah for sharing and reliving his bittersweet story.

Melody Antillon, Ben Brown, and Maren Farnum for meticulous research assistance.

Bob Doran and Hank Sims of the *North Coast Journal* for publishing an essay (18 June 2009) based on a chapter in this book.

Bob Benson for painting such an evocative image of Tsahpekw (Stone Lagoon) and allowing me to use it on the cover.

The staff at Heyday, especially Jeannine Gendar and Malcolm Margolin, who from the start expressed unseemly enthusiasm for this book and gave it loving care from conception to birth; and Lillian Fleer, Natalie Mulford, and Lorraine Rath, who made this collaborative experience a pleasure.

My fellow members of the Coalition to Protect Yurok Cultural Legacies at O-pyúweg, who are working to commemorate and preserve Big Lagoon's native past.

Definitions

Archaeologist: a person who engages in the scientific study of ancient cultures through the examination of their material remains, such as buildings, graves, tools, and other artifacts dug up from the ground.

Collectible: an object of a type that is valued or sought after by collectors; one of a group of objects prized by fanciers.

Collector: somebody who collects objects of a particular type for their interest, value, or beauty.

Excavate: to make a hole in, hollow out; to remove by digging or scooping out.

Grave (n): a hole dug in the ground for a dead person's body, or the place where a dead person's body is buried; the end or destruction of something.

Grave (adj): solemn and serious in manner; very important and with serious consequences, and therefore needing to be thought about carefully.

Grave (v): to fix something firmly in the mind.

Grave robber: somebody who steals things from graves or tombs, usually either valuable artifacts or corpses for dissection.

Home: where somebody was born or raised or feels he or she belongs.

Homeland: the country where somebody was born or where somebody lives and feels that he or she belongs.

Memento mori: an object, especially a skull, intended as a reminder of the fact that humans die; a reminder of the fact that humans fail and make mistakes.

Native (n): one born in or connected with a place by birth; one of the original inhabitants or lifelong residents of a place.

Native (adj): existing in or belonging to by nature; of, belonging to, or characteristic of the original inhabitants of a particular place.

Repatriate: to restore or return to native land.

Salvage: to save something of worth or merit from a situation or event that is otherwise a failure.

Savage: not civilized, barbaric, lacking polish.

Sightline: a line of vision between a person and an object or place.

ONE
Between the Lines

If you cannot see
istilleat
between the lines
allofmymeals
then your collected facts
witha
will never constitute
musselshell
knowledge.

—Shaunna Oteka McCovey,
Yurok/Karuk, 2005[1]

You can come to a place time and time again, year in and year out—as I've been coming to my getaway in Humboldt County on California's northwest coast for some thirty-five years—and not see for so long what a serendipitous experience suddenly makes obvious and impossible to ignore. My relationship with Big Lagoon first changed as a result of a personal tragedy. But it was my belated recognition of a social tragedy embedded in the landscape that triggered a journey that would become this book.

Visiting Big Lagoon has always been a life-affirming experience for me, an opportunity to slow down my citified pace and take small pleasures in the everyday. The Yurok refer to the lagoon as Oket'o, or Where It Is Calm, a name they give to any large body of enclosed water. Oket'o seems especially appropriate for placid Big Lagoon, only a stone's throw from the volatile Pacific Ocean. I typically escape here to luxuriate in the present. But out of the blue, about three years ago, I found myself propelled into the "cool sepulcher of the past" when I discovered that my bucolic retreat was a short walk away from an unmarked Yurok cemetery that had been plundered early in the twentieth century.[2]

1.1 Oket'o (Where It Is Calm), or Big Lagoon

I thought I was familiar with every nook and cranny of Big Lagoon until this new information expanded my sightlines. Bob McConnell, Tribal Historic Preservation Officer for the Yurok, taught me to imagine the thousands of people who lived, worked, and died here long before the region became a mecca for tourists. Gene Brundin, Chairman of the Yurok Tribe's Repatriation Committee, introduced me to Big Lagoon's botanical diversity—its herbs, plants, and roots once regularly used as medicines, teas, and materials for baskets. And archaeologist Janet Eidsness encouraged me to look at the ground in new ways in order to appreciate how a midden of rocks cracked by heat from fire, oily dark-stained soil, and broken shells reveals stories about everyday native life.

It's an interesting paradox of the creative process, as choreographer Twyla Tharp observes, that you need to exercise rigorous control over a project, "but good planning alone won't make your efforts successful; it's only after you let go of your plans that you can breathe life into your efforts."[3] Unlike my previous work, this is not an investigation that I carefully thought through and planned before starting the research. The topic came to me head-on and demanded my attention. And once I agreed to go off into uncharted territory, I stumbled into fissures that run deep beneath the ground.

Humboldt County is typically described in tourist guides as an "outdoor paradise" and "ecotourist's heaven," with "legendary giant redwoods," "stunning beaches," "rugged cliffs," and "picturesque coastal villages." It's a place "where you can connect with Nature." I am very familiar with this narrative. It's what draws me to Big Lagoon. But beneath this imagery of a pristine landscape is a messy social history of people divided by warfare, antagonisms, and disillusionments. From the perspective of the Yurok and other native peoples in the region, "much of the land has been wounded, broken or lost."[4] As some historians have acknowledged, northern California in the mid-nineteenth century was one of the bloodiest places in the country, deserving of a vocabulary that we usually associate with other countries and other times: pogroms, ethnic cleansing, apartheid, even genocide. What happened in California did not presage Nazi Germany or mimic Boer-ruled South Africa, but there are resemblances and affinities that demand serious consideration.

Thanks to the post-1960s generation of historians, we've made considerable progress in complicating the rosy-hued story of northern California as a place celebrated primarily for economic daring and individual initiative, peopled by "men with empires in their purposes / And new eras in their brains," as Sam Foss put it in 1894. Now we know much more about the brutal underside of the Golden State, and about the micro-histories of people who were typically omitted from the master narrative of evolutionary progress—native communities, Chinese immigrants, women pioneers, Latino miners, and white workers who didn't strike it rich.

And yet it's still so easy to visit Humboldt County and be

oblivious to its troubled history: there are few public memorials or monuments or preserved sites that shock us into remembrance of tragedies not-too-long past or juxtapose the grandeur of the region's scenery with its killing fields. Nobody seems bothered that a well-visited elk refuge in Prairie Creek Redwoods State Park is named in honor of one of the country's most notoriously racist ideologues.[5] We seem to have a hardwired capacity to deny and compartmentalize painfully disturbing information. For many years, I could separate my knowledge of Big Lagoon's troubling past from its pleasurable present. In this sense, I was no different from my parents, who refused to visit Germany because of its murderous legacies but didn't think twice about vacationing in what had been Vichy France, happily visiting towns where Jews had been rounded up for transportation to concentration camps.

Death changes the meaning of a place. Until a few years ago, I'd never associated Big Lagoon with the end of life. But since the summer of 2006, when we followed our son's wishes and launched his remains into the lagoon, it's been impossible for me to separate the living from the dead. And about a year later, answering the Yurok Tribal Council's call to protect the cultural legacies of their ancestors who had been uprooted from Big Lagoon, I decided to learn more about this "place of ceremonial renown."[6] As a historian interested in public history and memory, how could I ignore this past literally buried in my own backyard?

What I initially thought would be a personal exploration of mortality and a brief investigation into local events in a small place led to an investigation of big issues that resonate in the history of anthropology and archaeology, and in contemporary debates about patrimony and repatriation: Whose cultural meanings speak for a place? Whose history prevails in the public domain? What can be done to repair the damage and atrocities committed by long-gone generations? To answer these questions, I had to leave the rural quiet of Big Lagoon and travel to museums in London, Berlin, and Washington, D.C., and to a cemetery of slaves in New York; and delve into long-forgotten archives, shuttered cabinets, and basements stacked with human remains. I also had to learn to see between the lines.

TWO
Present and Alive

> "The tectonic layers of our lives rest so tightly one on top of the other that we always come up against earlier events in later ones, not as matter that has been fully formed and pushed aside, but absolutely present and alive."
> —Bernhard Schlink,
> *The Reader*, 1995

Second Home

I arrived in Berkeley in 1963, a twenty-one-year-old immigrant from the provinces of northern England. I was here for graduate school, temporarily I thought, ready to climb the first rung into the meritocracy and then return to the homeland. But the magnetism of the student movement and seduction of an expanding academic job market in the United States quickly changed my mind. By 1968, after two years on a fellowship in Chicago, I was back at Berkeley as a junior professor, married with two kids, a mortgage, and an occasional fantasy about a getaway place on California's northwest coast.

It wasn't until the late 1970s, now divorced, that I found a property by the ocean that my girlfriend and I could afford, and even then we had to recruit another couple to split the costs. In 1978 we paid $25,000 for a small, two-bedroom cabin—about 700 square feet—in Big Lagoon, Humboldt County. The previous owner had bought the place four years earlier for $2,000, plus $50 for some appliances, from a local Native American family. Today, even with a shaky housing market, the cabin has increased its value about fifty-fold in the last thirty-five years.

The place called Big Lagoon encompasses a county and state park, a public elementary school, the thirty-eight-acre Big Lagoon Rancheria on the southern shore of the lagoon, and the Big Lagoon Park Company, a sixty-acre private recreational community in Big Lagoon's southwest corner, where I co-own one of seventy-six cabins. The rancheria houses about eighteen family members of Yurok and Tolowa descent on tribal land a half-mile northeast of our cabin. For the last decade, it has been trying, so far unsuccessfully, to build a Vegas-style "gaming facility" at the lagoon's edge. As you can imagine, it's a topic of endless arguments, pitting defenders of the environment against advocates of economic development and native self-determination.

With its intimate mingling of ocean, lagoon, and forest, Big Lagoon is a unique habitat with what a popular local guidebook describes as a "wilderness feeling."[1] Recognized by the California Coastal Commission and the Save-the-Redwoods League for its distinctive ecosystem, Big Lagoon's habitat includes many special-status plant and animal species, among them Coho salmon, rainbow trout, and peregrine falcons. There are about thirty species of fish in the lagoon, plus crab, soft-shelled clams, and bay mussels. The surrounding marshes, forests, and hills are home to Roosevelt elk and black bears, and thousands of migratory birds make the lagoon a stopover on the Pacific Flyway.[2] And a twenty-minute drive takes you to the Redwood National Park, where you can wander amazed through what's left of "the most wood-laden forest on Earth."[3]

Big Lagoon is a mixed-use, commerce-free village, bounded by the Pacific Ocean on its west and Highway 101 to its east. Its northern boundary ends with a three-mile lagoon, covering close to fifteen hundred acres in California's state park system. To its south, buffered by a subdivision along the cliffs, is Patrick's Point State Park, which is linked to Big Lagoon by Agate Beach, a destination for collectors of semiprecious stones. Many a day you'll find me on the beach, along with other penitents, moving slowly at water's edge, head down, scouring the millions of rocks for the rare black-green glint of jade that surfaces naturally polished by the confluence of the Klamath River and Pacific Ocean. One of my ritualistic pleasures on this daily pilgrimage is to stop, face the ocean, and look out with eyes wide open. There's always movement, always something to watch: whales, otters, and sea lions, the lights of the crab boats, herons and pelicans skimming the water.

Winters at Big Lagoon tend to be short on light and deep in rain, averaging sixty-five inches annually. By the end of the year, we keep a wood fire going twenty-four hours a day, sealing our refuge against the chilly damp nights and roiling storms; it's when the Pacific takes its best shots at the long stretch of beach that goes from the northern point of Big Lagoon down to jagged rocks at Patrick's Point. In December and January, a huge section of the beach is impassable and most locals keep their dogs on a short leash. Up and down the coast, the sheriff's search and rescue team are kept busy looking for the remains of visitors who underestimate the ocean's power or ignore the warning, DANGEROUS UNDERTOW. Spring comes as a relief of verdant foliage and vibrant blooms.

In addition to the few year-round residents, many visitors come to Big Lagoon in the summer to swim and boat in the lagoon, to walk a long beach that rims the fierce ocean, and to camp in a scenic copse at one of the state's most picturesque campgrounds.[4] The land that once was home to many long-term native settlements and a site of historical significance is unprotected and unmarked. Unknowingly, many day-trippers park their cars on top of O-pyúweg, or Where They Dance, once a large Yurok town.

I've been coming to Big Lagoon for more than thirty years, first with my children, and then their children. Even on a calm night, in our cabin some two hundred yards from the Pacific you can hear the kettledrum booming of waves hitting the shore. At the coast, a barrier beach runs for about three miles north of our cabin until you reach a place where Big Lagoon, fattened by streams and rain, occasionally leaks into the Pacific, and where the ocean at extreme high tide turns the lagoon brackish. For most of the year, however, these two extraordinarily different bodies of water coexist a stone's throw apart. If you stand exactly in the middle of the beach, one ear is deafened by the ocean's roar, while the other can hear the whoosh of brown pelicans as they alight clumsily on the placid lagoon. And this détente has lasted for a long, long time, as we know from tales passed on by the Yurok.

It's three hundred miles from our house in Berkeley to our second home, now co-owned by my wife, Cecilia, and myself, and two other couples—close enough to make it there by car in six hours, but far enough to make me feel as though I'm getting away from it all. Once you get beyond Santa Rosa and the sprawling exurbia of the Bay Area, Highway 101 winds through Sonoma's overdeveloped wine country and corporate farmland until you reach Humboldt's largest city, the once-prosperous Eureka.

During the 1950s, about one of every two working people in the county was involved in lumber production, and families were better off than most folks in the country. During the 1960s, however, as the housing boom receded, Eureka began its steep decline into hard times. And by the 1990s, more people were leaving than moving to Humboldt. As of August 2009, home sales in the county were down almost 40 percent from ten years earlier; and the official unemployment rate, which almost doubled in two years, reached 11.4 percent, one of the highest in the country. In December 2009, a few days before Christmas, some twenty-five hundred people lined up at the mall to receive free toys and food from the Salvation Army.[5]

Prior to the recent economic crash, there were some signs of revival: a large, charmless mall was built at Eureka's southern, funky edge and the old downtown reborn as a lively, mixed-use destination. But now the city is a hardscrabble place, with one out of five people living below the poverty line, and many others just hanging on.[6] And like the rest of the county, it's overwhelmingly white and English-speaking, much different from what it was like in the nineteenth century, when it was a babble of multilingual native peoples, migrants, and immigrants.

Beyond Eureka, heading north, is the People's Republic of Arcata, a college town and bastion of progressive environmentalism and participatory democracy. On Saturdays in the summer, you'll usually find me at the farmers' market in the plaza, watching the tie-dyed hula-hoopers and jugglers swaying trancelike to Grateful Dead wannabes. In 2004, Bush-the-Clear-Cutter received only 16 percent of the presidential vote. It was

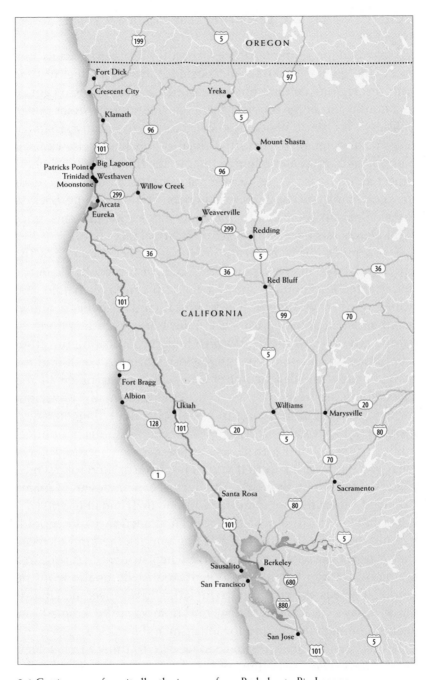

2.1 Getting away from it all—the journey from Berkeley to Big Lagoon.

a surprise to me four years later that McCain was able to get even 13 percent.

I love coming to the northwest coast for its natural beauty and peace and quiet, but it's an unexpected bonus that I feel in sync with the region's cultural life and politics. Humboldt is receptive to a quirky and noisy activism that challenges the expectations of pollsters who like to divide up the electorate into neatly separated red and blue regions. Here, the polarization found elsewhere is blurred, with the center edging closer to the fringe. Bucking what's expected of poor, white, semi-rural counties, Humboldt tends to vote Democratic in decisive numbers. You have to go back to Ronald Reagan's campaign to find a plurality for Republicans; since 1984 Democrats have won all six presidential races here.

A few miles north of Arcata is Trinidad, once a center of the Yurok universe, an entry point for Gold Rush speculators in the mid-nineteenth century, and a twentieth-century whaling and fishing port. Now, aside from a few locals and residents of a low-income trailer park, it's mostly a stop for tourists heading north or for the city folks who can afford to look for a vacation or retirement home in this pricey setting. Most mornings you'll find me hanging out at the Beachcomber Café, catching up on email and succumbing to fresh pastries. The environmentally conscious owners frown upon ordering to go—"You will be flogged if you insist on a paper cup," it says on the menu—and make you feel guilty if you use more than one paper napkin. But they know what you like to drink even if you've not been around for a while. "Here's Tony from Berkeley, small coffee with foam." Obama trounced McCain more than three to one in Trinidad in 2008.

Further north, in a sparsely populated section of Humboldt County, hugging the coast, is Big Lagoon. It's the kind of place that *National Geographic* had in mind when it identified this area as among the top twenty "unspoiled" tourist destinations in the world.[7] There is a temptation to think that here, enveloped in rusticity, today's vacationers and second homers are striking a blow against commercialism, and for localism and modesty.

But we're more mainstream than we like to think of ourselves; people have been searching out and recording places like Big Lagoon for a long time. The lure of California as an "unspoiled" tourist destination was a foundational element of the state's earliest economic development. "We have a territory that is blest by Nature beyond all the world," wrote historian John Hittell in 1878.[8] Some 120 years later, the same idea is enshrined in popular histories of the state. "American tourists discovered California's natural beauty in the late 1800s and early 1900s," proclaims a typical museum blurb. "The sparkling lakes, Alpine peaks, rapid rivers, rugged canyons, exotic animals, Native American cultures, and sandy beaches entranced them."[9]

Look carefully and "natural beauty" reveals a great deal of human initiative. Peel back layers of a landscape and you'll unearth many histories. Which ones we remember are a matter of choice, morality, and clout. For most of its social history, northwestern California was not a refuge from the world, but where the action was. Long before Big Lagoon became a cultivated wilderness, it was a workplace to thousands of people.

First Home

It's easy to forget, given the dearth of public memorials and prompts, that today's recreational landscape was once a human homeland.[10] The western terrain may be filled with mundane references to the prehistoric past—in Trinidad you can go down to the beach via the "Primary Trail to Indian Beach"; in Ashland, you can drive along "Dead Indian Memorial Road"; in northwest California, you can visit Burney Falls, a reminder of a pioneer "killed by local Indians," or raft down Oregon's Rogue River, named after rebellious Karuk—but the icons referred to in this signage rarely rise above ground as fully developed human beings.[11] We're used to seeing Native Americans frozen in the past, as Rebecca Solnit observes, like "insects in amber."[12]

Prior to becoming generically stuck somewhere between the "exotic animals" and "sandy beaches," the people now known as "Yurok" lived prosperously for many generations in some seventy villages upriver and along the Pacific, along the Klamath River down to Humboldt Bay. There is no agreement about when and how the Yurok arrived here.[13] But archaeological evidence supports the claim that native peoples lived inland for many thousands of years, and on the coast for at least seven thousand years. The Yurok often use the term "from time immemorial" to denote a long past and deep roots in an "ancestral territory" that, according to the tribe's website, "ranged from their sacred high country in the mountains of southern Siskiyou, to the banks and terraces above the Klamath River, where most villages were located, onto the Pacific shoreline lagoons, and even out into the numerous rocks and sea stacks miles from shore. The Klamath River was the people's highway, as well as their source of food, inspiration, and cultural fulfillment."

The Yurok, who were spread out in small, extended families over a large territory, did not imagine themselves a coherent tribal entity until government officials in the second half of the nineteenth century began to herd native communities into reservations, and anthropologists in the early twentieth century constructed a classification of tribal types.[14] The term "Yurok" is a relatively recent term, notes anthropologist Thomas Buckley, reflecting "an objective entity that could be militarily supervised, bureaucratically managed, and ethnographically inscribed."[15] For many years, the US attempted to contain the various Yurok groups in the Hoopa Valley Indian Reservation, created in 1864, where they struggled to maintain an identity independent of the more powerful and economically resourceful Hupa. Most of their ancestral village sites were declared "surplus" and opened up to homesteaders and, eventually, lumber companies.

An elected Yurok government and written constitution were not formalized until October 1993. And some groups with strong family ties to the Yurok nonetheless opted out of membership in the tribe, which doesn't allow for "dual enrollment." The tiny Big Lagoon Rancheria, for example, whose land was originally purchased by the US government for "homeless Indians" in 1918, was federally recognized in 1985 and has the same legal and political status as its northern neighbors, the 116,000-acre Hoopa Valley Reservation (Hoopa Tribe) and 63,000-acre Klamath River Reservation (Yurok Tribe).[16]

The Yurok, according to the tribe's constitution, for most of their history were known by a variety of names—Pohlik-lah, Ner-er-ner, Petch-ik-lah, and Klamath River Indians—and spoke different languages on the river and coast, a reflection of their decentralized identities. Moreover, there was such an overlap of trade and marriage with other local native communities in the

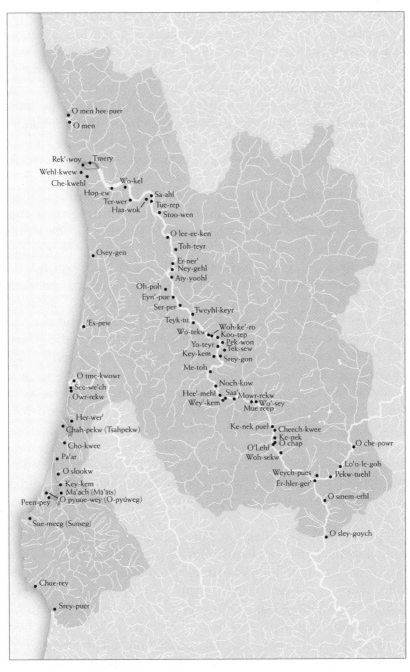

2.2 Precontact Yurok settlements.

northwest—especially Hupa, Karuk, Tolowa, and Wiyot—that even before white Americans were added to the mix by force and consent, native identities were forged through family and place rather than by tribe. Until the Yurok and other native groups became politically organized late in the twentieth century, mixture and hybridity were the norm. Even today, the small Blue Lake Rancheria, located a few miles from Arcata, includes Wiyot, Yurok, Tolowa, and Cherokee in its membership; and the Trinidad Rancheria acknowledges its "ancestral ties to the Yurok, Wiyot, and Tolowa peoples."[17] Membership in the Yurok Tribe requires only a biological parent who is a tribal member and proof of at least one-eighth "Indian Blood." It's not surprising, then, that many young native activists continue to struggle, in the words of Yurok-Karuk poet Shaunna McCovey, with life as "a series of measurements" and questions of "what it means to be whole."[18]

There are currently more than fifty-three hundred members enrolled in the Yurok Tribe, but the largest tribe in California owns less than one percent of its ancestral territory. Of the sixteen hundred natives and whites who still reside on the Klamath River Reservation, some 80 percent live in poverty, with most homes lacking access to basic services.[19] "My siblings and I," recalls McCovey, "grew up here in this remote area without electricity or a telephone."[20] In their heyday—long before there was a meth problem and a dearth of essential community facilities[21]—the Yurok led what one descendant of Tsurai (today's Trinidad) described as an "elegant lifestyle."[22] In 1775 the commander of a Spanish expedition checking out Puerto de Trinidad was impressed that the local Indians practiced "a well-ordered economy."[23]

The main Yurok village at Big Lagoon—one of the largest coastal settlements—was known as O-pyúweg, or Where They Dance, to signify its importance as a ceremonial center. At one time, there may have been as many as nine villages scattered around the lagoon.[24] Some anthropologists claim that the Yurok were among the groups who "arrived first and staked out the best living areas," but this is fanciful speculation.[25] The site is "certainly very pleasing to the eye," conceded Thomas Waterman (1885–1936), an influential Berkeley anthropologist who mapped the area in 1909, "and Indians are not at all insensible to scenic

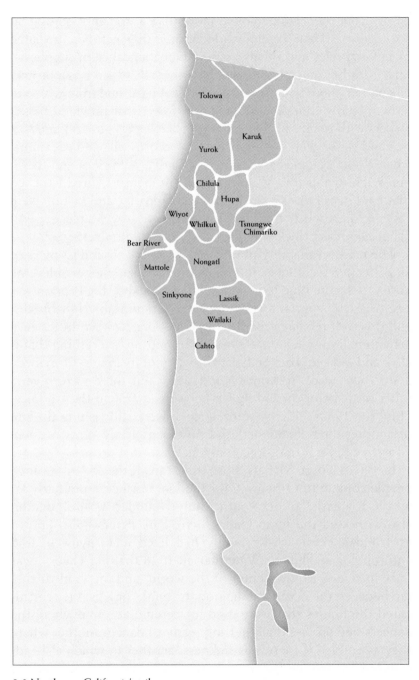

2.3 Northwest California's tribes

beauty." But the Yurok enjoyed more than a "romantic setting" at Big Lagoon.[26] Their "carefully honed harvesting methods, mediated by cultural rules and rituals," ensured an abundance of supplies—timber for housing and fire; nearby redwoods to serve as a protective barrier, more than three hundred feet high, and from which to fashion sturdy canoes; a Sitka spruce forest that provided basket makers with tough, pliable roots to make watertight containers; a rich and varied diet of salmon, mussels, acorns, elk, and occasional whales; and wetlands as a source of herbal medicines and teas.[27] Yurok informants told Waterman and his mentor, Alfred Kroeber, that mud hens grew so fat that they couldn't fly, and salmon were easy pickings when they got trapped in nearby Maple Creek.[28] "The lagoon was thick with ducks," noted a visitor in 1850.[29]

The ready availability of material resources around O-pyúweg and effective techniques for managing food supplies enabled the Yurok to devote time to ceremonies and rituals.[30] Big Lagoon was one of a few "special areas" that were "comfortably inhabited"[31] and it is well remembered for the Jump Dance, a world-renewal ceremony lasting ten days, devoted to putting "everything that is alive and in need" back in balance.[32] Two of its towns, O-pyúweg and Pi'npa, were "reckoned good size," and there were several other settlements, including Mä'äts, spread around the lagoon.[33] Until the 1950s, elderly Yurok women were still visiting the site of another long-abandoned and now densely overgrown town, Pa'ar, to carry out traditional prayers.[34]

In 1902 George Mahats, born in Mä'äts in the 1830s, recalled people coming to O-pyúweg for the Jump Dance "from fairly far up the Klamath." In her youth Fanny Flounder, a Yurok doctor, also witnessed the Jump Dance here. Pete Peters—also known as Trinidad Pete—whose family had lived in O-pyúweg, told anthropologist Thomas Waterman in 1928 that Big Lagoon was once imagined as "the center of the world" and the sandbar that ran between the ocean and lagoon its "omïl," or legs. He remembered the houses that were used for ceremonies: one where the dancers tied up their hair, getting ready to dance; another where they assembled if there was sickness; another in which a "headman lived whom people would ask when they were to have the Jumping Dance." And between these houses was "the ancient sweathouse for cleansing the world."[35]

2.4 Pete Peters (Trinidad Pete) at his home in Trinidad, 1928.

In the early 1970s, Yurok elders described O-pyúweg as a "ceremonial ground."[36] According to a Hupa story, it was at Big Lagoon that Creator "placed a sweat-house and a house in which the people should dance. 'Here,' he said, 'they will dance if anything goes wrong with the ocean. If the water rises up they will dance here and it will settle down again.' Then he went back to the northern world beyond the ocean."[37]

Their towns may have been sedentary and settled "since time immemorial," but this doesn't mean that the Yurok lived in a closed or static world. Prosperous towns, like the one at Big Lagoon, were a hubbub of exchange: the Yurok traveled far and wide in the northwest region, trading redwood, elk antlers, and seafood for dentalia shells, obsidian, and woodpecker feathers.[38] There's a popular tendency to think of the Yurok as both spatially insulated and culturally insular—"the boundary of [their] world," observed Waterman, "was not far beyond the area of which [they] knew the place names."[39] To anthropologist Alfred Kroeber (1876–1960), the worldview, as well as the world of the Yurok, was "snug, known, [and] unchanging." They identified "with this shrunken core of a universe intensely and passionately."[40] Of "adjacent tribes...there was only the dimmest knowledge," and beyond them "only the end of world, or a strange unsighted ocean, and perhaps things that no one wanted to see."[41] Writing for *Sunset* magazine in 1910, Kroeber described California Indians as being "vehemently attached to the particular locality where they have been born."[42]

But it's just as likely, proposes an anthropologist who worked for the Yurok Tribe for many years, that native coastal groups were in touch with vast regions of North America over a long period of time through a series of interconnected trails.[43] Even Waterman recognized that the Yurok journeyed quite a distance from their homes, until they reached "open country where no one exercises any claim of proprietorship [and] thus [they] know a good deal of country besides their own."[44] There were extensive economic ties between tribes, involving considerable traveling.[45] "It was not unusual for a messenger to travel forty miles in a day," says Karuk medicine woman Mavis McCovey. "I don't care how isolated we look, the tribal people did move around and trade all the way out to the East Coast."[46]

The first Spanish expedition to enter Trinidad harbor, in 1775, reported that the local Yurok carried knives made out of iron that they had acquired "from more northerly places."[47] When a British expedition captained by George Vancouver sailed into Trinidad harbor in May 1793, the flagship *Discovery* was "visited by two of the natives in a canoe; they approached us with confidence," wrote Vancouver, "and seemed to be friendly disposed." The Yurok, who "traded in a very honest and civil manner," were already accustomed to dealing with Europeans. "They sang songs in approaching the ship, by no means unpleasant to the ear."[48] No party to this trading, though, could have imagined that functional elk-antler spoons acquired by Vancouver's crew during this stopover in Trinidad would be displayed more than two hundred years later as objets d'art in a prestigious British museum.

By the late eighteenth century, several decades before the Gold Rush, northern California was already incorporated into regional and global economies. The Yurok and other native groups in northern California regularly traded "through a long-distance prestige-goods network" that stretched far north.[49] In the 1770s, Spain belatedly tried to defend its interests and aspirations in the region by shoring up its "pitiful defenses" against Russian and British competition.[50] When Spanish ships stopped at Trinidad on Trinity Sunday in 1775 in search of supplies and a northern port, they stayed nineteen days. They planted a cross as a "sign of possession" on the Indian settlement of Tsurai's highest hill and prematurely claimed "all these lands, seas, and its landmarks" in the name of Charles III and their Catholic god.[51] By the time that Vancouver's expedition scouted Trinidad in 1793, the cross—not unlike the Spanish empire—"was in a certain state of decay," and when another European ship visited Trinidad in 1817, the crew found what was left of the cross on the shore.[52]

In the early nineteenth century, the Pacific was the site of multi-national hunting expeditions for lucrative pelts to be sold on the China market. In June 1806, the coastal Yurok were trading otters for iron tools and other implements with the crew of a ship captained by a Bostonian, financed by Russians, and manned by indentured Kodiak and Aleut natives from Alaska. This joint venture was set up to exchange otter skins in Canton for teas, silks, spices, and nankeen cloth. Captain Winship didn't stay long in Trinidad. He thought it "most prudent to withdraw and retreat to the ship as the natives were collecting from every quarter."[53]

But venture capitalists returned less than half a century later and stayed this time, displacing longtime native settlements in the rush for gold. The descendants of those who inhabited the region during that cataclysmic moment of turmoil and warfare sometimes refer to it as "the time when the stars fell." To scholars, what happened in northern California was emblematic of "the greatest human demographic disaster in the historical record."[54] Statewide, the Native American population was reduced by about 90 percent within a hundred years; the Yurok population declined by more than two-thirds between 1770 and 1910.[55]

Big Lagoon was an early target of destruction and looting because it was en route to mining sites. Prospectors loaded up on provisions in Trinidad and headed north or inland. During the 1850s, the Yurok of Big Lagoon and other coastal settlements were defeated by superior technology, relentless numbers, and infectious diseases. "As many as half the Yurok population died from measles, smallpox, and tuberculosis passed on from settlers. Many others," notes the Yurok Tribe, "were killed by settlers, miners, and loggers over the balance of the 19th century. Several Yurok villages were subsequently burned by settlers." Between 1850 and 1950, Yurok life expectancy halved.[56] "We lost most of our ancestral lands and many aspects of our culture," says Shaunna McCovey, "and our language took a severe beating."[57]

Some historians now call this encounter in northern California "genocide,"[58] and all would agree with Alfred Kroeber that "the white man came and irreparably tore the fabric of native life to pieces."[59] The first detailed map of Big Lagoon, completed in 1876, does not identify any Yurok villages remaining in the region.[60] When Kroeber visited Big Lagoon in the early 1900s, he found "all the Indians gone except one family." O-pyúweg had been "ploughed over."[61] An elderly Yurok told him that "when a rancher took up the land at Oket'o and was about to wreck the sacred sweathouse there, the Indians offered him ten dollars to let it stand. 'We do not like to see it torn down,' they told him, 'because it is for the dance, and has been there a long time. We would be sorry if it were gone.' But he refused."[62]

There was survival and adaptation, as well as defeat. Inland, where "the unforgiving terrain" served as "a barrier from the outside world," riverine groups not only survived but also were able to preserve cultural traditions.[63] Despite the sale, plunder, and destruction of regalia, even in the worst of times, such as the 1890s, the Yurok and Hupa carried out White Deerskin Dances and Brush Dances in all their finery at ceremonial sites along the Klamath. And on the coast, where there was no place to hide, we know from public records that native peoples always had a presence. In 1904 the Northern California Indian Association reported fifteen people living in a native community at Big Lagoon.[64] In 1928 Pete Peters posed for a photograph close to the pit marking his ancestral house at O-pyúweg with Oket'o in the background. Today there are more than 650 descendants of Big Lagoon Yurok enrolled in the Yurok Tribe.[65]

Throughout the northwest, survivors hired themselves out as beasts of burden or went to work in canneries and the nascent lumber industry; many women lived with miners and settlers, some purchased or captured, some voluntarily. The Yurok also figured out how to market themselves—first selling their specialized knowledge of the terrain to argonauts seeking to know the fastest trails, where to cross rivers, and how to avoid predatory bears. Later, around the turn of the century, some sold their stories and recollections to anthropologists, their artifacts to collectors, and their own images to photographers eager to feed a nationwide nostalgia for a "vanishing race."[66] In 1893 participants in a White Deerskin Dance at Hoopa charged A. W. Ericson $5 for permission to take photographs.[67] A decade later, Kroeber

2.5 Pete Peters at O-pyúweg, 1928.

was paying $1.50 per day, plus traveling expenses and lodging, to Indian guides and informants.[68]

As Modern as Tomorrow

Meanwhile, Big Lagoon became an important site of people and goods in transit, and of continual and varied entrepreneurial activities. For a long time it was a place on the way to somewhere else. In December 1849, an expedition searching for a harbor to service the needs of the American economy on the northwest coast stumbled into "a small lake" (Big Lagoon) before heading south to Trinidad, where they carved their discovery into a tree.[69] Two years later, the talented artist and topographer J. Goldsborough Bruff observed "perpendicular clay-cliffs" at the ocean's edge and "numerous wild fowl" in the lagoon.[70] Until they were rounded up and expelled from Humboldt County in 1885, it was quite common to see Chinese immigrants passing by Big Lagoon on their way to gold strikes on the coast.[71]

Many adventurers traveled through Big Lagoon to make their fortune in gold mining or off gold miners, but many stopped to camp or to look and listen. Several travelers with literary aspirations took notes for posterity about the local inhabitants and environment. Thomas Gihon published his recollections of how he was seriously injured here in 1850 when his companions attacked the Yurok settlement at O-pyúweg, forcing him "to fight, to save my own life, on the side of men that I now detested and believed altogether in the wrong."[72] Ernest de Massey, a French businessman hoping to recoup his fortune with a gold strike, documented his positive experiences with the Yurok of Big Lagoon and his appreciation of the "booming" sea and "gigantic tree trunks half buried in the sand."[73] And Carl Meyer, visiting from Switzerland, also was impressed by the "sweet water lake, with an abundance of fish, only separated from the sea by a sandbank," and by "the enormous tree trunks scattered about the shore."[74]

After the Yurok were driven out and their settlements destroyed, Big Lagoon attracted even more traffic. Greenleaf Curtis, a Civil War soldier, and his men wandered into Big Lagoon in 1862 and helped themselves to an absent miner's pigs and chickens. The next day, they "got a canoe and crossed the Lagoon at two trips. Some of the men in going around shore found a dead Indian."[75] From the late 1890s through World War I, many travelers and traders took a risky shortcut between the lagoon and ocean. Cattle drivers herded their stock along the beach to save time but often ended up losing stock, their wagons, or their lives. "Big Lagoon claims one more victim," noted a local historian in 1893.[76] In 1908 Shirley Hannah, a young schoolteacher heading to his first job, teaching Yurok kids up the Klamath River, walked along the beach at Big Lagoon on his way from Trinidad to Orick—a ten-hour hike—with a suitcase full of clothes and books after he missed the stagecoach.[77]

But many people also stayed or worked in Big Lagoon. By the 1850s newcomers established ranches and farms in the region, and some were living with native women. In the late 1870s, the Big Lagoon Mining Company tried to extract gold from the sand but quickly failed. In 1892 another would-be miner created "a novel machine for abstracting fine particles of gold from the beach sand" but gave up when it was swept away in the fierce surf.[78] Other entrepreneurs had similar bad luck at opening a hotel, starting a commercial nursery, and building a model town.

By the turn of the century, the lumber industry was already big business, with redwoods "entirely in private hands" and "in universal use on the California coast," as *National Geographic* noted in a piece boosting the value of the new wonder commodity. "At the present rate of cutting, the supply will probably last for three hundred years."[79] With some four hundred sawmills along the coast busily producing all the necessities of life and death, from redwood cradles to redwoods coffins, it took only sixty years to clear-cut about 95 percent of the old-growth redwoods.[80] It had taken even less time to deplete the supply of salmon, so critical to native economies. "The appearance of the white men," wrote a member of the US Fish Commission in 1873 about the American and Feather rivers, "has been followed by the *total destruction* of the spawning beds of these once prolific streams, and the spoiling of the water, so that not a single salmon ever enters these rivers now where once they used to swarm by the millions."[81]

In the early 1920s, the small farmers and ranchers who owned land at Big Lagoon sold off their holdings to corporate interests that dominated the area's economy for many years ahead. Ownership of the land, as a state report later observed, was "marked by a bewildering array of absentee landlords, banks, trusts and lumber companies," including the Lagoon Lumber Company in 1920, the Little River Redwood Company in 1923, the Hammond Redwood (later Lumber) Company in 1931, and Georgia Pacific in 1956.[82] In 1929 the Little River Redwood Company leased some of its land to Humboldt County to create a park and recreational area, including construction of vacation homes.

By the mid-1940s, the Hammond Lumber Company had set up a company village near Big Lagoon, equipped with prefabricated "bachelor cabins" and a mess hall that could serve 120 men at one sitting. The camp, noted a local newspaper, was "as modern as tomorrow."[83] One of Hammond's employees and his family lived in our cabin, which they called "Sea View." As a child, Billy Dean Hill remembers, he played softball on a nearby square until dusk drove him home, and sat on our porch shooting at birds. "Good job he was a bad shot," says his wife.[84]

Hammond's successor, Georgia Pacific, replaced the donkey engine with caterpillars and more efficiently tore into the earth. You can witness their impact at Big Lagoon in *Logging the Redwoods*, an oversized book composed mostly of photographs

2.6 Log pond at Big Lagoon, 1949.

that celebrates Man's conquest of Nature and how California harvested timber "without seriously depleting the supply."[85]

A few years later, the nearby forest of old-growth redwoods—once so central to the Yurok's "well-ordered economy"—had been clear-cut. In the early 1960s, with the profitable extraction of trees in the area now exhausted, the lumber company sold off its Big Lagoon properties to the county and to the newly incorporated "cabin colony" known as Big Lagoon Park Company. A decade later, one of its cabins became my second home. [86]

The seemingly pristine qualities of Big Lagoon that attracted me in the 1970s were recognized by some of the first settlers who traveled through Humboldt in the 1850s. A San Francisco newspaper urged city folks to head north to Trinidad, a "paradisical" region of "natural loveliness," its climate "superior perhaps to that of any other part of California."[87] Another correspondent recommended the "balmy atmosphere" and "picturesque" countryside.[88] In 1851 a traveler from Basel, Switzerland, was as impressed as I am today by "the constant roar of the sea" and the "many lovely bits of stone and shells" along the beach around Big Lagoon.[89] Some ninety years later, Alfred Kroeber appreciated "the flash of sunset, the distant streak of land horizon from far out at sea, the breakers or rapids ahead at which one pauses before venturing on them."[90]

Humboldt County was first promoted as a commercial tourist destination in the 1890s, when "rusticating" became popular in the area. As early as 1893, the county was using an image taken by the well-known local photographer A. W. Ericson of hunters on the water in Big Lagoon to promote tourism to the "by-ways of wild nature."[91] By the turn of the century, the duck-hunting season brought a thousand sportsmen to the lagoon.[92] Thomas Waterman, like many visitors, took note of "the contrast between the heaving Pacific with its broad line of surf, and the quiet, still lagoon."[93] In 1915 a papier-mâché relief map created for the Humboldt exhibit at the Panama-Pacific International Exposition in San Francisco highlighted Big Lagoon and other tourist attractions.[94]

California's state government first got involved in marking historical sites and marketing tourist attractions in the 1920s. In southern California, a therapeutic climate, restored missions, and

2.7 Rusticating at Big Lagoon, c. 1893.

luxury hotels attracted wealthy visitors. Up north, the "redwood highway" was promoted to travelers who appreciated the rugged outdoors and wanted to witness what was left of old-growth redwoods, typically described as "true living fossils" and "isolated remnants of a once robust lineage."[95] The Save-the-Redwoods League began buying up what was left of the old-growth redwood groves that would form the core of the state's redwood parks.

Newton Drury, the first executive director of the league (and later head of the National Park Service), played a key role in preserving and promoting redwoods as tourist attractions. Together with his brother Aubrey, who organized the state's first inventory of historical resources, and his father, Wells (who headed the Berkeley Chamber of Commerce), he was a pioneer in the emerging field of public relations. In 1913 Wells and Aubrey Drury coauthored the *California Tourist Guide and Handbook*.

The Drurys' clients included the Ford Dealers Association, Southern Pacific Railroad, and Save-the-Redwoods League. Aubrey Drury regarded "historic sites primarily as resources for tourists," argues historian David Glassberg. When Drury was put in charge of the state's historical marker program in 1931, he worked closely with automobile associations and local business organizations to make sure that the only places designated as historic sites, including redwood groves, would be accessible from the road. "It was a public program in name only," says Glassberg. "In reality, control remained firmly in the hands of the state chamber of commerce."[96]

The automobile helped to put Big Lagoon on the map. As a consequence of state-sponsored tourism, by the 1920s Big Lagoon was popular with day-trippers, campers, sportsmen, and pothunters looking for "Indian relics."[97] In 1929 motorboat races on the lagoon attracted some three thousand spectators.[98] In the 1930s, visitors could try their hands at golf—on a course dotted with sand traps twenty-five yards from the beach—oblivious that O-pyúweg was beneath their feet. Aside from a brief period during World War II when the area was used for military target practice, tourism and recreation gradually prevailed.[99]

In less than a hundred years, Big Lagoon's economy went from hunting and gathering to subsistence farming, to corporate capitalism, and to public recreation—an accelerated version of what took centuries to develop in other parts of the world. By the time that I started visiting the area in the mid-1970s, Big Lagoon's native, agricultural, and commercial histories were erased from public memory. It had become the kind of rural haven that folks like me were seeking as a respite from the metropolis.

But it is difficult to purge the landscape of its ghosts. The past never rests in peace; it is always in motion, subject to revision and reinterpretation.[100] The tectonic layers of Big Lagoon's troubling, panoramic history—formed by the present absences of natives and settlers, victims and survivors, homesteaders and lumber barons, visitors and residents, collectors and collected, buried and excavated—continue to shift and reverberate here and now. The history of this place inextricably links the lives and deaths of many people—albeit divided by race, class, gender, and beliefs—in much the same way that blacks and whites in the American South, and Africans and Native Americans during the colonization of the Americas, were intimately interconnected.[101]

* * *

Memento Mori

For me, this history is personal as well as public. My son Daniel had four close calls and one final call in his forty-year life—all stemming from a brain tumor the size of a small orange discovered when he was a teenager—so I had plenty of opportunities to rehearse his death. In the spring of 2006, he managed to get away by himself for a weekend at our family cabin in Big Lagoon. He'd been coming here since he was a child and his deep love of this area is one of the reasons that I've held on to my share of the property. Before he left for the last time, on May 28th, he wrote in the cabin's journal: "I've had a weekend of beautiful weather and salvation. The jade gods have been good to me on this trip. Walked down to the point yesterday. Saw whales from the beach today. So many great memories from Big Lagoon. When my well-used body gives up, which I hope is not for a while, I'd like a Viking funeral."

Six weeks later he was gone, no *deus ex machina* this time. On July 22, the family gathered in Big Lagoon to fulfill his written request. Together we all made a raft from long pieces of buoyant driftwood washed up on the shore, lashed together by strands of twine. At twilight, we built a small pyre to hold the cedar box

2.8 Nathan and Jonah Platt looking out at Big Lagoon shortly after their father's Viking funeral, 2006.

2.9 Big Lagoon memorial: marking the spot, 2008.

containing his ashes on top of the driftwood. There were rose petals for us to scatter, and two bouquets of herbs to accompany the ashes: rosemary, oregano, lavender, sage, yarrow, thyme, and a little bit of forget-me-not. "And we never will." We carried the three-tiered edifice to a promontory jutting into the lagoon, a sanctuary of calmness facing the treacherous ocean. The pyre lit up immediately and moved gradually off shore.

I've been back to Big Lagoon regularly since then, enough times to hone my rituals. I collect black-green jade on the beach to place on a memorial bench—made by a local artist from reclaimed redwood—that sits in our cabin. During each visit I walk along the western shore of the lagoon to pay my respects to Daniel's launch site, marked magically and no doubt temporarily in 2008 by three sentry-like limbs of a beached tree sprouting through the sand.

I often chat with my son here, not unlike the Yurok who used to visit nearby Nrgr'i-o-il (As-Far-As-It-Comes), where the cliffs and beach meet, the site of a spirit who helps you "if you go and talk to him." On warm days, I sit by the lagoon, propped up against a log, and imagine the place where, according to the Yurok, disembodied souls started their journey into the underworld.[102] I get a sense of comfort from these fixed reminders, though as a historian I know that there's nothing more chameleon-like than memory.

About eighteen months after we said farewell to Daniel's Viking spirit, other ghosts surfaced from the past. Two of my fellow cabin owners wanted to cut down a forty-five-foot-tall Sitka spruce that threatened to topple over in a winter storm and damage their property. The Yurok Tribe's Culture Committee of elders raised objections since the tree's roots are very likely covering an ancient burial ground. It was a classic battle between property rights and cultural patrimony that stirred up longtime animosities. The dispute was eventually settled by a compromise in which the tree was topped down to fourteen feet and protected by a fence.

But the event sparked my curiosity about Daniel's companions in death. Wanting to learn more about Big Lagoon's Yurok past and the subsequent layers of history embedded in the landscape, I did some research, starting with technical archaeological reports on the region. To my surprise I came across a brief reference, in a report on hazardous trees and a water tank replacement, to an allegation that in the 1930s local collectors had been digging up Yurok graves and taking away their contents, body parts and all.[103] This supposedly took place within a quarter-mile of our cabin.

I am fortunate that my son is well remembered at Big Lagoon, a place he deeply appreciated and that is meaningful to me. Some of my fellow cabin owners who have died are also well remembered, their names etched onto a bench that looks out from a choice spot on a cliff facing the Pacific Ocean. John Svenson Field (1941–2005), a regular visitor to Big Lagoon, is similarly well remembered by his family: they have erected a handsome bench in his honor on a grassy perch overlooking the lagoon.

But there is no public honor roll, nor are there memorials or benches, naming the thousands of people who lived and died here over the course of several millennia. At the lagoon, visitors can learn from an educational plaque that the Yurok "first came to this area hundreds of years ago" and that "ceremonies are important to Yurok life." It's the kind of bland, comforting nugget of information that typifies most public acknowledgments of native peoples' histories. What's omitted is why and when the Yurok left Big Lagoon—the sorrowful, disturbing stuff about massacres, arson, diseases, kidnappings, thievery, and the diaspora that occurred when the stars fell—and how survivors and their descendants continued to live at Big Lagoon even as the world they had known imploded.[104]

Moreover, there is another insulting, albeit well-meaning feature of the plaque at Big Lagoon: a reproduction of a 1918 photograph that portrays a woman and a young boy holding up two large, recently caught salmon. A text identifies the white boy as Harry Roberts, while the second subject—Alice Spott, the celebrated Native American leader, known for her skills as a hunter, canoe handler, and warrior—is reduced to a generic "Yurok woman."[105]

When I started doing research for this project, I met skepticism and resistance from some Yurok elders who have a long memory of petty and grand humiliations committed in the name of science, history, and anthropology. By the time that I finished reading a sizable literature and viewing a portfolio of images about the Yurok, I had a better idea why they felt and feel the way they do, and understood that trust would have to be earned.

THREE

It Is Not Gone Into Here

"The people that came here, that went
through here, they killed us. They
murdered us, they stole our regalia...and
the stuff to dance with and everything
so that it was almost impossible for the
people to do it again. That's the kind of
stuff we put up with. What do they call
it, genocide?"
—Walt J. Lara Sr., Yurok, 1990[1]

Purely Aboriginal

The young Harry Roberts, pictured on the plaque at Big Lagoon,
was one of the few outsiders to be given a rigorous education in
Yurok practices. "I have been in close association with the Yurok
Indians since my childhood, as a friend and a student," he wrote
in 1973. He made pilgrimages with them to sacred areas "on foot
over the old Indian trails before there were any roads"[2] and went
on to lead an extraordinarily creative life as a botanist and horti-
culturist.[3] He grew up on the northwest coast. His father worked
as an accountant for the Klamath River Packers' Association,
which operated a salmon cannery in Requa, at the mouth of the
Klamath; his mother, Ruth (1885–1967), an advocate for native
rights, was an important source of local information for Alfred
Kroeber in the 1920s and 1930s.[4]

3.1 Harry Roberts and Alice Spott, Klamath River, 1918.

Harry's training under the tutelage of Yurok leader Robert Spott—Alice Spott's brother—left him "not in the middle of society, but in between white and Indian worlds, an outsider to both."[5] He was reluctant to put his experiences with the Yurok into writing because, as he noted near the end of his life:

> It was just too personal [and] too hard to get out. It's hard to say because I worry that I won't be understood. That's what the old people used to say: "We just want to be understood." That's *all* they wanted, but when they realized that the anthropologists and psychologists couldn't understand them, they stopped speaking of personal things or developed things and only gave them what they could understand. That's the Law: don't give people what they can't understand.[6]

Many Yurok shared Harry Roberts's views on this topic. In 1916 Lucy Thompson, the first Yurok to publish a book, wrote, "Our traditions and religion are too sacred to be expounded before strangers of another race."[7] No wonder, then, that Kroeber regarded "the Indian [as] a notoriously suspicious animal,"[8] or that his protégé Thomas Waterman, the anthropologist whose 1920 *Yurok Geography* is still used today as the definitive guide to Yurok towns, ran into all kinds of recalcitrant subjects when he was trying to reconstruct a history of Yurok marriages and families.[9] Waterman's field notes written between 1909 and 1922 are filled with exasperated asides:

> Mrs. Frey, who is a good friend of mine, enlightened and emancipated in every way, and married to a white man, refused to tell me anything about her own people. Nor would any other Indians tell me about Mrs. Frey's family. I tried both persuasion and bribery, which were met by bland forgetfulness and obstinate evasiveness. Nobody cared to offend her by talking about her people.

> I could not in 1928 get...to say a word about the details of their ancestry. This town (Srégon) contained the wealthiest families in the tribe. Its citizens were notoriously overbearing, and intolerant of the least slight. The people themselves were too "high toned" to talk for pay, and doubly unwilling to talk without it. Nobody else cared to talk about them, and their marriages, for fear of offending.

> Mrs. Marks is a very intelligent woman, and one of my informants on my last visit, but she would not tell me her Indian name.

> Tuley Creek Jim, who lived here (Kenek), also refused to talk to me, for reasons of his own, which he did not enlarge upon. I never found an Indian who was willing to embroil himself with these people by giving me information about their family and marriage arrangements.

> With every desire and motive to complete my notes, I could learn nothing about the details of marriage in Espaw. The present writer sat for some days observing this site, with an informant at his elbow, but no information worth the name could be obtained concerning the people here."[10]

The distrust of academics, especially anthropologists and archaeologists, among Yurok elders has deep roots.[11] For a relatively small tribe—one of a hundred or more throughout the state—that lived for a long time in an inaccessible place, the Yurok received an inordinate amount of attention from a wide variety of intellectual and creative notables of the nineteenth and twentieth centuries. This attention, according to many Yurok, has been a mixed blessing, if that. The problem is neither with the attention nor with the search for knowledge and information, but rather with relations of power between the investigator and subject, and with how the products of knowledge have been used and misused.

Northwest native Californians were central to the development of UC Berkeley as "one of the world's great research museums and teaching departments of anthropology."[12] Beginning in 1900, under the leadership of Alfred Kroeber, Berkeley sent a cadre of anthropologists into Wiyot and Yurok territories: Kroeber himself did his first fieldwork with the Yurok in the 1900s; under his direction, Thomas Waterman roved throughout Humboldt in 1909, doing extensive research for *Yurok Geography*; Kroeber's iconoclastic apprentice Llewellyn Loud carried out the first serious ethnography of the Wiyot in 1913; during the 1920s, Berkeley anthropologist Edward Gifford measured the skulls of living and dead Yurok—as well as other native Californians—for his research on anthropometry; a collaborative project between Kroeber and Robert Spott over many years generated a book of Yurok tales and myths (with Spott as lead author); and when Berkeley launched the University of California Archaeological Survey in 1948, Robert Heizer and his colleagues supervised several student digs in Humboldt.[13]

It wasn't only anthropologists who were interested in extracting knowledge from the Yurok. The journalist Stephen Powers had traveled on foot and horseback along the West Coast in the summers of 1871 and 1872, writing about the Yurok and other native groups for national magazines.[14] He also amassed "four boxes of Indian collection" that he shipped to the Smithsonian, and seven human skulls that he sent to the Army Museum.[15] In the summer of 1922, photographer Edward Curtis took an extensive journey along the West Coast to document and preserve the

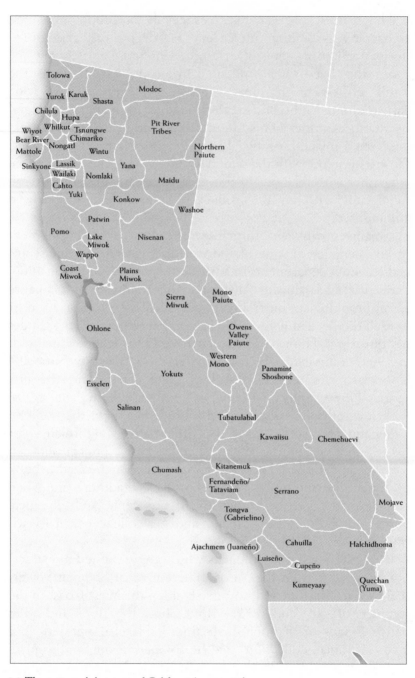

3.2 The major subdivisions of California's many tribes

experiences of "one of the great races of mankind [before] the opportunity will be lost for all time."[16] Also, renowned psychologist Erik Erikson accompanied Kroeber in the early 1940s to the Klamath, where the "resistive and suspicious temperament of the Yurok" did not stop him from psychoanalyzing their childrearing practices.[17]

So, not surprisingly, when I started doing research for this project in 2008, I was greeted with skeptical wariness. I asked a Yurok elder if he had any advice for me. "Never believe the first thing that comes out of a Yurok's mouth," he told me straight-faced before cracking a smile. "Yet another author who wants to write about the Yurok" was how an official with the Yurok Tribe greeted my initial inquiry. "People are grinding axes that have nothing to do with you," he advised. I was just the latest in a long line of investigators and recorders who have claimed the Yurok's attention. The burden, I quickly realized, was on me to demonstrate that I wasn't one of those academics who, in the words of singer Floyd Red Crow Westerman, "go to write their book and tell the world there's more / but there's nothing left to write, it's all been done before."[18]

An assessment of past intellectual projects involving the Yurok begins inevitably with Kroeber, who looms biblically large in the anthropology of the Yurok as redeemer and nemesis—the man who helped to "salvage" the cultural experiences of "savages" from likely oblivion; and the man who kept his "silence about the costs of white conquest."[19] His significant body of work deepened our understanding of the Yurok, as it deepened resentments among the 1960s generation of Yurok activists. As one of his admirers puts it, Kroeber was not particularly interested in the applicability of his ideas to "human welfare problems."[20]

Alfred Kroeber was twenty-four years old when he arrived in San Francisco in 1900 to take what would be a short-term job with the California Academy of Sciences. A year later, now the recipient of Phoebe Hearst's patronage and the first doctorate in anthropology to be awarded by Columbia University (where he studied with Franz Boas), he took on the challenge of building both the UC Berkeley Department of Anthropology and the university's Museum of Anthropology in San Francisco (now located in Berkeley and known as the Phoebe A. Hearst Museum of Anthropology, or PAHMA).[21] While Harvard's Frederic Ward Putnam was nominally in charge during the early 1900s, it was Kroeber who taught some of the university's first anthropology classes in Berkeley and worked for years at a furious pace in San Francisco to create a functioning museum. "Practically every specimen that is catalogued," he wrote Putnam in 1905, "has to be handled, placed, and named by me."[22]

On his arrival in California in 1900, Kroeber was immediately drawn to the northwest coast, much as I was in the 1970s, especially its "creeks and rivers, bays, inlets, lagoons, and the shore of the sea."[23] And like me, he ended up living most of his life in north Berkeley and buying a cabin on the coast (a few miles from mine), which he owned for several years. From his two-acre lot at Sigonoy,[24] close to the Yurok settlement of Oreqw (now known as Orick), he had views to the west of "sea-stacks, sacred objects in Yurok lore, a bit off-shore, and with coastal freighters passing outside the stacks; to the south were Dry and Big Lagoon and the distant lights of Eureka, while to the north the view was to the lighthouse at Crescent City." Close to his cabin lived Orick Bob, who became one of his informants about Yurok culture and language. And when he went inland, Kroeber would easily switch from car to redwood canoe and hiking. "It was leisurely and sociable," recalled his wife, Theodora, about Alfred, "to go up the Klamath with three or four Yurok aboard, with stops at each village along the way and at each of the sacred praying places on the river banks."[25]

Kroeber was lucky to be on the ground floor of American anthropology, surrounded by young, innovative intellectuals able to find their bearings in new situations. His first colleague, Pliny Goddard (1869–1928), was a Quaker whose missionary work on the Hoopa Reservation formed the basis of his doctoral dissertation on Hupa grammar. Goddard brought linguistics into the fledgling anthropology department, and at thirty-two was the old man of the group. Thomas Waterman—described by Kroeber as "extraordinarily stimulating" and "brilliant"—was twenty-two years old when he started working for Kroeber as a museum assistant in 1907, and twenty-five when he received his Ph.D. (also under Franz Boas at Columbia) and joined the faculty at Berkeley.[26] Kroeber met Edward Gifford (1887–1959) at the California Academy of Sciences, where as a teenage high school graduate

3.3 Theodora and Alfred Kroeber at their cabin at Sigonoy, near Orick, 1931.

Gifford was working as assistant curator of ornithology and already a "passionate collector." Kroeber recruited him in 1912 to become his right-hand man at the Museum of Anthropology, and later a researcher and professor at the university. Gifford received his anthropological training on the job and had a successful academic career without a college degree.[27]

The most idiosyncratic member of Kroeber's circle was Llewellyn Loud (1879–1946), who had worked as a longshoreman, miner, and laborer before he was hired at the museum as Kroeber's factotum. He took some classes at the university but did not complete a degree, and he was working as a janitor when Kroeber spotted his archaeological potential. It is to Kroeber's credit that he gave considerable responsibility to a self-described socialist who was not at all awed by his boss's credentials and signed one of his field reports "Yours for the Revolution." In 1913, when Kroeber inquired about research on the Wiyot he was expecting from his apprentice and intended to use for a paper he was writing, Loud replied:

> I am wondering if you are thinking of annexing my three months' work to your "half day's work with an Indian under a shade tree."...You have made your reputation by past work, you are considered an authority in your profession and your job is secure, while I have the reputation of being a crank and a fellow from whom it is easy to get a lot of good work for little pay. My responsibility is as great as yours because I am struggling to gain recognition.[28]

Loud worked for $2.75 a day, $1.25 more than Kroeber paid his native informants.[29] When the department's research on the Wiyot was eventually published in 1918—*Ethnogeography and Archaeology of the Wiyot Territory*—its sole author was Llewellyn Loud.

The reputation of the department was boosted by its relationship with Ishi, a Yahi survivor of massacres, bounty hunts, epidemics, and starvation, who emerged from hiding in the small California town of Oroville in August 1911 to become a big-time celebrity in San Francisco, until his death from pneumonia in March 1916. Learning from Waterman that "this man is undoubtedly wild" and would make a "good exhibit for the public," Kroeber quickly staked a claim to becoming Ishi's official guardian.[30] He housed Ishi in a room at the Museum of Anthropology, gave him a job as a janitor, and proudly displayed him to his colleagues and the curious as "the most uncivilized man in the world today."[31] Thousands of people showed up at the museum to watch Ishi using a drill to start a fire and making arrowheads, or vicariously followed his daily routines through sensational stories in the local press.[32]

Ishi certainly enhanced Alfred Kroeber's career in the short run, but the Yurok played a much more significant, long-term intellectual and personal role in the life of an anthropologist who authored some 550 published works, and under whose leadership Berkeley quickly became one of the six principal anthropological centers in the United States.[33] The Yurok were not the first nor last Native Americans that he studied, observed Theodora Kroeber, but they were "the people and culture who most engaged his curiosity and imagination."[34] It is not by accident that Kroeber's thousand-page, encyclopedic tome, *Handbook of the Indians of California*, published in 1925, begins with an account of the Yurok.[35] His survey of the Yurok takes four chapters and is "the most exhaustive of the descriptions within the book."[36]

In 1900 the Academy of Sciences in San Francisco sponsored Kroeber's first trip to the Klamath River. With one hundred dollars provided by David Starr Jordan, chairman of the board

3.4 Alfred Kroeber's view of Big Lagoon, 1907.

of directors, Kroeber set off to purchase artifacts and cultural information.[37] Most of his fieldwork with the Yurok took place in the 1900s, but he continued to visit the area in the 1920s, staying at the cabin he bought in 1923.[38] He kept in touch with his informants and some, like Robert Spott, came to Berkeley to collaborate on projects.[39] Kroeber later fondly recalled Weitchpec, a hub of the Yurok world, as "an old home of mine. I have lived there half a dozen times, once or twice for a month or so. I used to know all the inhabitants and every shack and tree and trail in and around the village. Please give my regards to the old town," he wrote to a teacher there. "All the old Indians are gone," she replied.[40] "Are you ever coming this way any more?" Weitchpec Frank wrote Kroeber in 1920: "All or nearly all your friends in Klamath are dead now. I would like to hear from you."[41]

Kroeber went out of his way to try to find local jobs around the Klamath for his Yurok contacts, and not only as guides and informants. In the early 1930s, for example, he explored with Ruth Roberts the possibility of getting Yurok hired in canneries and garages, and in the growing business of recreational fishing.[42] Ruth Roberts, a graduate of Mills College, was an influential member of a network of white, middle-class women who acted as

3.5 Two unnamed native women in the backyard of Kroeber's cabin, 1928.

informational entrepreneurs for anthropologists such as Kroeber, advocated for social services for native groups, and introduced white audiences to Native American cultures. She felt equally at ease among the matrons of her hometown Piedmont in the Oakland hills and in the backcountry along the Klamath River, where she camped and fished with her Yurok friends during the summer. She spoke out against "the ever increasing intruders who swarm over and defile the sacred places" and was not at all intimidated by academics. "My first conversation with Mrs. Roberts was awesome," recalled anthropologist Arnold Pilling after her death. "I left feeling as though I had gone for a shower and found myself beneath Niagara Falls."[43]

While Kroeber was recruiting native men to meet with his students in Berkeley, Roberts brought young native women to the East Bay to live with and work for her society friends, and to participate in the East Bay Yurok Club that she organized to promote cultural activities. And occasionally the activities of

3.6 Alice Spott in an oceangoing canoe near Requa, c. 1917.

these gender-separated worlds would overlap. One of Roberts's recruits was eighteen-year-old Margaret Marks, whose mother, the "very intelligent" Josie Marks, had refused in the 1920s to tell Thomas Waterman her Yurok name (it was Sin-gi-wa, Seagull) and who herself, along with her brother Milton, would become a leading advocate of native rights. In 1930 Margaret Marks invited Kroeber to become an honorary member of the Yurok Club in recognition of his "effort to preserve the history and lore of the California Indians." Kroeber replied that he was "pleased and honored" to be recognized by the club.[44]

Many Yurok also respected Kroeber for his longtime advocacy of native land rights. "The solution of the California Indian problem," he told an audience at the Commonwealth Club in 1909, "lies above all in giving him land—property which he can call his own, and by which he can at least partially subsist and thereby be independent. For our own good as well as the Indian's, we do not want a class of homeless, property-less peons. Land of course means land that is good for something, not a quarter section on a granite hillside barely able to furnish pasture for a single cow. Where land to be worth anything must be irrigated, the Indian's allotment needs water rights. When this foothold of independence is given him, and he is no longer the football of circumstance or of the caprice of his white neighbor, he will become a useful if humble member of the community, instead of a squalid outcast."[45]

Almost half a century later, close to the end of his life, Kroeber testified for the plaintiffs in California Indian Land Claims Commission hearings. The federal government had asked him to back up their case, but "he chose instead," his son noted, "to testify at length *for* the Indians."[46] It was awkward because some of his ex-students testified for the government, but "especially my old friends among the Indians," said Kroeber, "would not have understood if I had been nominally 'against' them." By all accounts, Kroeber gave a "masterful performance" in court, arguing that "native possessory rights" went beyond material needs: "You have got to have your food and you have got to have sleep and shelter, but that isn't the whole of life to an Indian any more than it is to us. I see it always as a larger whole in which the subsistence is basic and they pyramid up into the sunshine and supernatural." In a pyrrhic victory for the plaintiffs, the Indian

Land Claims Commission (established by Congress in 1946) sided with Kroeber and determined that California Indians had been illegally dispossessed of 64,435,000 acres of land. The case was settled in 1963 for $29.1 million, which after lawyers' fees amounted to forty-five cents per acre.[47]

After his death, Kroeber was gratefully and respectfully acknowledged by the Council of California Indians for his "inspired enthusiasm to learn all there was to know about the present and past history of Indian people," and for serving as an expert witness in the land claims hearings. "Members of the Council," observed an obituary on December 15, 1960, "feel that they express the conviction of every California Indian when we say that we will be forever grateful to the Great Spirit, who must have guided Dr. Alfred Louis Kroeber from Hoboken, New Jersey to California where he soon became our friend and in later life our greatest hope for long delayed justice."[48]

In his introduction to *Yurok Narratives*, coauthored with Robert Spott in 1942, Kroeber modestly expressed the hope that the book might "help to perpetuate the qualities of a culture into

3.7 Alfred Kroeber and Robert Spott in Requa, 1939.

which one of us was born and which the other gradually learned to sense and value."[49] Kroeber apparently intended to write a "more personal, psychological, and biographical" history of the Yuroks, but he never did so. "Perhaps I cannot write of the Yurok this way," he told his wife. "I feel myself too much a Yurok."[50]

It would have no doubt pained Kroeber to be so disparaged by the generation of native activists who by the 1960s had supplanted his confidantes, and who constitute today's elders. Theodora Kroeber remembered that "when I went up river with Kroeber, his old Yurok Indian friends, recognizing him as our canoe came close, hurried to greet him, often to embrace him, the rush of words, his and theirs, coming first in Yurok."[51]

Kroeber and his colleagues are widely appreciated as ethnographers who painstakingly recorded and preserved ceremonies, language, and stories. "I don't put Kroeber or any of those anthropologists down," says Joy Sundberg, a Yurok leader with the Trinidad Rancheria and longtime activist, "because there's a lot of things that would not have been documented if it hadn't been for him to come up and interview these people."[52] Without the assiduous work of that "good Doctor Kroeber," another Yurok elder once told Thomas Buckley, "we wouldn't know a thing today about who we really are."[53] An authority on folk tales considers *Yurok Myths* "a timeless memorial to the creative imagination of the Yurok people and the tireless labor of one of the giants of anthropology."[54] To this day, anybody seriously interested in Yurok settlements and place names has on hand a well-thumbed copy of *Yurok Geography*, researched by Waterman in 1909 under Kroeber's close supervision.

While Kroeber is acknowledged, sometimes reluctantly, for these contributions, most Yurok "generally resent the way they have been depicted in the literature of anthropology," observes Richard Keeling, "and—whether he deserves it or not—they focus their bitterness on Kroeber."[55] Why does his legacy leave a bad taste among some of today's Yurok?

As Karuk scholar Julian Lang has noted, Kroeber was so preoccupied with precontact cultures that "he never introduced us to the living people."[56] This is not just a critique of Kroeber's chronology, but also of his failure to report on how native peoples survived against all odds and lived to fight another day. The northwest Yurok, Hupa, and Karuk were able to sustain them-selves longer than most tribes after 1849 because they were close to food supplies, and the terrain made guerilla warfare viable; until the 1890s, access to the Hoopa Valley was possible only on foot or by mule.[57] Activists looking for inspirational accounts of struggle, organization, and resistance find little solace in Kroe-ber's work, which has a tendency to be read as nostalgic for the good old days rather than forward-looking.

New developments in cultural studies since Kroeber's death in 1960 make us aware also of how he tended to essentialize the Yurok—not necessarily in negative ways—and how he reduced complex human relationships to a monolithic, unchanging core, fixed and immutable, evocative of eugenic imagery about racial types. Drawing upon research on the Emeryville shellmound, in 1909 Kroeber ruled out the possibility that there had been any significant cultural changes over time in native groups.[58] Many years later, in a widely read essay, he was still making sweep-ing and often derogatory generalizations about "Yurok National Character": the Yurok are "touchy to slight, sensitive to sham-ing, quickly angered...They hate wholeheartedly, persistently, irreconcilably...They are acquisitive, but even more avaricious and retentive...The men seemed to me bitter and withdrawn, and some were of terrifying mien; but the old women made an impression rather of serenity."[59]

From early in his career, Kroeber rejected prevailing views about a multiplicity of human races, hierarchically organized into a natu-ralistic pecking order. Influenced by his mentor Boas, he dismissed simplistic views about racial difference in favor of cultural relativ-ism. "Most of the alleged existing evidence on race endowment is likely to be worthless," Kroeber argued in his 1923 textbook. "Racial inferiority and superiority are by no means self-evident truths....In short, it is a difficult task to establish any race as either superior or inferior to another, but relatively easy to prove that we entertain a strong prejudice in favor of our racial superiority."[60]

Yet Kroeber harbored racialized attitudes and imagery that surfaced in his observations about native peoples. "By tempera-ment," observed Kroeber in a speech in 1909, the "California Indian is docile, peaceful, friendly, sluggish, unimaginative, not easily stirred, low-keyed in emotion, almost apathetic."[61] And he publicly compared Ishi with a "puppy" that "comes running when you call him, and if you were to tell him to stand in the corner or stand on his head, if he were able he would do it without hesitation."[62]

Alongside Kroeber's reductionist view of culture and his tendency to derive his information from older, male leaders runs the surprising fact that almost nowhere does he explore the extent to which his subjects' recollections were mediated by their age, and direct or indirect knowledge of the catastrophe that swept through their lives in the second half of the nineteenth century. Kroeber tended to rely on what Erna Gunther, in a different context, described as "the fading memory of the old men from whom anthropologists in the twentieth century and even the nineteenth century have had to pry their information."[63] Not surprisingly, given their knowledge of a calamitous past, many of his informants gave an impression of being "most often melancholic, punctuated by choler," their tales suffused with an "almost elegiac emotion."[64] What Kroeber considered to be inherent in Yurok culture from time immemorial was no doubt survivors' depression, or realistic accounting of dreadful times.

Kroeber was not particularly interested in sociological or historical approaches to anthropology. He favored methodologies that were "free of any motivation of applicability or social control."[65] "What happened to the California Indians following 1849—their disruption, losses, sufferings, and adjustments—fall into the purview of the historian," wrote Kroeber in 1954, "rather than the anthropologist whose prime concern is the purely aboriginal, the uncontaminatedly native."[66] Margaret Mead similarly defended her life's work as "the preservation of the record of a vanishing culture for whose loss, we believed, the world would be poorer." It was not the job of anthropologists, she added, to concern themselves with "the immediate welfare and well being of the Indian people on a particular reservation."[67]

In 1976, writing about the observations made by Stephen Powers a hundred years earlier, Berkeley anthropologist Robert Heizer chided the journalist for commenting "unfavorably on the character of the [native] people themselves" without taking into account that "these were the broken, dispirited and decimated survivors of a series of independent tribal nations."[68] You could substitute "Kroeber" for "Powers" here, though Heizer would never have been so impolite or impolitic.

To Joy Sundberg, Kroeber's problem was typical of attitudes expressed by "people when they get into academia. You know, everything's got to fit into a certain slot, and they can never, ever think of how people really are; to them, if it doesn't fit into the little slot, it's not right."[69] Thomas Buckley attributes Yurok antagonism towards Kroeber to his perceived insensitivity to religious and spiritual practices, his lack of attention to Yurok culture after 1849, and his "historical obliviousness towards genocide."[70] It is not so much that Kroeber was oblivious to the relentless attacks on native groups in northwest California after 1849 as that he rarely spoke out or provided leadership about what he knew. "Far more Indians than fell in battle were massacred, or exterminated almost without resistance, merely through fear, suspicion, or because they 'were in the way,'" he told a San Francisco audience in 1909 in a rare moment of bluntness.[71]

In his landmark 1925 *Handbook of the Indians of California*, Kroeber discusses the decline in native populations after contact in a thirteen-page chapter on "Population," some 880 pages into the book. You have to read between the lines and beyond his subdued tone to appreciate the horror of what happened. "There is one Indian in California today," he wrote," for every eight that lived in the same area before the white man came." The Yurok went from 2,500 in 1770 to 700 in 1910.[72]

"The causes for this decline," noted Kroeber, "are obscure": perhaps the result of diseases and changes in diet among a variety of "obvious organic or physiological" factors. Cultural factors too, he suggested, were at work. Here he provided examples from different parts of the state. In the missions, the fathers "were saving souls only at the inevitable cost of lives... The brute upshot of missionization, in spite of its kindly flavor and humanitarian root, was only one thing: death." Why inevitable? A number of poor hill tribes "vanished completely in 60 years...The maladjustment caused by even a light immigration of Americans was enough to push them over the precipice." Why were they standing so close to the edge? "Where [American] cities sprang up, there was soon not an Indian within miles." Where did they go? Reservations for the most part did not help much because "Indians kept running away even faster than they could die." Why did they want to leave?

Kroeber, who could be quite soulful and expressive when describing precontact Yurok culture, is coldly restrained about the human impact of the decline. "The decrease is saddening" was the most emotion he could summon in 1925.[73] By this time, it would have been impossible for Kroeber to ignore the cacophony of moral outrage that preceded and surrounded him, expressed not so much out of sympathy with native peoples as alarm that the civilizers were stooping to the level of the uncivilized.

Carl Meyer, traveling through Humboldt in 1851, was shocked that native people "were being constantly more or less persecuted. A war of destruction was being carried out against them."[74]

"We can conceive of no palliation for women and children slaughter," wrote journalist Bret Harte about the massacre of Wiyot families on Indian Island in February 1860. "We can conceive of no wrong that babe's blood can atone for. Perhaps we do not rightly understand the doctrine of 'extermination.'"[75]

"Never before in history," wrote Stephen Powers in the early 1870s, "has a people been swept away with such terrible swiftness, or appalled into utter and unwhispering silence forever and forever, as were the California Indians by those hundred thousand of the best blood of the nation."[76]

"Early California history is not for babes, nor for sentimentalists," warned historian Josiah Royce in his book *California*, published in 1886. "Nowhere else were we Americans more affected than here, in our lives and conduct, by the feeling that we stood in the position of conquerors in a new land."[77]

"The history of the United States Government's repeated violations of faith with the Indians," wrote Helen Hunt Jackson in her 1881 call to action, "thus convicts us, as a nation, not only of having outraged the principles of justice, which are the basis of international law; and of having laid ourselves open to accusations of both cruelty and perfidy; but of having made ourselves liable to all punishments which follow upon such sins."[78]

"The savages were in the way," wrote Hubert Howe Bancroft, the paterfamilias of California history, in 1890. "It was one of the last human hunts of civilization, and the basest and most brutal of them all."[79]

"To a member of the present generation," wrote Llewellyn Loud in 1918, "learning only a few facts of the early history, it may seem that Humboldt county is preeminently disgraced by a blot of greater foulness than was ever attached to any other locality."[80]

"The principal outdoor sport of the settlers during the 50s and 60s," wrote Edward Curtis in 1922, "seemingly was the killing of Indians. There is nothing else in the history of the United States which approaches the brutal treatment of the California tribes."[81]

"The Indians, driven from their homes and from the lands of their fathers, fled like hunted beasts to inaccessible and desolate spots and secret lairs," wrote historian Rockwell Hunt in 1926. "It is a picture that stirs within the manly breast sensations of shame and remorse."[82]

Throughout the rest of his career, Kroeber rarely made public comments about the terror of the 1850s and when he did, his voice was as restrained as it had been in 1925 when he found the decline in native populations "saddening."[83] His most extensive statement was made in 1954: "No student working with living Indians could escape observing the shattering that their society underwent and listening to tales of their deprivation and spoliation. Briefly," Kroeber continued, "the Indians lost the overwhelming area of their lands; with these, their main habitual subsistence; and with the going of this they lost their way of life, their own culture. All this was taken from them generally without compensation, redress, help, or any but mere pittances of opportunities for readjustment and a new way of life."[84]

The transformation of everyday life after contact, Kroeber conceded in a 1959 article, was "traumatic for many Yurok," with American settlement of the region transforming them into "disadvantaged and second-class Americans." But, he added, "it is not gone into here."[85] This abrupt, unvarnished statement characterizes Kroeber's public posture. It wasn't that he didn't know. He just didn't go into it. Kroeber died in 1960, leaving it to his wife, Theodora, to express what he chose to mostly keep to himself. "The Anglo-Saxons made no place for the Indians in their dreams of wealth and expansion," she wrote with Robert Heizer in 1968; "they set out to enslave them, herd them onto reservations out of the way, let them die, or better, kill them, exterminate them. By and large, they succeeded."[86]

The hands-off tone set by Alfred Kroeber influenced anthropological discourse in California for the first half of the twentieth century. With the exception of the rambunctious Llewellyn Loud, Kroeber's colleagues toed his line by sticking to the "purely aboriginal."[87] One consequence of this moral cowardice was that until World War II a crude and racist imagery about native peoples dominated the public space in California, making it easier to frame their near extermination in the imagery of natural history, subject to inevitable processes of erosion and decline, rather than as the result of a human intervention by the nation's "best blood," a genocide. Many Yurok hold Kroeber accountable because he had resources and authority to influence public opinion. Of course, one person, even Kroeber, did not wield such power, but he became the personification of amnesia.

Grisly Statistics

The "grisly statistics" of changes in the native Californian population tell the story: from an estimated 300,000 in 1769, to 200,000 in 1821 under Spanish occupation, to 30,000 in the 1850s, to a low point of 15,000 in the 1900s.[88] In a period of 150 years, the original population had declined by 95 percent.

It's difficult to know exactly how many died face-to-face—murdered, massacred, or killed as a result of what Governor Peter Burnett called "the irregular mode of warfare"—and how many died from infections, starvation, and despair. Unlike typical expectations of what constitutes genocide, there was no master plan drawn up to identify all who had one drop of Indian blood, or to round them up to be butchered in designated abattoirs. Burnett did not issue secret orders for a "war of extermination," but rather publicly observed "with painful regret" that such a war "must be expected."[89] What is apparent, however, is that the decimation of native peoples in northwest California was bloody, rapid, and different than what happened in most other parts of the United States. The sudden discovery of gold and, soon after, the lure of "sequoia gold" brought hundreds of thousands of miners, settlers, lumber men, and entrepreneurs to the coast within a few years. And they were in a hurry to make their fortunes.

According to a recent study, fifty-six massacres of native

people took place in the Humboldt region from 1850 to 1864.[90] The most heinous massacre—a coordinated affair carried out on Indian Island and at other locations by some of the county's leading landowners and businessmen on February 25, 1860—resulted in the murder of as many as two hundred innocent Wiyot people. Mostly women, children, and elderly were hacked to death with "quiet weapons."[91]

The violence of the 1850s and early 1860s typically involved skirmishes, ambushes, and outright murders. In 1850 a group of prospectors camped near Big Lagoon on their way to the Trinity River goldfields. Overnight, several items were stolen from their camp. Next day, they walked down to O-pyúweg and "came upon a group of miserable huts. My companions," recalled Thomas Gihon, "at once began firing their guns. I protested strongly against this cowardly and wanton murder of poor naked savages, but I knew there were several killed." Gihon's fellow travelers "were all quite jubilant at what had happened, and said that was the way to serve Indians. I bore [the Indians] no ill will—the first aggression came from our side." A few weeks later, a vigilante force returned to Big Lagoon, burned the main Yurok village, and took prisoners back to Trinidad, where they were executed by a firing squad. "I was associated with men who thought nothing of murder," lamented Gihon. "My heart was heavy. I had never seen such an affair before, and it made me sick at heart."[92]

Other attacks and killings followed at Big Lagoon. The Yurok recount the massacre of all the inhabitants of Mä'äts except one young child.[93] In another incident, a local newspaper reported in 1855 that a "private war party" killed several Yurok and burned their homes around the lagoon. But there was resistance as well as victimization. The surviving "Indians of the Lagoon," noted a letter in the *Crescent City Herald*, "are well concealed in the redwoods and are not easily reached, if they can be reached at all."[94] Skirmishes persisted for years "in the vicinity of the big lagoon." In 1862 a group of whites traveling from Gold Bluff to Trinidad via Big Lagoon was "fired on from an ambuscade—about seven or eight shots being fired." They "retraced their steps in quick time, being pursued and fired at by the Indians."[95]

Relations between settlers and natives, even at the height of the conflict, were not always based on violence and terror, nor did all whites act as racist predators. Shortly after Gihon's traumatic experience, Ernest de Massey had a much more peaceable encounter. Eager to document "this primitive man who is now here before my eyes" before he became "mythical and legendary," the French explorer observed the Yurok at work, "tanning the skins of wild animals, making arrows, quivers, and fishing equipment, and weaving excellent baskets." He was especially impressed by their agility and keen senses of hearing, sight, and smell. When de Massey returned to Big Lagoon from a short trip, he found his "comrades who had remained behind visiting with several Indians who were going out on the lagoon to fish in the evening."[96] Similarly, Carl Meyer, who passed through Big Lagoon early in 1851, camped temporarily at O-pyúweg and left with "a young Rhäkwa Indian girl, a prisoner of war whom we received from the Lagoon Indians in exchange for several presents and who we expected to bring back to her tribe as a sign of our peaceable intentions."[97]

Most of the good pioneers who, unlike Gihon, de Massey, and Meyer, dismissed the humanity of the Yurok as they stomped through the land did not benefit from their own racism.[98] The journey from Trinidad to the goldfields was "tedious and expensive,"[99] and the narratives of travelers brimmed with complaints and disappointments: about being price-gouged for necessities, becoming ill and miserable from the rigors of "very hard traveling" along the coast, and being swindled by "speculators and charlatans" promoting the lure of "tinsel gold."[100] And once they reached the mines, they were more likely to get sick than find gold "lying around loose" on the beach or by the river.[101] A local newspaper warned that mercury poisoning could cause "severe sore mouth, spongy gums, tremblings, ulcerations, and swelling of limbs, paralysis and death."[102] Most of the pioneers who expected to get rich quickly "returned impoverished," observed Meyer, "and harvested only regrets and bitterness from their most brilliant hopes."[103]

But whatever hardships newcomers to Humboldt encountered, they paled when compared with the catastrophes suffered by its longtime residents. A decade of massacres, bounty hunting, and epidemics was followed by several decades of forced labor, incarceration, and systematic efforts at cultural annihilation. "With the exception of the Civil War and the military occupation of the

South during Reconstruction," notes historian Clyde Milner, "the U.S. Army throughout the nineteenth century was largely a western army, manning posts and pursuing native peoples."[104]

Around the state, tens of thousands of native people were forced by the rule of law or coerced by economic necessity into what historian James Rawls calls "varieties of exploitation"—as domestic servants, casual laborers, ranch hands, agricultural workers, and gold diggers. The 1850 "Act for the Government and Protection of Indians"—and its amendments in 1860—paralleled the Black Codes of the post–Civil War South, subjecting "vagrant Indians" to debt peonage and indentured slavery, and tribal youth to kidnapping and unpaid labor in the guise of apprenticeship.[105] "Have I not with my own eyes seen Americans steal Indian women and girls for slaves, and compel the men to serve them as guides and burden bearers?" asked Carl Meyer in 1851 as he traveled north from Trinidad.[106]

For those without work, there was confinement. The few Wiyot survivors of the 1860 massacres were locked up in a cattle pen at Fort Humboldt. By the turn of the century, the descendants of the thousands who had lived close to Humboldt Bay numbered fewer than three hundred.[107] After Congress authorized the creation of five reservations in California in 1853—among the first in the country to be built on government land, surrounded by white settlers, and subject to oversight by government agents[108]—thousands of local native people were forced into impoverished misery, first at the Klamath reservation in the 1850s, and after it was abandoned in 1862, at the Smith River and Hoopa Valley reservations.[109]

With the failure of the reservation as an institution of containment and economic development, policy makers and politicians decided that separating native children from their families was the best means to break the bonds of tribal cultures and indoctrinate a new generation into the values of individualism, capital accumulation, Christianity, and American citizenship. By 1902 there were several off-reservation boarding schools throughout the country—including three in California, at Greenville (1895), Fort Bidwell (1898), and Riverside (1902). At the Sherman Institute in Riverside, the lesson plan included unpaid, backbreaking labor harvesting melons and oranges for local farmers.[110] "Our girls learned to sew and set Emily Post's table," says Shaunna McCovey, "while our boys were taught to weed and manicure lawns to prepare for great futures in menial labor."[111]

But rather than produce conformity and assimilation, the boarding school generated persistent resistance in the form of escapes, arson, and recalcitrance. More significantly, as historian David Wallace Adams has observed, "the very institution designed to extinguish Indian identity altogether may have in fact contributed to its very persistence in the form of twentieth-century pan-Indian consciousness."[112] Likely it was at the Sherman Institute that Milton Marks, a Yurok from the village of Morek, developed a political consciousness that would serve him well as a leader of the regional movement to stop the desecration of native graves in the 1970s.

Making History

To Josiah Royce and other concerned reformers of the late nineteenth century, what happened during the shock and awe of the Gold Rush era and its aftermath was a repudiation of "reverence for relations of life" as the new state "entered into the valley of the shadow of death."[113] The widespread moral condemnation of what Bancroft called a "human hunt" was typically rooted in religious imagery. Aggression against Indians, noted Edward Curtis "by those who claim to civilization and Christianity is worse than criminal."[114] But the argument between exterminationists and assimilators, militarists and do-gooders, was a matter of tactics, not principles. Hard-liners advocated better dead than red, while reformers preferred the reservation and the boarding school as instruments of deracination. Even the best "Friends of the Indian" advocated cultural, if not physical extermination, through separating children from their native families and cultural institutions. "All the Indian there is in the race should be dead," Richard Pratt told a social work conference in 1892. "Kill the Indian in him, and save the man."[115] The Protestant reformers' "peace policy," as Richard White has wryly noted, had a "ferocious edge."[116]

From early in the 1850s until well into the twentieth century, public criticism of how the Indian Question was handled in California was interwoven with racialized images of native peoples as doomed by their own degeneracy. "The almost black swar-thy Yurok creeping on all-fours out of their round door-holes" reminded Stephen Powers of "black bears as often as anything."[117] According to a well-regarded historian of northwest California, writing in 1881, "the chief characteristics of all these Indians are filth, superstition, ignorance and degradation. There are a few exceptions as regards intelligence, but even the most intel-ligent among them do not rise above the level of the lowest of the whites."[118] Bancroft, known for his critique of settlers run-ning wild with "money-making" taking precedence over "nation-making,"[119] similarly popularized the prejudice that "taken as a whole the Northern Californian is not such a bad specimen of a savage, as savages go, but filthiness and greed are not enviable qualities, and he has a full share of both."[120]

Occasionally, a lone voice, such as C. E. Kelsey of the North-ern California Indian Association, would make a provocative observation. "We are so familiar," he said, "with the idea that the Indian race is fading away before our own that inquiry is seldom made into the details of the process by which we fade them."[121] But as the first decade of statehood receded into the past, racist views about native people became more flagrant, and in retrospect the brutality of settlers seemed more justifiable. Violence against peaceable Indians was to be deplored—so went the emerging California Story—but as an inferior civilization stuck in the past they were destined to extinction anyway. It was just a matter of time before they dropped off the precipice, to use Kroeber's met-aphorical image, to which they were precariously clinging. Even if American settlers had acted like gentlemen, the thinking went, extinction was predestined; if the settlers were guilty of anything, it was only speeding up the clock. This revisionist view of the past quickly became incorporated into the teaching of history in schools and museums, the commemoration of significant events and people, and the development of the state's cultural identity in magazines, travelogues, adventure stories, and public gatherings.

In the nineteenth and early twentieth centuries, the production of California history was a popular enterprise, regularly incorpo-rated into grandly produced "theatres of memory" in statewide celebrations such as the Columbian Exposition in 1893 and the 1915 Panama-Pacific Exhibition and well-attended local fairs and fiestas.[122] It was not the work of professional historians or a master political authority, but the product of independent writers, journalists, boosters, and businessmen.[123] Most of the early chroniclers of the California Story were not academics: William Henry Brewer was a geologist (before teaching at Yale); Louise Heaven and Helen Bandini, popular writers of fiction; John Hittell, a journalist; and Hubert Bancroft, a businessman who turned a profit off his scholarship. The "astonishing social energy" of multinational, post–Gold Rush California, noted Carey McWilliams, generated a vigorous publishing industry; San Francisco produced more books than the rest of the western United States and by the 1850s surpassed London in the number of its newspapers.[124]

In California, history was a topic of considerable interest, a staple feature of widely read magazines such as *The Land of Sunshine* (founded in 1894) and *Sunset* (1898). And the earliest travel guides included capsule histories and sites of historical interest, just as they do today.[125] Many writers willingly tried out new genres in an effort to reach a wider audience: novelist Louise Heaven wrote *A Youth's History of California* for children in 1867, and Theodore Hittell, an attorney and editor, produced his primer, *Brief History of California*, in 1898. Well into the twentieth century, professional historians took time to write children's textbooks or popular versions of their academic work.[126] In addition to widely read, first-person accounts of exploration, travel, and adventure, such well-known authors as Helen Bandini, Phil Hanna, Gertrude Atherton, Henry Norton, and John McGroarty made California history popular with nationwide audiences.[127] Henry Norton's *The Story of California*, first published in 1913, went through twelve editions by 1934. Bandini and McGroarty were influential in promoting the romantic, nostalgic, fantasy past made famous by Helen Hunt Jackson in *Ramona*, a past in which courageous Spanish missionaries did their best to uplift the backward Indians, and blue-blooded Californios left a legacy of genteel living and Old World romance.[128]

Native people did not fare well in this sanitized version of California's history: they were "all equally stupid and brutish,"[129] backward, a drag on progress, blind to California's largesse, overindulgent and lazy, in need of a firm hand. "There are some forms of savage life we can admire," wrote a commentator in

Land of Sunshine in 1894. "There are others that can only excite our disgust. Of the latter was the Californian Indian."[130] If these charges sound familiar it is because they paralleled and echoed widely distributed claims made about African Americans after the collapse of Reconstruction.

"Our American experience," said Governor Peter Burnett in his address to the legislature in 1851, "has demonstrated the fact that the two races cannot live in the same vicinity in peace....The two races are kept asunder by so many causes, and having no ties of marriage or consanguinity to unite them, they must ever remain at enmity....the inevitable destiny of the [Indian] race is beyond the power or wisdom of man to exert."[131]

Native people were presented as inherently indolent, happy-go-lucky savages. "They are, from habit and prejudice, exceedingly averse to manual labor," said Burnett.[132] "After sleeping and eating, the principal amusement of this primitive people was gambling," observed Henry Norton some sixty years later. "Dancing was another popular amusement, and both sexes indulged. Their festivals began with dancing and speechmaking and ended in the wildest debauches. Everywhere the most prominent characteristic was laziness."[133] Decades later, the same image persisted. "The Indians did not learn to make better tools than the first Indians had made," instructed a book for young children published in 1941.[134] "They were great thieves, wore little or no clothing, and loved music and dancing," observed one of California's most influential historians in 1946.[135]

The alleged failure of California's first inhabitants to endure was explained not by conquest and terror, but by their inherent unfitness and inability to create prosperity. They were so "ignorant and barbarous," observed Louise Heaven in 1867, that they could not even "use or appreciate the blessings by which they were surrounded."[136] Their lack of civilization was evident in their incapacity to develop "the fixed and permanent character of their communities."[137] Whatever worthwhile history predated statehood, it certainly was not to be found in the native past. "No red man living at the Mission of San Francisco," wrote journalist John Hittell in 1878, "founded a family that still exists, or ever distinguished himself sufficiently to deserve special mention of his name in local history." They left "no arts, no literature, no legend, no institutions, no durable monuments of their own designing. The natives of California," continued Hittell, "were as savage in A.D. 542 as they were a thousand years later."[138] Their inability to keep up with the "stern march of progress" meant, sadly, that they had to "give way to another and all-conquering race."[139]

Native people were portrayed as childlike, stuck in the premodern past, unwilling to change or make the most of their environment unless strictly supervised. The Spanish missions that exploited the labor of some sixty thousand neophytes between the 1770s and 1830s figure prominently in this history.[140] Unlike Kroeber, who equated "missionization" with death, the architects of the California Story gave the Spanish period a makeover and blamed Mexico's secularization of the missions (1821–1846) for native Californians' alleged reversion to savagery. Just as Reconstruction had given former slaves too much freedom, they argued, under Mexican rule the California Indians, "free from restraint, soon sank to a low depth of barbarism and vice."[141]

To the author of a typical children's history published in 1908, the missions were a "fairy tale, wonderful and unreal," an oasis of civilization in a "wilderness inhabited only by savage men and wild animals."[142]

According to John McGroarty, "very few of the California Indians occupied a plane of civilization higher than that of beasts when the first white men first found them....They had no names for themselves, no traditions and no religion." When the Franciscans took on the "hopeless task" of their salvation, they confronted "the most mentally slothful human creatures on the face of the earth."[143]

"The natives," wrote Gertrude Atherton in 1914, "proved docile and willing to be baptized." Secularization of the missions was a grave mistake because "in the first place, the Indians had neither the intelligence nor the energy to cultivate even a small estate and make a living out of it; and in the second, they were still the weaker race."[144]

A 1922 high school textbook written by two leading academics provided a familiar, comforting gloss on the missions' deadly policies: "The friars treated the Indians kindly, as if they were children. But sometimes the Indians ran away because they did not like to work, and preferred the free life of the mountains and valleys."[145]

The coastal natives, suggested another 1922 textbook, "had so much in the way of nature's bounty that there was no inducement to struggle for a living.…Although they had made no progress for themselves in civilization, they were capable of learning readily all the mission fathers taught them." Under the instruction of the Franciscans, they learned how "to build their homes, to earn their food, to grow their crops, herd their flocks, and to be clean, and, above all, they were Christianized." The "sad story" began when the missions ended and Indians were prematurely propelled into freedom. "They still needed care as a child needs careful watchfulness and training before he can become a self-supporting man."[146]

"It cannot be denied," observed the authors of a popular history in 1929, "that the aboriginals of California stood lower in the scale of humanity—physically, morally, and mentally—than any of the other tribes of North America.…The Dons were not hard masters, and life went on happily enough for the original owners of the land."[147]

By the 1930s, when amnesia had become an acceptable way to deal with the genocidal past, a popular textbook could relegate the ruin of California's native peoples to a footnote.[148] Moreover, their characterization as racially inferior, predestined to doom, and salvageable only by an authoritarian regime prevailed well into the twentieth century in popular literature. The eugenic movement of the 1920s refueled the racial argument made by John Hittell in 1878 that there was a "physical weakness in the Indian blood."[149] The Europeans no doubt hastened the demise of California's Indians, observed journalist Phil Hanna in 1935, but they "would have perished just the same had the Spaniards not come to these shores" because "within them was the ineradicable germ of disintegration."[150] Even Sherburne Cook, whose 1943 book documented in great detail the devastation caused by settlers and militias, speculated that "their possibly inferior physique" predisposed native people to disease.[151]

And so this barrage of racialized insults continued. "The depressing story began with the secularization of the missions," observed Robert Cleland in 1944. "After the mission communities were dispersed, nothing was done by individuals or institutions to improve the lot of the California Indian. No attempt was made to raise his standard of living, provide him with even the rudiments of an education, or save his immortal soul—if, indeed, he had an immortal soul to save."[152] Native peoples on the West Coast were "very primitive," noted a 1953 guide to California. "Lacking a challenge in life, they lived like drones and evolved no culture worthy of the name. Actually, they seemed to be moving backwards culturally as the centuries passed....On occasion, when a brave was killed in battle, they did not hesitate to eat each other."[153]

The notion of the Far West as a site of natural beauty, a Sleeping Beauty awaiting Prince Charming's manly hand to whip it into alert shape, is an enduring motif in California's historiography. It took the right kind of racially constituted settlers to discover and exploit its "undiscovered glories."[154] "They came! And waked me from my sleep," wrote poet Clifford Trembly in 1905.[155] "The history of the state begins in 1542 when the first white man set forth on the shores of California," noted one of the first comprehensive high school textbooks.[156] This cultural invention, and wishful thinking about the purity of Spanish blood, became a standard view by the early twentieth century, though the chronology often shifted. For Grace Dawson, the arrival of "white men" occurred a couple of centuries later "with the ringing of Father Serra's mission bells in 1769."[157]

When Robert Cleland observed in 1930 that "by origin and tradition California is essentially an Anglo-Saxon state," he reflected a prejudice that was widely shared by two generations of writers, journalists, editors, and academics.[158] By this time, whether depicted nostalgically as romantic curiosities or racially as a precursor to modernity, native peoples had become a footnote to history. The hundreds of pages of relatively nuanced anthropological observations made by Alfred Kroeber and his colleagues in the 1920s hardly made a dent in the public arena. As for the "tale of disgrace to our people"—as Josiah Royce described California's "blind nativism" in 1886[159]—it would not be until the rise of the Red Power movement in the 1960s that the issue of genocide would get a public hearing.

* * *

After completing the research for this chapter, I felt weighed down—as you may after reading it—by the accumulation of racialized and racist images, and accounts of commonplace violence that saturated public media for so many decades. But we need to feel and ponder this weight in order to appreciate what follows. Of course, as we shall see, there has been longstanding opposition by native people to these images, and occasional voices of sanity can be heard in the chorus of prattle about the "vanishing race." But the overwhelming impression of a century of public information about the Indian Problem is one of dehumanization and inferiority, swaddled in romanticism. So it is not surprising to me that the Smithsonian's National Museum of the American Indian—the first national cultural institution "about Indians run by Indians," authorized by Congress in 1989 and opened to the public in 2004—for the most part sidesteps the history of physical and cultural subjugation, choosing to focus on everyday life before contact, and to emphasize the point that the disappeared not only have been found, but are a vital and diverse presence on the continent.[160] "We are not a museum of history or anthropology or archaeology," a guide told me when I visited the museum in 2010. "We are a museum of living peoples."

Meanwhile, native peoples face not only a long struggle to humanize and add complexity to the remembrance of their ancestors, buried in misinformation and amnesia, but also the challenge of what to do about the unauthorized excavation of hundreds of thousands of gravesites in which their ancestors' remains were buried. Throughout the West from the late eighteenth to late twentieth centuries, there was a brisk trade in native body parts and funerary artifacts, propelled by the popularity of commercial and recreational "collecting," scientific curiosity, and the rise of the heritage industry. What happened in northwest California was a small part of an international enterprise, a realization I stumbled into during a family trip to England a few years ago.

FOUR
Unpleasant Work

"And so they are ever returning to us,
the dead."
—W. G. Sebald, 1993

Trivial Articles

"Oh no, we haven't visited the British Museum," said Cecilia as she reviewed our checklist of things to do with our ten-year-old grandson, Nate, on the last full day of his first trip to London, in June 2009. So with lunches packed, we walked over from our flat in Fleet Street to the museum. Our strategy was to expose him to the variety of museums and galleries, give him a taste of a particular exhibition or display, stop before he got bored, and discuss the experience over food.

Our first stop at the overwhelming British Museum was an easy decision: the display of Egyptian funerary materials. The two-thousand-year-old mummies, as they are popularly known, are a big attraction to kids. The display of preserved human bodies or even skeletons is not common in the United States, unless expressly permitted by donors or as part of an exhibition dealing with the origins of the species.[1] The remains of Native Americans used to be a staple of American museums not too long ago, but today only models are displayed. The Museo Nacional de Antropologia in Madrid, however, still shows off skulls of "primitive peoples," the skeleton of a nineteenth-century "giant," and a tableau of "racial types," including cartoonish reproductions of thick-lipped Africans.[2] And in London, the British Museum displays its star-power attraction in a large, refurbished, and well-organized room with expansive cabinets and clear explanatory texts. You would think Egyptians would be picketing the place and demanding repatriation, but the only controversy during our visit was whether or not the Elgin Marbles should be returned to Greece.

Cecilia, Nate, and I joined the procession of teachers and mommies shepherding their charges in blazers and pleated skirts past the shrouded bodies, surrounded by objects needed to "ensure the transition of the individual from earthly existence to immortality." I found the whole experience unnerving and troubling, but it was a teaching moment. Over tomato and cheese sandwiches we discussed issues of patrimony. I was ready for a long discussion about the ethics of displaying the dead to strangers, but it was over fast. "They should give them back to Egypt," said Nate succinctly. "Can I have dessert?"

After lunch, Cecilia and I agreed to a division of labor: while she took Nate to check out the samurai exhibition, I popped into the JP Morgan Chase Gallery of the North Americas to see how the British Museum deals with its trove of Native American artifacts. The room is stuffed with objects from all over the United States, displayed artistically. It is a familiar hodgepodge of stuff that you would find in most Indian rooms of museums, beautifully displayed and minimally linked to historical contexts.[3] In the California section what immediately caught my eye were two elk-antler spoons familiar to me from the research I have been doing on the history of the Yurok in Humboldt. They look exactly like artifacts I have seen in collections back home.

A few days later, after we had sent Nate back to California, I returned to the Centre for Anthropology to do research on the two spoons and the museum's other Yurok artifacts. While the museum's description of the objects and their uses is shaky, its evidence of provenience and provenance is compelling.[4] The spoons were almost certainly acquired from "friendly disposed" Yurok traders by the Vancouver expedition when it was in Trinidad harbor in May 1793. The Yurok were eager to do business for iron—"in their estimation the most valuable commodity we had to offer," recalled Captain George Vancouver, who was not at all impressed by the "trivial articles" that his crew received in return.[5]

While the journals and diaries kept by the men who led expeditions to the Pacific Coast in the eighteenth century were closely guarded and edited by the governments who paid the bills, the accumulated "curiosities" for the most ended up in personal collections and family cabinets, at auctions, and eventually dispersed to museums throughout Europe, often without information about provenience.[6]

The trading in curiosities by European expeditions of the late eighteenth century was secondary to their military, diplomatic, and scientific objectives, but nevertheless was important to the mission and to many individuals who were avid collectors. When the imposing Royal Museum of Ethnology (Königliches Museum für Völkerkunde) opened in Berlin in 1886, it was already too small to house its collection of forty thousand items.[7] Alejandro Malaspina's expedition for Spain, as well as Vancouver's, carried instructions to gather native artifacts.[8] During Vancouver's 1790–1795 Pacific expedition surveying the North American coast for the British government, six of his leading officers, plus Archibald Menzies—the *Discovery's* surgeon and naturalist—a couple of midshipmen, and George Hewett, surgeon's mate, all amassed their own personal collections, most of which have disappeared into other private collections or been lost or destroyed. A few inventories survived to give us a sense of how important the artifacts were to the expedition and how much interest they later generated in England.[9]

Menzies described several native items he acquired in "Port Trinidad," including "baskets of different kinds, some curiously variegated & so closely worked as to hold water."[10] George Hewett, like any serious hobbyist, recorded his haul of more than five hundred objects, item by item, in a small notebook. There are eighteen items listed under "Trinidada," including "horn spoon" and "bone box."[11] "Mr. Hewett was evidently fond of natural history, and made note of anything that struck him as remarkable," observed archaeologist Charles Read in an 1891 talk about the Vancouver expedition.[12]

After Hewett's death, his family preserved some of his

collection and the small quarto volume in which he had listed his acquisitions. Many of his "Pacific curiosities," noted a relative, were lost or had disappeared. But in 1891, almost one hundred years after the *Discovery* docked in Trinidad Bay, a resourceful British Museum curator, Sir Augustus Wollaston Franks, bought what was left of Hewett's collection, including his inventory and Yurok items, for 150 English pounds, not a small amount of money in its day.[13] "Collecting is a hereditary disease and I fear incurable," Franks once admitted.[14] Today spoons made of elk antler—two of the "trivial articles" collected by Vancouver's crew in Trinidad in 1793—are elegantly displayed in one of the world's most famous museums, where they are reverentially described as "very fine carving" with "finely incised decoration."[15]

Over time, the British Museum has stocked and exhibited many Yurok items. In 1891 Charles Read examined a bow of cedar wood, bound in a leather thong—"an undoubted example of the bow used by the Indians residing around Trinidad Bay in Vancouver's time."[16] In 1952 American archaeologists Robert Heizer and John Mills identified a purse made from elk antler in the museum's collection.[17] And when California anthropologist Travis Hudson visited the British Museum in 1983 to 1984, he found several Yurok artifacts that I could not find in the museum's database in 2009.[18] Perhaps the rest are somewhere in storage, uncatalogued, or have been exchanged for other items. This tendency to lose track of native artifacts was quite common in museums before electronic record keeping became prevalent. Berkeley's Hearst Museum too seems to have lost some of its native heads and body parts over the years.[19]

As a result of numerous expeditions to North America in the late eighteenth and nineteenth centuries, hundreds of thousands of native artifacts were transported to Europe. Ferdinand Deppe, a former gardener for the Royal Court of Prussia, sold native baskets that he had collected in California to the Zoological Museum in Berlin in 1836. A few years later, the Royal Museum of Ethnology acquired a large collection of artifacts from the Smithsonian and from German collectors.[20] "Our excavations of ethnological material were particularly rich," reported Paul Schumacher after excavations of Chumash and Tongva (Gabrielino) graves in southern California, "and we collected about four thousand skeletons, which we brought into daylight."[21] A skull collected on

Santa Rosa Island was included in the United States display at the Columbian Historical Exposition in Madrid in 1892.[22]

By the late nineteenth century, "a staggering quantity of material," notes historian Douglas Cole, had "left the hands of their native creators and users for the private and public collections of the European world." Researchers and scientists were unable to keep up with the avalanche of materials that filled up the basements and display cases of museums.[23]

The drive to accumulate curiosities in the late eighteenth century was motivated in part by trade and exploration of the so-called New World, as well as "natural inquisitiveness,"[24] but it also continued a longstanding tradition of amassing and displaying natural, found, and made objects regarded as exotica or subjects for scientific investigation. The nineteenth-century museum popularized the "cabinets of curiosities" that had been reserved for men of wealth and status since the Renaissance. Instead of hundreds of items crammed into a room or display case to impress a small circle of friends, the modern museum could now store and show off to huge public audiences some of the millions of native artifacts imported from the Americas.

Compared to their European counterparts, American museums—in particular the Smithsonian Institution (founded in 1846), California Academy of Natural Sciences in San Francisco (1853), Army Medical Museum (1862), Harvard's Peabody Museum (1866), American Museum of Natural History in New York (1869), and Chicago's Field Museum (1893)—got a late start in the business of collecting, but once they joined the fray, they made up for lost time.

By the second half of the nineteenth century, government officials and wealthy private entrepreneurs had amassed huge collections, some of which made their way into museums through donations and bequests. Collecting became more comprehensive, deliberate, and competitive.[25] Some collectors were well informed about the materials they collected. "These Indians made objects that would deserve praise even in Europe," observed Vasily Golovnin, the Russian navigator, about baskets and hats that he acquired in the San Francisco Bay Area in 1818. "In my collection of curiosities I have many items made by them...They are not only well made but are very attractive."[26]

Museum directors and curators worldwide traded items with each other like baseball cards in order to achieve "a kind of Noah's ark collection, two from each area, two of each type."[27] In 1910 Berlin's ethnology museum paid Alfred Kroeber six hundred dollars to collect "something from all cultural property of a tribe, namely the cultural goods characteristic of the relevant tribe." Kroeber's first shipment included some fifty artifacts from northern California—including twined burden baskets, cradleboards, and pestles.[28] When I visited the Ethnologisches Museum Berlin, as the Museum für Völkerkunde is now known, in October 2010, I found several familiar materials from California—including a soup basket sent by Kroeber and an elk-antler spoon—displayed in a cabinet filled with "objects of value and prestige."

As a result of donations and institutional exchanges, Yurok artifacts can be found in museums all over the world: the Naprstek Museum in Prague, Museum für Völkerkunde in Vienna, Nationalmuseet in Copenhagen, National Museum of Finland in Helsinki, Naturhistorische Gesellschaft in Nuremberg, Göteborgs Etnografiska Museum in Sweden, Indianermuseum der Stadt in Zurich, Auckland Institute and Museum in New Zealand, and several regional museums in addition to the British Museum in England.[29] The only museum in California that collected ethnographic material prior to 1900 was the California Academy of Sciences, and the 1906 earthquake destroyed most of its collections and documentation.[30]

The Fresher the Better

Between the early 1780s—when Thomas Jefferson tried his hand at digging up a huge gravesite near his home—and the 1970s, when the Red Power movement began to put amateur and professional archaeologists on the defensive, the discovery and removal of native remains was promoted as good sport, entrepreneurial initiative, and sound science.[31] It is difficult to know exactly how many native skeletons were dug up in the United States during these 190 years, but estimates range from the Native American Rights Fund's conservative figure of six hundred thousand to the one million suggested by other experts.[32] It was a common practice by the 1790s, when Alejandro Malaspina's expedition dug up burial grounds in a Yakutat village in Alaska and took away ceremonial materials for the Royal Museum in Madrid.[33]

Captain George Vancouver, who was under orders to be "a diplomat as well as an explorer" and to develop relations with tribal groups on the West Coast, prohibited the looting of graves, a rule which was "not entirely" respected.[34] During the expedition's survey of Puget Sound in 1792, it was so common to see skulls, bones, and "other vestiges of the human body...promiscuously scattered about the beach in great numbers" that Vancouver considered the possibility that the area was "a general cemetery for the whole of the surrounding country." He witnessed and described the burials of natives in canoes, in trees, and underground but told his men to respect even abandoned cemeteries. "The general knowledge I had obtained from experience of the regard which all savage nations pay to their funeral solemnities," Vancouver wrote in his memoir, "made me particularly solicitous to prevent any indignity from being wantonly offered to their departed friends."[35] Next year, he reported the discovery of "a sepulcher of a peculiar character," probably on Vancouver Island:

> It was a kind of vault, formed partly by the natural cavity of the rocks, and partly by the rude artists of the country. It was lined with boards, and contained some fragments of warlike implements, lying near a square box covered with mats and very curiously corded down. This we naturally conjectured contained the remains of some person of consequence, and it much excited the curiosity of our party; but as the further examination could not possibly have served any useful purpose, and might have given umbrage and pain to the friends of the deceased, should it be their custom to visit the repositories of their dead, I did not think it right that it should be disturbed. Not from motives of superstition as some were then pleased to sup-pose, but from a conviction that it was highly proper to restrain our curiosity when it tended to no good purpose whatever.[36]

But some of Vancouver's men, according to George Hewett, were unable to restrain their acquisitiveness. They dismantled funeral sites and even used a burial canoe for a sentry box.[37]

Vancouver's sensitivity to the native dead was the exception to what soon became the widespread practice of indiscriminate exhumation.

As a child Thomas Jefferson witnessed a group of Indians taking a detour from their journey to visit a barrow—a large mound of earth above a cemetery—near the River Rivanna in Virginia, where they "staid about it some time, with expressions which were construed to be those of sorrow, [before] they returned to the high road, which they had left about half a dozen miles to pay this visit, and pursued their journey."[38] Some thirty years later, Jefferson excavated the barrow, knowing such sites to be "repositories of the dead," but curious about the people that had been buried there, and how and why they had been buried in this way. By contemporary standards, his digging was careful: he took notes and measurements on his findings as he unearthed the skulls, jawbones, teeth, and ribs of children and adults. "I conjectured that in this barrow," he wrote, "might have been a thousand skeletons," but he did not conjecture about whether anybody might be offended by his excavation of a place that had "considerable notoriety among the Indians."[39]

The practice of excavating native gravesites was rooted in the furious competition that took place among the country's leading museums during the nineteenth century as they vied to become showplaces of American progress through scientific study. Medical schools also hired grave diggers—ironically known as "resurrectionists"—to dig up the recently dead in the thousands so that students could perform and learn from autopsies. It was mostly the bodies of the black dead, poor and powerless, which were victimized by this practice.[40] Scientists were more interested in the bodies of Indians, who, it was believed, had been frozen in time, unchanging since the Stone Age, and whose remains were therefore thought to hold the key to the "secrets of human origins," as well as provide physical evidence for claims about European superiority and native degeneracy.[41] The notion that native peoples had resisted progress or only experienced change as a result of migration or external disruption was also a common assumption of early anthropology. Any creativity on the part of natives peoples, notes historian Bruce Trigger, was only "grudgingly admitted."[42]

Some scientists were interested in finding evidence for the doctrine of polygenesis, which assumed the existence of multiple races, hierarchically organized, the result of either divine creation or human development. The body was supposed to reveal and provide proof of the essential biological differences between superior and inferior civilizations. Even those who subscribed to the doctrine of monogenesis—a belief in a single human race—also promoted racist concepts of evolution by arguing that the more civilized societies became, the more they would approximate modern Europeans.[43] "The most primitive were doomed to vanish as a result of the spread of civilization," says Trigger in his interpretive history of archaeological thought, "since no amount of education could compensate for the thousands of years during which natural selection had failed to adapt them biologically to a more complex and orderly way of life." So what in fact was a political and social activity—conquest and repression—was rationalized as "natural" and "biological."[44] Or in the words of an 1841 article in the *American Phrenological Journal*, the "ultimate extinction [of Indians] is an event which is approaching, and whose accomplishment nothing earthly can prevent."[45]

The publication of *Crania Americana* (1839) by Samuel Morton, a Philadelphia physician considered the "father of American physical anthropology," became a rationale and apology for scientific racism and this widespread view that native peoples were biologically predestined to extinction.[46] Morton was the first scientist in the United States to engage in the systematic collection and classification of crania. By the time of his death, he had amassed close to one thousand skulls. He believed that cranial capacity was racially determined—the bigger the better—and races could be ranked by the sizes of their brains.[47] Morton encouraged doctors and military personnel on the frontier, where collecting became a cottage industry, to send him skulls, and they did in such numbers that his laboratory acquired the reputation of being an "American Golgotha."[48] This collaboration between local collectors and established scientists would become the foundation of modern anthropology and last well into the twentieth century.

Excavation of native gravesites in the nineteenth century was not the monopoly of racist scientists or museums eager to display freaks and oddities. Many archaeologists and collectors genuinely believed that they were making a contribution to the salvage and protection of a "vanishing race."[49] When the French traveler Ernest de Massey came through Big Lagoon in 1850, he made a point of "trying to learn everything I can [because] another fifty years more and this civilization will be gone."[50] Another explorer, traveling along California's northwest coast in 1851, came across the corpse of a "dead old Indian" that he considered sending to an "anatomical museum."[51]

Even antiracist anthropologists insisted on digging up native remains because they wanted to prove the commonalities of a single human race. "It is most unpleasant work to steal bones from a grave, but what is the use, someone has to do it," Franz Boas noted in his diary in 1888. "Yesterday I wrote to the Museum in Washington asking whether they would consider buying skulls this winter for $600; and if they will, I shall collect assiduously."[52] The going rate for a skull was between $3 and $5, depending on its condition.[53]

In 1897 Boas provided housing at the American Museum of Natural History for six Eskimos whom the arctic explorer Robert Peary imported at Boas's request to New York from Greenland like an exotic commodity. When one of them, Qisuk, quickly died from tuberculosis, Boas (and his young assistant, Alfred Kroeber) presided over a mock funeral, orchestrated for the benefit of Qisuk's son, Minik.[54] Meanwhile, Qisuk's bones were surreptitiously incorporated into the museum's collection and his brain sent to Aleš Hrdlička (1869–1943), a Czech physical anthropologist on the staff of the National Museum in Washington, D.C.[55]

A few years later, when Kroeber was in charge of "the last wild Indian in North America," housed in the Museum of Anthropology on Parnassus Heights in San Francisco,[56] he faced a dilemma following Ishi's death (also from tuberculosis): whether to preserve his remains in the interests of science or give the man he considered a friend a dignified burial. Kroeber was out of town when Ishi died. "I must ask you as my personal representative," Kroeber wrote his assistant Edward Gifford the day before Ishi died in March 1916, "to yield nothing at all under any circumstances. If there is any talk of the interests of science, say for me that science can go to hell. We propose to stand by our friends." But science trumped humanity: an autopsy was performed and

Ishi's brain removed before he was cremated and given a Christian burial. "What happened," Gifford informed his boss, "amounts to a compromise between science and sentiment with myself on the side of sentiment."[57]

In October, after Kroeber's return to San Francisco, he wrote to Hrdlička, offering to send Ishi's preserved brain to the National Museum. "There is no one here who can put it to scientific use," Kroeber wrote Hrdlička. "I hardly need say," Hrdlička replied, "that we shall be very glad to receive and take care of Ishi's brain." He instructed Kroeber that the brain should be "packed in plenty of absorbent cotton saturated with liquid in which it is preserved." Kroeber complied.[58]

Hrdlička made a career out of amassing a "racial brain collection" and developing the Smithsonian into one of the country's largest warehouses of crania, especially after it absorbed the Army Medical Museum's collection. Hrdlička himself had dug up an Indian burial ground at Larsen Bay, Alaska, in 1900 and taken away the remains of eight hundred Konaig natives.[59] By the time of his death in 1943, he had collected close to twenty thousand skulls.[60] There was nothing secretive in this kind of enterprise; the public display of skeletons was popular, as was the exhibition of living Indians. During the 1890s and 1900s, international and commercial fairs held in major American cities routinely included tribal groups on display and at work, a popular entertainment posing as ethnological science.[61]

Warren Moorehead, a "notorious collector," ransacked hundreds of graves in Ohio in the early 1890s, excavating native remains for display at the World's Columbian Exposition in Chicago in 1893, where they appealed to "the morbid curiosity of the public."[62] In 1897 thousands of New Yorkers paid a quarter each to scrutinize the six Eskimos that Robert Peary had brought from Greenland for Boas. And when the local sheriff put Ishi in a padded cell in the country town of Oroville in 1911, he drew the attention of three thousand visitors.[63] Kroeber may have rejected the crassly commercial aspects of Indian sideshows, but he made Ishi into a popular Sunday attraction at the Museum of Anthropology in San Francisco; and, despite his knowledge of Yahi taboos involving death, he apparently didn't think twice about housing Ishi in a building that also was a depository for the university's large collection of human remains.

In 1914 Hrdlička showed off some of his collection of skeletons and crania in San Diego at the Panama-California Exposition, all neatly arranged into a tableau of racial hierarchy, from "thoroughbred" white Americans to "full-blood American negro," and so on.[64] By this time, Hrdlička was well known in the emerging field of anthropology. His main claim to fame was a how-to manual for collectors of "specimens for physical anthropology," published in 1904.

Hrdlička encouraged "every intelligent person to call attention to the discovery of an ancient burial place or cemetery." Of course, collectors needed to get "proper consent or legal authorization" and approach their task "with the greatest delicacy and with profound respect" because "the savage as well as the civilized" holds "reverential beliefs concerning the dead." Meanwhile, Hrdlička advised his readers where they could find native gravesites. Look for "protruding slabs of stone, or numerous potsherds of better class of pottery." Look for "signs of sedentary people" because you will find "at least a part of the burials somewhere near, and clustered."[65]

Hrdlička was particularly interested in acquiring bodies before putrefaction set in because he believed that the brain was the key to understanding the "different grades within the human species itself." He noted that already by the turn of the century "Indian skeletal constituents" were "more abundant and comparatively easy of collection and transportation," but "the brain of a North American Indian has never been described, nor is there, so far as known, a good specimen of such a brain in existence." While recognizing that the harvesting of native brains was a "delicate and difficult matter," he nevertheless provided detailed guidelines about how to remove, preserve, and transport a brain—mailing costs to be paid for by the Smithsonian. "Open the tentorium as you come to it wholly, and, helping with one hand from within, receive the brain into the palm of the hand."

Better still, urged Hrdlička, "whenever possible all work connected with removing the brain may be obviated by sending the entire head...The fresher the product, the better."[66] So much for consent, delicacy, and respect.

The Collecting Bug

Throughout the late nineteenth century and the early part of the twentieth, anthropologists of every political tendency got in on the search for artifacts and skeletons "like bargain hunters at a fire sale," in the words of historian Steven Conn.[67] Exhumation of native people's remains also became a recreational fad, driven partly by a romantic nostalgia for the past, and partly by a mania for accumulating objects for prestige or profit. Digging became an end in itself, a pastime and preoccupation for everybody from boy scouts to country doctors, men's clubs, philanthropic ladies, wealthy collectors, and amateur archaeologists.[68] "The collecting bug seized me," admitted George Gustav Heye, who needed to build a museum to contain his collection, "and I was lost."[69]

The sons of privilege at Yale even named themselves after their hobby. In 1869 a Yale alumnus asked a colleague at the Smithsonian if he could acquire a "spare human cranium" to present to his club, the Order of Skull and Bones.[70] In the early twentieth century, rumors circulated that members of the hush-hush society had broken into the grave of the Indian leader Goyathlay, popularly known as Geronimo, who had died in captivity in 1909 and was buried at Fort Sill, Oklahoma. A recent failed lawsuit, which claimed that the club kept the Apache warrior's cranium in the Tomb, their hangout at Yale, relies on a letter written by a senior Bonesman in 1918 in which he informed a colleague, "The skull of the worthy Geronimo The Terrible, exhumed from its tomb at Fort Sill by your club...is now safe inside the T[omb] together with his well worn femurs, bit & saddle horn."[71] One of the alleged conspirators was Prescott Bush, grandfather of a political dynasty, who may have taken his penchant for headhunting too literally when he was based at Fort Sill in 1918.

Experts on the case are divided. Judith Schiff, an archivist at Yale, thinks "it has a very strong likelihood of being true, since [the letter] was written so close to the time."[72] David Miller, a history professor at the University of Oklahoma, is convinced that the Bonesmen "could not have located Geronimo's grave in 1918 since it was unmarked at the time."[73] It's plausible that the Bonesmen dug up an anonymous Indian or soldier from Fort Sill and made up the story that the remains were those of Geronimo to impress the lads back at Yale. It is not hard to imagine Prescott Bush and his chums trying to come up with an action that would enhance their Tomb cred. Or maybe they purchased the skull from a trader and, back at Yale, somebody made up the name Geronimo as a stand-in for the generic Indian: "Say hi to Geronimo, he's our mascot. Charge!"

Whether the claims about the fate of Geronimo's skull are true or not, there is no doubt that for the countless middle-class men who joined fraternal clubs in the second half of the nineteenth century, notes historian Curtis Hinsley Jr., "backyard archaeology served as a field for male play."[74] By the time that Kroeber's team started acquiring native materials in California in the 1900s, European expeditions, self-taught archaeologists, and enterprising collectors had already amassed millions of items. Looting and theft certainly played a role in this process of extraction, but there was also an enterprising market in which savvy Yurok and other native groups traded artifacts, as well as knowledge, for cash and resources.[75]

Some of Kroeber's first purchases of baskets and knives, collected for the California Academy of Sciences, were destroyed in the San Francisco earthquake.[76] With funding from philanthropist Collis Huntington and oversight by Franz Boas, in 1902 he collected many artifacts, of which some two hundred and seventy, including deerskin dance regalia, eagle feathers, and elk-antler spoons, ended up at the American Museum of Natural History in New York.[77] Much of what he collected stayed closer to home, stored at the Museum of Anthropology in San Francisco. Kroeber felt an urgency to salvage evidence of "uncontaminatedly native" cultures, to successfully compete with other museums for "two of everything," and to put on exhibitions that would attract popular and financial support. Berkeley's department of anthropology and the museum were the first to be established west of the Mississippi, and Kroeber carved out the region as his sphere of influence. "I do not want to collect in this state for any institution but our own," Kroeber wrote Boas in 1905. "I should very much like to keep you out of the state altogether."[78] He had similar advice for his colleagues in Berlin: "abandon the California field altogether. We cannot secure specimens for you that no longer exist," he lied.[79]

When Thomas Waterman left the Bay Area for Humboldt County in 1909 to begin mapping Yurok geography, Kroeber gave him his marching orders in a twenty-five-page memo titled "Specimens." He was primarily interested in "old pieces that have seen use."[80] Here are some of the items he instructed Waterman to buy:

> A small forehead band of fine condor feathers worn
> by the doctor women so as to hang over the eyes....
> The entrance door to a sweathouse [in] an abandoned
> rancheria about six miles below Johnsons, belongs to a
> hunchback Indian named Thompson...An old Indian
> house—the whole house, a couple of miles downstream
> from Knipeu, where the old woman without a nose
> lives....The old man [owner] said that next time he would
> be ready to sell the whole house.

Kroeber was a shrewd dealer and had not the slightest shred of sentimentality when it came to haggling with the Yurok. He didn't trust one of his dealers in Woxtek because "he does too much bargaining in advance." He told Waterman to pay no more than one dollar for the ceremonial feathers. As for the sweathouse door, another important artifact, "two or three dollars should be high pay for this piece, as it is absolutely no more use to owner, but we must have it whatever the cost." And he hoped to get the whole house for fifty dollars, plus another twenty-five for transporting it to Requa. It was important, Kroeber told Waterman, to negotiate the whole transaction at the same time. "If you bought the house and then arranged for transportation, the Indians would undoubtedly stick you for transportation."

Already a veteran anthropologist at age thirty-three when he gave Waterman these instructions, Kroeber had no compunction about trying to hustle native men twice his age or dismissing their desire to preserve their past. "The intrinsic value of an old house is practically nothing these days, and the people are attached to them chiefly for sentimental reasons."[81] Waterman learned well from his cagey teacher. "Please buy Old Charley's house," he wrote an aspiring amateur anthropologist in Klamath a couple of years later, "and ship it down to us by steamer. Say as little about it as possible, and hire some Indian to fill his canoe full of planks."[82]

Kroeber was particularly interested in purchasing ceremonial regalia, and he had his contacts on the lookout for likely acquisitions. Writing from her home in Requa in 1919, Ruth Roberts told him about "a carved stone figure of a man that Lagoon George dug up at Peckwan," and two "devil's costumes."[83] Many years later, a missionary working with the Yurok informed Kroeber that "an old Yurok Indian lady" wanted to sell "a large collection of rare Indian relics." The now senior academic took time to personally reply, still interested in the possibility of buying "valuable objects which the old people used in dances and like treasures."[84]

Today you can find legacies of this early twentieth-century

4.1 Door of Yurok house, 1907, collected by Waterman and photographed by Kroeber.

penchant for digging and collecting throughout California. There are pre-1850 native artifacts from Humboldt and Del Norte counties on show or in storage at several places in the northwest region, from professionally curated displays to funky tourist stops: the Clarke Historical Museum in Eureka, the museum of the Trees of Mystery in Klamath, Chapman's Gem and Mineral Museum in Rio Dell, the University of California's Hearst Museum in Berkeley, and the Favell Museum in Klamath Falls. And if you are in the market, say, for "Big Lagoon Yurok Indian artifacts," you could go online and purchase for less than one hundred dollars a "large and colorful pendant with fine serrations between 800-1,000 years old,"[85] or visit a trade show specializing in antiquities to buy rare Wiyot items for thousands of dollars.[86] A foot-long ceremonial zoomorph in good condition can be sold for as much as thirty thousand dollars on the private market.

What you typically will not be told is that many local "Indian relics" preserved in university labs, museum display cases, private collections, and tourist attractions were taken from inside graves; and that often collectors also removed skulls and bones to show off to their friends or ship off to anthropologists in Berkeley in exchange for scientific advice or fraternal recognition.

Today it is a crime in California to engage in the "willful injury, disfiguration, defacement, or destruction of any object or thing of archaeological or historical interest or value," but until the 1970s digging up native burial sites for pleasure, science, or profit was for the most part authorized and popular, despite longstanding and persistent native protests. Sleuthing the locations of gravesites and carrying out exhumations was a thriving enterprise that yielded hundreds of thousands of native body parts and millions of artifacts, to which northern California contributed more than its fair share.[87]

FIVE

Joint Ventures

"White people came through this area in
the 1920s and '30s and took everything
Indian they could get their hands on.
Every college, every souvenir hunter
wanted Indian artifacts. Back then there
was no way to stop them. Now we can at
least try to protect our ancestors."
—Joy Sundberg, Yurok, 1981[1]

The Living and the Dead

The Yurok observe taboos and carefully honed rituals with respect
to their dead, just as all social groups do, my own included. When
my parents died, my sister Sue shuddered at the idea of cremation, and my brother Steve and I respected her preference for
interment. When my son Daniel died at home in Chico in 2006,
he left written instructions about his desire for a funeral at Big
Lagoon, but we still had to make decisions about how to remember his life and observe his death. Our ceremony imaginatively
combined modern and ancient elements: cremation and a Viking
ritual in proximity to a familiar place. While I know of course that
Daniel's remains were absorbed into the waters of the lagoon,

streams, and ocean, I am comforted by visiting the exact place at the edge of the lagoon from which we launched his ashes on a burning raft. Since his funeral, each time I stay at Big Lagoon I search the beach for a piece of jade to place on Daniel's memorial bench, which sits in our cabin, and I do not feel at ease until I have done so.

Though my rituals are personal and idiosyncratic, they reproduce very old customs which mark death as "both familiar and near," in contrast to contemporary funeral practices in the United States which tend to sweep the dead out of sight and mind, and make death "so frightful that we dare not utter its name." My attitude to death is similar to that of the Yurok of O-pyúweg, who, as have most people for most of human history, developed ceremonies that reflected "promiscuity between the living and the dead."[2]

Yurok graves were always in or close to a town. "The Yurok conceive of a life as established on a spot," observed Kroeber. "Settlement there gives final repose and marks accomplishment of natural courses. This attitude is reflected in tale after tale; and in life by the custom of dying where one was reared."[3] In this sense, the Yurok were not unlike rural Americans of the eighteenth and early nineteenth centuries, when family and community were intimately involved in preparing and mourning the dead, and when it was not uncommon to bury people on family property.[4]

The Yurok buried their dead close to where people lived both for practical reasons of protection and from a sense that life and death are interdependent, taken-for-granted events. According to the Yurok writer Lucy Thompson, the location of burials was intended in part "to keep the wild animals away."[5] Also, proximity enabled families to take elaborate care of graves. Typically, recalled Thompson, mourners placed baskets upside down on graves and surrounded the cemetery with a picket fence. A post might be driven into the ground near a grave and festooned with deerskins. Often personal articles and valuables were placed on and around the deceased.[6]

When the journalist Stephen Powers documented native life in northern California in the 1870s, he assumed that the tradition of enclosing graves with "a neat, white picket fence" was "copied after the Americans, for they [Indians] are very imitative."[7] But as anthropologist Robert Heizer later noted, "since the picket fence enclosing graves was observed widely in northwestern California in 1849–1851, it is very unlikely that this is a feature learned from whites."[8]

One of the first foreigners to come through Big Lagoon, in 1850, witnessed a "graveyard, marked off with stakes, where the graves of parents and ancestors were decorated with the possessions they had used during their lifetime."[9] Yurok elders later told Alfred Kroeber during his fieldwork in northern California in the 1900s that "cemeteries adjoined towns; often lay in their very heart. Large settlements sometimes had two or three graveyards....At present each plot is neatly fenced with pickets and posts; but the Yuroks say that even in the old days their graves were enclosed with boards. The clothing and some of the personal belongings of the dead were set or hung over the grave."[10]

The Yurok funeral rites ensured that the living were not contaminated by the dead. When a Yurok died, his or her body was passed out from the house through a hole in the wall made by removing planks. A dead body was never carried out through the doorway nor did the living go through the exit made for the dead.

5.1 Yurok sweathouse and family graveyard, c. 1920s.

Mourners and people who touched the corpse cleansed themselves with water, herbs, and rituals.[11] Once the dead were buried,
the community urged their spirits to find a resting place, never to
return. "The dead are said to go to a lake," reported Waterman.
"After going round and round and about they go down through
this water into the underworld."[12] Each Yurok community knew
of a specific place that led to this underground river of the dead.
Any violations or interruptions in this journey predicted the
worst of luck.[13]

The Yurok shared with many communities from time immemorial a fear that the dead might return to haunt the living, and
they took steps to make sure this did not happen.[14] Typically,
relatives would guard a grave for several nights until "the soul
of the deceased was believed to have moved on elsewhere."[15] In
Theodora Kroeber's version of "The Inland Whale," a famous
Yurok tale, the son "made a fire on his mother's grave to warm her
until she should have had time to make her journey to the land
of the dead."[16] A person who returned from the grave was considered a "monster."[17] In a Yurok story told by Pekwon Doctor—also
know as Mä'äts-kus-egor after his mother, who was from the Big
Lagoon area—a young man from Turip with help from Weasel
went to the world of the dead and returned with his sweetheart.
"Then he had children by her," and neighbors told the children,
"She has come back from the dead, has your mother." The woman
decided to go to Pulekuk, the downstream edge of the world.
"And the man followed, followed...And she told the man (when
he overtook her), 'Go back, go back. I cannot return. I am going
to Pulekuk and will never come back.' Then he did that, the one
who grew up at Turip. From there she went on to Pulekuk, but he
did not go on."[18]

As a way of keeping the dead in their place, the practice of not
referring to them by name was widely observed. According to
Robert Spott, traditional Yurok showed "the greatest resistance
to touching on this topic."[19] They were "loath to discuss this subject," confirmed Waterman.[20] The Navajo were similarly reluctant
to discuss their funeral practices with outsiders.[21] And anthropologists involved in studying Ishi in San Francisco reminded each
other that for the Yahi "it was dangerous to speak of the dead; bad
even to think too much about them."[22]

By the 1900s, it was widely recognized by everybody "attempt-ing to handle Indians" that funerary practices and "intercommu-nion with the spirits of the dead" required sensitive attention. "The Indians continually make offerings to the names of their deceased ancestors and friends, especially at the annual feast of the dead," observed a representative of the Northern California Indian Association in 1904, "and they expect to receive in return protection from all manner of spiritual and earthly terrors. The desire of the Indian to remain by the bones of his ancestors is therefore much more than a mere sentiment, and the feeling is still strong."[23]

In 1902 Kroeber could not get Srä'mäu (also known as Sregon Jim) to talk about his past, because it "involved mention of dead relatives," and family "would be offended if they learned that he had discussed them.... This would only stir up fresh troubles and liabilities."[24] Waterman's Yurok informants also would not tell him the location of So'o-o-gúr (Corpse Water), a small lake near Big Lagoon that disembodied souls entered on their journey to the underworld.[25] In 1928 he tried bribery and pleading to get two of his informants to provide him with details of their ancestry. "The young Indians," he observed in his research notes, "defer to the old, and the old for the most part regard the taboos too highly to talk. The young people are my informants, but on these matters would not inform."[26]

"No act was regarded as more degraded or spiritually dangerous to all," notes a Karuk scholar, than 'insulting the dead.'"[27] When the Yurok buried the deceased, recalls a present-day leader, they also buried with them their ceremonial items, broken or destroyed "so that it couldn't be used again." These items would demon-strate that "he or she was someone of distinction here on earth... When you dig these things up and remove them from the grave, you're actually ripping them off of their inherited right with the Creator."[28] Dry sand was often sprinkled around a burial area so that the Yurok could detect if anybody had disrupted a grave.[29] "We bury our individuals with the trappings of their life," says the Yurok tribal historic preservation officer, "in order to show their status in the afterlife. To separate the dead from their artifacts is to separate them from their identity."[30]

From at least the time of Vancouver's voyage to the Pacific

Coast in the 1780s—when the captain issued an order prohibiting his crew from digging up native graves—to the rise of modern archaeology, it was widely recognized that many valuables would "ultimately find their way into a grave."[31] Some of the first fortune hunters traveling along the northwest coast on their way to the goldfields knew it was dangerous to violate a native cemetery. "Anyone who dares defile the graves," observed Ernest de Massey as he passed by Big Lagoon in the spring of 1850, "would be swiftly punished by a deadly arrow shot quietly from behind some tree. Knowing this, we approached the sacred burial-place with the deepest reverence. Though well-prepared to put down any aggression on their part, yet we did not want to anger them and cause trouble."[32]

But a few weeks after de Massey's respectful visit to Big Lagoon, a group of vigilantes swept through O-pyúweg—its main settlement—killing some Yurok residents, taking others as prisoners to be executed the next day.[33] Before burning down eleven houses, they took "all the curiosities out of them,"[34] thus initiating the area's long history of appropriation.

Many Archaeologies

Beginning in 1854, California enacted legislation to "protect the bodies of deceased persons," making it a crime to "disinter, mutilate or remove the body of any deceased person," but native bodies were in practice exempt from protection of law.[35] The excavation of tribal sites around Humboldt County was carried out over many decades by a wide range of professionals and amateurs—some acting alone or in small teams on the spur of the moment, others working in large-scale, well-planned, and resourceful operations. Early anthropology was the work of many minds and hands, and from the beginning was a hybrid, interdisciplinary endeavor.[36]

There has been a tendency to blame local "pothunters" for their irresponsible and unscientific desecration of sacred lands for fun and self-aggrandizement, but the responsibility for ignoring the longtime record of native opposition to excavations, for profiting off sorrows, for suspending humanitarianism in the name of science, and for crass insensitivity can be distributed among a wide array of respectable individuals and established institutions.

There were three primary groups involved in excavations: local collectors—many of whom considered themselves self-educated archaeologists contributing to scientific knowledge—who were involved as traders and hobbyists; teachers and museum curators, who encouraged sales and donations of artifacts to build up collections for educational purposes; and academic researchers—first as solitary forays and later as large-scale expeditions—whose surveys and digs in Yurok and Wiyot territories were important to Berkeley's development as an anthropological powerhouse.

An important distinction, however, must be made between the people who conducted excavations—most of whom for most of the twentieth century were small-time collectors and academics—and nationally celebrated patrons of culture with big pockets and large egos, men and women such as George Gustav Heye, Collis Huntington, and Phoebe Hearst who imagined themselves to be making and not just collecting history. Heye, a New York banker, acquired the largest number of Native American artifacts collected by a single person—eight hundred thousand items, enough to fill his own museum in New York, the Museum of the American Indian, which opened in 1919. Heye commissioned archaeological expeditions around the world, paid dealers to look out for unique objects, and bought up collections from regional collectors.[37]

At the bottom of the collecting pyramid were local entrepreneurs, such as the Reverend H. C. Meredith, a pastor who worked in central and northern California communities before becoming director of the Northern California Indian Association. He bought "curios" from his native contacts and sold them at a profit to collectors such as Henry Deisher, a businessman from Pennsylvania who displayed his large collection of seventeen thousand artifacts in the gallery of his Victorian mansion. In 1915 George Heye bought up Deisher's Pacific Coast Collection. Included in the two tons of artifacts were all kinds of grave goods that Meredith had either excavated himself or bought from his contacts. The collection's inventory listed pestles from graves in Stockton and Arcata, "polished charm stones from grave" in Butte City, "obsidian ceremonials from grave" in Calistoga, "skull with obsidian arrowpoint" from Napa, skulls "found eight feet below surface" near Sacramento, and "skeleton of a child" in Stockton.[38]

Whereas it was George Heye's desire to own "the biggest collection of Indian things anywhere,"[39] academics wanted to document and preserve what they regarded as a historically valuable and soon-to-be-extinct culture. Alfred Kroeber was primarily interested in cultural anthropology and, according to his wife, Theodora, "never dug in California nor did he take students on archaeological field trips."[40] But although he may not have been comfortable working with human remains, he "did what he had to do," notes one of his biographers.[41] Long before Berkeley created an anthropology department, it had a collection of skeletons donated by Charles Voy, a wealthy amateur naturalist who excavated a mound in Vallejo in 1872.[42] Kroeber himself reported finding "midden and bones" close to his cabin on the coast near Freshwater Lagoon.[43] According to federal records, in 1924 he deposited the "human remains" of one person in the University of California's anthropology museum.[44] And in 1936, he was on hand at the Miller site in Colusa when a Berkeley team dug up forty-seven human remains.[45] While Kroeber may not have led

5.2 Alfred Kroeber surrounded by excavated graves at the Miller site, Colusa, July 1936.

any digs in California, he certainly participated in digs, took a keen interest in archaeological expeditions, encouraged his staff to collect human remains, and trained Edward Gifford to become one of the country's leading experts on physical anthropology.[46]

It was quite commonplace for people from all over the state to send Berkeley's fledgling department of anthropology requests for advice and information about native remains. The publicity surrounding the housing and display of Ishi at the museum gave Kroeber and the university cachet among aspiring archaeologists. Some amateur collectors sent photographs of skulls, others sent skulls or remnants of bodies in return for expert advice or payment.[47] "HAVE DISCOVERED OLD INDIAN GRAVES SKELETONS BEADS AND ARROWHEADS NEAR SONORA TUOLUMNE COUNTY PLEASE ADVISE IF OF SCIENTIFIC VALUE" read a cable sent to the "Department of Archaeology" in 1939.[48] Some petitioners treated the department as a lending library of body parts. As late as 1959, the Department of Anthropology received a request to borrow a native skull. "Any Apache would do."[49]

During the department's formative years, Kroeber was personally involved in the details of the department's administration and all of its projects, including the collection and analysis of crania. In 1911 he contacted the president of the California State Dental Association for help in recording information about the teeth and jaws in native human remains collected by the university. Dr. Chappel promised to come over to the museum as soon as he had some free time and to "bring a suitcase full of material from the Santa Rosa mounds home with me...and will work it over, returning it to you afterwards."[50]

Kroeber sent one of his staff members, Llewellyn Loud, off to Humboldt in the summer and fall of 1913. Most of Loud's archaeological work was done at Indian Island (then known as Gunther Island) in Humboldt Bay, an important location to the Wiyot, who abandoned it after the bloody massacre that took place there in 1860.[51] Kroeber was actively involved in the planning of Loud's expedition, instructing him by mail in exacting detail to the point of thoroughly irritating his outspoken apprentice. "In general I will say that you appear to be misunderstanding the situation very thoroughly and to be doing work which I have not authorized you to do," Kroeber admonished Loud. "I am perhaps misunderstood and not appreciated and *certainly* not getting the *'full product of my toil,'"* replied Loud, giving as good as he got.[52]

Kroeber wanted Loud to devote all his time on Indian Island to purely archaeological matters—"I know of no reason why...you should be planning to work up a historical paper"[53]—but Loud insisted on including in his final report an acknowledgement that the place was associated with the massacre of 1860, "a climactic act of barbarity and inhumanity on the part of a half dozen vicious whites....Mercilessly the hatchet descended on all alike, old and young, women, children and infants. Their skulls were cleft, their spines severed, their bodies thrust with bowie-knives."[54]

After Loud had set up "housekeeping" on Indian Island, Kroeber reminded him to report on "whether you have found any skeletons" preexisting the 1860 butchery. Loud let Kroeber know that "relics seem fairly abundant" and that he had "dug out" several human remains.[55] Loud's final report did not mention any previous disturbances of gravesites, but it included detailed descriptions and locations of artifacts and twenty-four skeletons he found in twenty-two graves pre-existing 1860.[56] After he published his findings in 1918, Indian Island became a popular site for local hobbyists and entrepreneurs, who now knew for sure that its cemeteries contained collectibles as well as skeletons. Dr. H. H. Stuart, the most prolific collector in Humboldt County, noted in 1931 that he had used Loud's study "as a basis for my own data."[57]

Kroeber stayed involved in the collection and analysis of crania for many years. In 1921 he authorized payment of ten dollars for "the skull of an Indian" dug up near Goose Lake in Kern County.[58] A few years later, he was excited about the possibility of examining a skull unearthed by a Santa Barbara physician and self-taught archaeologist—"an amateur who likes to know." Dr. Ousdal's find was reported in the *San Francisco Chronicle* as an example of early man who "could have [not] done more than grunt" and whose "face was much like that of the gorilla." Kroeber asked for and received photographs of the skull, which he speculated was characteristic of people from Catalina Island. "If at any time I come to Santa Barbara I shall esteem it a privilege to be allowed to examine your specimen."[59]

Kroeber responded quickly to an inquiry in 1931 about two skulls found on state land. "We would be interested in knowing their probable age and also as to whether you believe them to be Indian skulls or not." On the basis of the fragments mailed to him, Kroeber was hesitant to offer an opinion. "Most Indian and Caucasian bones do not differ so markedly that one can be certain of distinguishing them in fragmentary condition."[60]

In 1932, when an amateur archaeologist, Harry Sanford, informed Kroeber that he had "uncovered a very definitely planned out graveyard" near Stockton with many skeletons "placed in tiers or one directly above the other to a depth of about eight feet," Kroeber quickly replied: "The Museum of Anthropology would be very pleased to receive the skeletal materials and to make the necessary measurements." Kroeber asked anthropologist Ronald Olson to "perhaps coax some skulls out of him [Sanford]."[61] When a physician from Twin Falls, Idaho, inquired about the likely provenience of a native skull excavated by a friend, Kroeber took time to educate him about "normal Indian materials."[62]

Kroeber was knowledgeable about the science of human remains, but Edward Gifford eventually became the expert on anthropometry to whom Kroeber deferred. By the early 1920s, Gifford had visited several museums to measure "skeletal remains," and he had completed the measurement of "several hundred living Indians" as well.[63] He also was the department's point man for trading in skulls. "Will you be so good as to inform me of the most reliable firm to deal with for such specimens?" he asked the dean of the College of Dentistry in San Francisco. "Our collection is abundantly supplied with American Indian skulls, but lacking in Caucasian, Negro, and Mongolian material." In return for information about how to purchase skulls, Gifford made the museum's "collection of aboriginal American crania" available to researchers and visiting professors for study. The dental school's Dean Millberry thanked Gifford for his kindness towards his graduate students. "They are even willing to get the trays of skulls out and put them back if your assistants are too busy to do it for them."[64]

When high school students, encouraged by their teachers to collect and analyze native remains, sent inquiries to the department of anthropology, Kroeber assigned the replies to Gifford. Kroeber was eager to educate and co-opt students, and to enlist them into the ranks of amateur archaeology. In 1925 Golda Williams, a biology student at Oakdale Union High School in

Riverbank, sent a box of teeth, shell beads, pendants, and a scale drawing of a skull to the university. "It appears a typical Indian skull," responded Gifford. "If at any time it is decided that the school is not a safe place for the skull, the University would be very glad to receive it as an addition to its collection of California crania."[65]

It was Gifford that academics increasingly consulted about technical matters, such as the relationship between cranial lesions and syphilis.[66] And by the 1930s, requests for information about human remains were usually routed to Gifford. "We have found on our property a skull," a typical letter reported, "which my father thinks is not altogether human. It was found with innumerable other things, which have been dug up since we have bought the property. Mortars, pestles, arrowheads and whole skeletons have been unearthed at different times." Gifford asked the correspondent to send the skull and "we shall be glad to report on it."[67] He was always on the lookout for skulls, especially if he knew that they had been removed from native gravesites.[68]

In its early days, the university's department of anthropology and museum took every opportunity to expand their sphere of influence. Each member of the department became a proselytizer promoting anthropology, sharing expertise and taking part in recruiting a broad network of informants. Early twentieth-century archaeology was very much shaped by enterprising, self-educated collectors who knew their local communities and had access to native confidantes.[69] Initially, the relationship between academic and local archaeologists was cooperative and mutually self-serving. For example, the "untrained and uninformed" Jeremiah Lillard, president of Sacramento Junior College, was "extraordinarily perceptive and energetic," recalled anthropologist Robert Heizer about his weekend excavations in 1932, "and saw in some fashion which I could not, and can never divine, that one could recover the story of the Indian past by digging and studying the materials recovered."[70]

Berkeley's anthropologists received information on the names and location of native sites, access to records that could help them map settlements, and human remains for evidence of diet, health, and racial typologies. Enterprising locals received advice and expertise from academics, as well as professional legitimization of their activities. For the most part, this division of labor was carried out without rancor or battles over turf: the locals were given advice and encouragement; and the academics were given tips and amassed a huge collection of crania. To this day, Berkeley's anthropology museum stores thousands of native remains in the cavernous basement of the Hearst gym.[71]

California Crania

One of the main suppliers of native skeletons from Humboldt County was the prolific collector mentioned earlier, Eureka dentist H. H. Stuart (1885–1976), known as "Doc." A bon vivant, avid outdoorsman, and larger-than-life character, he was a charter member of the Humboldt Historical Society and a board member of Eureka's Clarke Memorial Museum. Local newspapers boosted his reputation as "one of the few authorities" on "the discovery and documentation of tribal skills, customs and knowledge of the first citizens of Humboldt County."[72] He was lauded for his "deep appreciation of the life and culture of the early Native Americans."[73]

Beginning in the early 1920s when he moved to Eureka, Stuart's lifetime avocation netted him ten thousand Indian artifacts, which he preserved, traded, and sold.[74] In 1923, inspired by Loud's published work, Stuart secured a lease from a private landowner on Indian Island and became the legal occupant of the Wiyot site. "I had no trouble getting permission to dig in it," he later recalled.[75] During his extensive excavations on the island, started in 1923, Stuart dug up 382 graves.[76] And his field notes on 141 graves later became the basis of a study by Berkeley anthropologists of Wiyot culture.[77]

Big Lagoon was also an important archaeological site for Doc Stuart, as it was for high school teachers, weekend hobbyists, and academics. By 1920, Thomas Waterman's *Yurok Geography*, with its detailed mapping of O-pyúweg and other settlements in the area, was published and widely available. But what brought Stuart and others collectors to Big Lagoon were press reports a few years later that highway construction crews had uncovered "an ancient Indian village and burying ground on high land above the lagoon." Some "relics" were sent off to Berkeley for identification, but locals were on hand to get first pick.[78]

The highway trestle over Big Lagoon was begun in April 1926 and dedicated in August, a media event marked by the presence of Miss Redwood Highway, a "comely Indian girl."[79] During four months of construction in 1926 on the eastern side of the lagoon, Doc Stuart was busy excavating a Yurok cemetery north of Maple Creek at a place that locals called Digger Point. Very likely this was Mä'äts, identified by Waterman as a town with five houses,[80] and remembered by the Yurok as the site of a notorious massacre. "Doc would go up there after the work of the construction crews was over for the day," recalls Tom Hannah, who was introduced to archaeology by Stuart. "It wasn't a formal excavation. The main site was by the lumber mill. There was a substantial village site there, disturbed by construction at the bridge. Doc told me it was the most important site at Big Lagoon."[81]

Stuart did not use Waterman's study as a reference for Yurok settlements at Big Lagoon as he had used Loud's report for Wiyot settlements on Indian Island. Instead, when asked by his Berkeley contact for "the exact provenience of the skeletal material you so kindly donated to the Museum," he drew a crude map, on which he identified Big Lagoon (O-pyúweg) and Digger Point (Mä'äts) as the main sites of his excavations. From all accounts, Stuart kept extensive, if spotty, field notes on many of his digs, but most of them were destroyed or lost, or perhaps remain in the personal collections of his confidantes. Searching through old accession files at the Hearst Museum in Berkeley, I was lucky to find some of Stuart's original field notes and a handwritten sketch in which he clearly identifies the locations of his excavations at Big Lagoon.[82] I am very familiar with the main site, O-pyúweg, that he plundered; it's a few hundred yards from my cabin. This evidence would later prove helpful in convincing skeptics about the need to protect Yurok cultural legacies at Big Lagoon from looters, neglect, and amnesia.

The notes that have survived from Stuart's excavations are cryptic, difficult to decipher, and incomplete.[83] They tell us, though, that from 1926 to 1931, at Mä'äts and at O-pyúweg, Stuart dug up at least sixty-three graves; and another sixty-one at O-pyúweg in the 1940s.

Stuart worked out a deal in 1926 with officials in charge of road construction and the county superintendent of schools that he

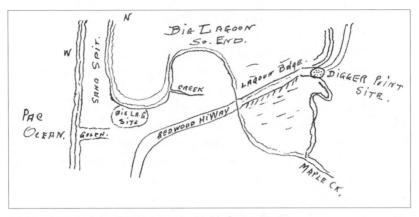

5.3 Handwritten map of Big Lagoon by H. H. Stuart, 1931.

would turn over to Eureka High School a percentage of artifacts he found at Mä'äts. Records indicate that he donated only two obsidian knives, while his personal notes report that he excavated dozens of items.[84] Stuart kept or sold most of the artifacts he found in graves, with the exception of some mundane items, such as grooved stones, which he donated to the University of California's museum.[85] According to his field notes, among the items he recovered were "some beautiful red and black obsidian blades" and "nose plugs of ivory from Alaska and at least one wax effigy of a squaw with baby on back, showing a trade relation with Alaska." In addition, he recorded finding abalone shells, salmon spear tips, harpoon heads, "a pipe bowl of steatite," and "ancient wampums made from lip of olivella shell."

During one of his excavations at Big Lagoon, Stuart found a zoomorph, an important ceremonial artifact shaped like a mythic animal, popularly known as a "slave-killer" because it was wrongly thought to have been used by northwest natives to execute slaves. Stuart clumsily glued together and restored his trophy with what appears to be plaster of paris before selling it in 1936 to a fellow collector. The zoomorph was eventually sold or donated to the University of California's Museum of Anthropology by Jeremiah Lillard.[86] Stuart also sold two zoomorphs that he had excavated from graves on Indian Island to a member of Franklin D. Roosevelt's cabinet, who in turn sold them to a dealer in native artifacts. They were bought by the Museum of the American Indian in

New York in 1962 and later transferred to the National Museum of the American Indian in Washington, D.C.[87]

Doc Stuart kept the human remains that he dug out of graves in his home until University of California archaeologists expressed an interest in acquiring them. In February and June 1931, he shipped three cartons containing "31 skulls and various human bones" to Edward Gifford at the Museum of Anthropology. Occasionally, he asked the museum to return body parts that interested him, such as some "teeth and jaws and fragments of bones I should like to have identified...I have a checklist with what I think them to be and I'm curious just how far wrong I am on some of them."[88] Stuart kept several crania for his personal collection, and years later was glad to show off to a local newspaper his "fabulous collection," including "jaws and skulls of some of the members of the extinct tribe."[89]

The university was encouraging and grateful to Stuart for his donation of Yurok remains. "In shipping do not hesitate to send the specimens express charges collect," Gifford wrote Stuart. The museum's curator in turn passed on the good news to the university's president about a "gift of thirty-one skulls from various shellmounds in Humboldt...excavated and donated by Dr. H. H. Stuart. They form a desirable addition to the collection of California crania."[90]

Gifford himself was particularly interested in this gift because of his scientific work in anthropometry, namely the measurement of apparent racial differences between peoples, as indicated by the length and breadth of heads, noses, and ears; the degree of slope in foreheads; the axis of nostrils; and whether or not "the fleshy lower margin of the septum is exposed."[91] Gifford's search for the biological basis of social differences was consistent with the ideas and assumptions of the racist eugenics movement that had a considerable following in California between the world wars.[92]

Some seventy-five years later, in May 2006, after the University of California published its inventory of human remains as required under the 1990 Native American Graves Protection and Repatriation Act,[93] thirteen of the skulls dug up by Stuart were repatriated to the Yurok Tribe.[94] There is no record of what happened to the missing eighteen skulls and "various human bones" shipped by Stuart to Gifford in 1931. The collections manager of the Hearst Museum (as the Museum of Anthropology is now known) attributes the discrepancy to poor record keeping and the tendency of museums, until recently, to "freely trade in crania."[95]

Stuart and a crew of friends continued to work in Big Lagoon through the 1930s and 1940s, excavating another sixty-one gravesites at O-pyúweg. There is no record of what he did with the human remains, including "an old adult, evidently male," covered by "the head and shoulder blades of an old elk"; "child on steatite slab"; and "child 8 yrs." Presumably, Stuart kept the many artifacts that he found in graves, such as "a perfect maul," "black obsidian knife," and "a walrus tusk from a head dress."[96]

At a minimum, Stuart excavated 124 graves at Big Lagoon. Together with his work on Indian Island, by his own count he unearthed more than six hundred crania and skeletons in Humboldt County.[97] "Over the past three decades," observed a Eureka reporter in 1952, oblivious to the living presence of native peoples, "he has dug up a museum of remains, discovered, for the most part, in the tribal burial grounds of this extinct race."[98]

By today's standards, Stuart's archaeological practices were of course unethical, as well as decidedly unprofessional and lacking in technical finesse.[99] And by any standards, his knowledge was uneven and his craft often shoddy. He kept records on some graves, but not on others; his field notes were often imprecise and undated; he did not seem familiar with Waterman's anthropological mapping of Big Lagoon; he did not include evidence of provenience with the human remains he sent to the university until asked to do so; and when he sold hundreds of his most valuable artifacts to Oregon collector Gene Favell in 1973 for $13,500, he turned over the collection without any field notes.[100]

When I visited the Favell Museum in Klamath Falls in June 2008, I found Stuart's Yurok collection dispersed throughout the exhibition, mostly without descriptive labels or information about provenience. Stuart himself is the star of the display: there is a framed newspaper article with a headline announcing "Dr. Stuart Rediscovered a Lost People," and his photograph is in the center of a display case, surrounded by his "treasures." Occasional labeling indicates that the bulk of the collection comes from Indian Island and Big Lagoon. It is a stunning exhibition of extraordinary artifacts in very good condition, including six zoomorphs, large obsidian blades, elk-antler spoons and purses, wooden pipes with stone inlay, and many other objects, all intermingled and displayed without any sense of historical context. Several items are clearly smoke-damaged and repaired, the telltale sign of grave goods. Given that the Favell has not received federal funds, it is not legally required to publish an inventory of holdings that constitute "funerary objects" as a precursor towards possible repatriation. Nor as yet does it feel ethically obliged—in accordance with the best practices of museums in the United States—to withdraw from public display any materials that have been plundered from graves.[101]

As for the human remains excavated by Stuart and others that ended up in Berkeley, even Alfred Kroeber admitted privately that they were of minimal scientific value. "We have hundreds of Indian skeletons that nobody ever comes to study," Kroeber wrote Gifford in a personal letter in 1916.[102] Similarly, a representative of the Southwest Museum in Los Angeles told Gifford in 1923 that it had "made no systematic study of the skeletal materials in our Anthropological Department."[103]

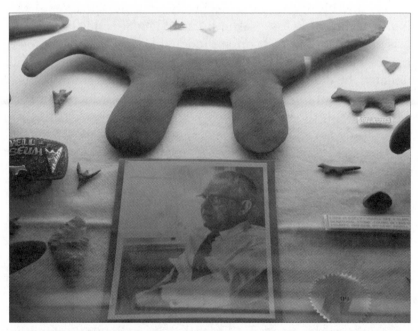

5.4 H. H. "Doc" Stuart displayed amid his "treasures" at the Favell Museum, Klamath Falls, Oregon, 2008.

Though the study of human remains, especially in the first half of the twentieth century, was often distorted by racist ideological assumptions, there is of course much to be learned about diet, health, injuries, and day-to-day life from autopsies and the scientific analysis of bones. And with the development of sophisticated DNA techniques, it is possible to reconstruct a great deal of information about personal and social life. The main problem with respect to Native American human remains is that the desirability of getting informed consent from or consulting with the lineal and cultural descendants of the subjects under study was disregarded until the 1970s.

But even on scientific grounds, the hundreds of thousands of excavations have ultimately provided minimal information: most harvested human remains were never studied, and documentation of provenience of bones and artifacts found in graves was often nonexistent. The racist Aleš Hrdlička dismissed the racist Samuel Morton's collection of skulls as scientifically worthless, but Hrdlička himself was a "careless man in the field," digging too quickly and taking insufficient notes.[104] George Heye meticulously catalogued his collection but threw out field notes that provided historical context.[105] Gene Favell was more interested in displaying a collection impressive for its size and uniqueness, jamming as much stuff as possible into display cases, than in documentation.[106] And even Alfred Kroeber, according to one of his students, "kept no journal in the field, and his notes were extremely sketchy."[107]

Cabinets of Curiosities

If Doc Stuart was representative of a cadre of serious collectors and dealers, Cecile Clarke (1886–1979) embodied the leadership of private, educational Indian museums. Born in 1886, within a year of Stuart and Edward Gifford, Clarke combined the interests of a forward-looking, modern professional with a social and political conservativeness rooted in Edwardian propriety. She was the fiercely independent New Woman, a devotee of self-reliance who chopped her own wood and put career before family. But she was also uneasy with egalitarian shifts in the power from which she herself had benefited. By the last decade of her life, she had become a Nixonian Republican, unnerved by "hippies" and repulsed by "the dirtiest bunch of Indians" that tried to sell her some baskets.[108]

While Llewellyn Loud was auditing courses and working for Kroeber, Cecile Clarke was studying California history with Herbert Bolton at Berkeley. Her first job after graduating with a history degree in 1908 was teaching in Mendocino. In 1915 she moved to Eureka High School, where she remained until her retirement in 1950. With wealth inherited from her family's successful sheep ranch, she bought a Eureka bank building and transformed it into a historical museum.[109] The Clarke Memorial Museum—now known as the Clarke Historical Museum—opened in 1960.

Single and without children, the young Cecile put her spare time and enormous energy into collecting and preserving native artifacts. Each week she set aside time for washing and mending "relics," preparing items for shows, and discussing her finds with fellow collectors. When her collection took up too much room in her home, she moved several cases of bowls, mortars, pestles, and other treasures to the high school, where she organized exhibits for students and staff.

5.5 Cecile Clarke with her collection of "Indian relics" at Eureka High School, c. 1950s.

5.6 Unnamed diggers on Indian Island, c. 1930s.

Clarke first became interested in Indian Island in the 1920s, when Doc Stuart sent her "a slave killer and two mended knives" for her collection via his son, who was a student in her class. By 1931 George Albee, superintendent of schools, had worked out an agreement with a landowner on the island to allow Clarke and her designated agents, including Doc Stuart, to excavate Wiyot sites.[110] About the same time, the Humboldt County Board of Supervisors approved a request by the school board (on behalf of Cecile Clarke) and the State Indian Museum "to excavate and preserve relics of Indian tribes native to this region."[111]

Clarke put up signs on Indian Island warning unauthorized visitors to stay away and hired a team of diggers to follow up on excavations done by Loud and Stuart. She focused primarily on searching for "relics" in graves, as she noted in her diaries: "Maul in loose earth and skull south of tree line…parts of skeleton lying with skull…fragments of hip bones…remains of child's or infant's skeleton…remains of a burial…only a few pieces of pelvic bones left of skeleton."[112]

When Clarke found it impossible to keep local collectors away from Indian Island, she made a deal with them, allowing excavations if they turned over half of their spoils to the school district. But most diggers did not keep to this agreement, and this included Doc Stuart. One of her hired hands reported to her that Stuart "got a bowl which he didn't think the dentist wanted him to see." Another amateur archaeologist "didn't turn in a thing to the school, hadn't lived up to any of the terms."[113] Eventually, Clarke felt betrayed by Stuart and told him that his "privileges were suspended." Quickly, though, Stuart worked his way back into her good graces, serving as her informal adviser on Indian Island. Later he joined the Clarke Museum's board of directors.[114]

As her ambitions grew, Clarke hired locals to carry out excavations on her behalf and spread the word that she would buy artifacts. She was issued a "permit" by the Little River Redwood Company to excavate "Indian burying grounds" on its property in Big Lagoon and Trinidad.[115] A typical Sunday in 1928 found a group of young men digging near Big Lagoon for mortars, pestles, and spears. "One of the interesting finds," reported the *Arcata Union*, "consisted of a string of beads made from abalone shell in a fair state of preservation, and other implements and trinkets made up a varied list."[116]

Some of the first and last artifacts that eventually made their way to the Clarke Museum came from Big Lagoon: a couple of Doc Stuart's finds were turned over to the school in 1926; a

5.7 Cecile Clarke's collection at Eureka High School, c. 1950s.

collector provided wedges and pestles in 1931; Cecile Clarke paid Henry Vicenus fifteen dollars for red and black obsidian knives in 1935; and in July 1967, Clarke welcomed a young collector who "brought in a pasteboard box of Indian artifacts from Big Lagoon, some good and some fragments."[117] Proud of the eight "slave-killers" in her collection, she asked Edward Gifford if he knew of any museum that had a larger holding. He did not have that information but was glad to identify four abalone pearls that Clarke had dug out of "cremation sites."[118]

Cecile Clarke's payroll spawned a cottage industry of diggers who scoured all the local native sites. In 1934 she paid one of her favorite agents $177, about $2,800 in today's dollars, for digging and filling holes and finding artifacts that Stuart had missed.[119] But Clarke was sloppier than even Stuart in her archaeological record keeping. While her diaries meticulously documented meals, chores, social outings, and meetings, her accession records were minimal, her field notes sparse and incomplete. Fortunately, Clarke allowed two Berkeley archaeologists, Albert Elsasser and James Bennyhoff, to review and take notes on her collection when it was housed at the Eureka High School Museum, on October 30, 1953. It is clear from this handwritten, eleven-page document that the most important items in Cecile Clarke's collection at that time—including zoomorphs, obsidian blades, and abalone ornaments—came from graves either on Indian Island or at Big Lagoon.[120]

Established as the city's first historical museum, the Clarke continued to be involved in archaeological projects through the 1960s. In 1961, the year after the City of Eureka acquired owner-ship of most of Indian Island, the city council granted exclusive permission to the Clarke to carry out excavations on Wiyot sites. Cecile celebrated the decision with two future board members, John Ham and Tom Hannah, whom she entrusted to carry out field research on behalf of the museum. The council was unani-mous in its approval, noted Cecile Clarke—there were "no open discussion or questions."[121]

Work on Indian Island began in the summer of 1963 and lasted until 1969. "Nothing of any significance was found," only frag-ments of organic and inorganic tools, reported Hannah, a self-taught archaeologist who at that time was assistant principal of Winship Junior High School in Eureka. Hannah—now retired

from a career as a high school teacher, community college adminis-
trator, and member of the Eureka city council—had close ties with
the Yurok when he was young. It was his father who walked by Big
Lagoon in 1908 on his way to his first job, teaching school upriver
at Johnsons. As a teenager Hannah had spent summers in the
important Yurok town of Morek, where his mother, Mary, taught
school. Here, Sam and Lizzie Smith, who had lived at Morek since
before the first white men came through, took Tom into their home
for overnight visits. "They treated me like family. I considered them
family." Sam taught him how to net salmon and catch eels in a
basket trap. "He did much without my realization to turn my life
around and head me in the right direction. My deep love for Indian
life comes from this experience," Hannah says.[122]

The Clarke's team carried out radiocarbon dating tests on Indian

5.8 Mary Hannah and Lizzie Smith
outside the school in Morek, 1948.

Island that confirmed the site's
original occupation as 880 A.D.,
a disappointment to local archaeologists who had hoped it would
be much earlier.[123] The press was
full of sensational references to
the search for evidence of a "lost
tribe" who "were advanced in their
culture and differed greatly from
Indians who followed them."[124]
Hannah's investigation paralleled
an earlier and similarly unfulfilled
quest by anthropologist Robert
Heizer for evidence of a "pre-
Yurok culture" at Sumeg, in Patrick's Point State Park.[125] No doubt
some archaeologists had difficulty
imagining that the ancestors of
impoverished, twentieth-century
Native Americans—the survivors
of epidemics, massacres, and dis-
placement—could have produced
desirable artifacts now sought
after by collectors, museums, and universities.

In 1969, not long after Hannah completed his dig on Indian

5.9 Tom Hannah holding a photograph of Sam and Lizzie Smith, Eureka, April 2008.

Island and presented his findings to the Humboldt County Historical Society,[126] the Eureka city council refused all further requests for excavations. The rise of a militant Native American movement, as we shall see, made public authorities nervous about being perceived as grave looters. In 1965 Hannah had proudly shown off to the *Humboldt Times* a collection of artifacts—including zoomorphs, ceremonial knives, and pipes—that had clearly come from graves.[127] The illustrated story reported that the collection belonged to Hannah; he later claimed that it was on loan from Doc Stuart and that he did not personally excavate his own "modest collection," acquired from Stuart, from graves.[128] By the end of the 1960s, collectors were reluctant to display their native artifacts to the press, whatever their source.

Many years later, in an acrimonious exchange, the tribal chairman of the Table Bluff Wiyot Tribe accused the Clarke, in particular Tom Hannah, of conducting "grave robbing and the mining of our dead" on Indian Island. In reply to these "libelous and slanderous" accusations, Hannah threatened legal action. "No burials of human remains of any kind were found," he replied.[129] In Hannah's view, his archaeological work on Indian Island had contributed "to the appreciation of the heroic past of the American Indian."

Their history, he reflected in a public essay, "should be part of our shared and remembered heritage."[130] But accusations of grave robbing continued to dog Hannah long after his retirement.[131]

The social movements of the 1960s shook up the kind of comfortable relationship that white "friends of the Indian," like the Hannahs, had developed with native individuals and families. Many of Tom Hannah's relatives had close ties with local Yurok. His uncle used to go on fishing trips with Trinidad Pete; his aunt took casual snapshots of her native friends; and his mother worked with local Yurok at the school in Morek. Despite the genocidal backdrop of the nineteenth century and systemic racial discrimination in the twentieth century, on a day-to-day basis, moments of respect and even friendship between folks on different sides of the color line sometimes transcended white romanticism and native survival tactics. And then there is the long, mostly unspoken, inflammatory history of widespread sexual relations between white men and native women that unsettles the region's fiction of pure bloodlines and racial separation.

The now eighty-year-old Hannah feels that the Native American movement of the early 1970s made him the symbolic fall guy for the looting of the region. "I was the last person there at Indian Island" before excavations were halted, he says. "I understand the antipathy. If I knew then what I know today, I wouldn't have done any work on the island."[132] It's also deeply troubling to Hannah because his digs brought him respect and admiration from his peers, and also because his childhood experiences with the Yurok in Morek still loom large in his memory. "Gathering in the wild crops, fishing, hunting, trailing and driving the deer, building the salmon weir, acorn gathering, this rhythm learned from nature was mixed with the human drama of living."[133] What Hannah did not know was that Morek, the place that had such a deep impact on him at an impressionable time in his young life, was also the birthplace of a Yurok family that decades later would lead the struggle to stop the excavation of native gravesites without authorization and collaboration.

During the first half of the twentieth century, the digging up of native sites was backed by the rule of law. When asked in 1932 about the legality of such excavations, Kroeber replied that permission should be sought from the Smithsonian if the excavation was on federal land and from the landowner if on private property. Otherwise, he said, a permit might be needed from county officials, but a local ordinance "is not likely to be invoked unless someone takes offense at the digging." If in doubt, consult an attorney, Kroeber advised.[134] And so local collectors signed contracts with the private owner of Indian Island to excavate Wiyot sites; they sought permits from the timber company to excavate Yurok sites at Big Lagoon; and they received the blessings of local governments to carry out excavations on public lands for the public good. "Everything we did was planned, open, and publicized," says Tom Hannah.[135] "There was a time," anthropologist Robert Heizer recalled in 1974, "when sending the heads of Indian leaders who had lost a war to Washington could be done without anyone criticizing such acts. There was a time, more recently, when prehistoric Indian graves could be dug up without anyone raising a fuss."[136]

Most archaeological projects in Humboldt County took place in the full light of day, involved leading citizens and some of California's most distinguished academics, and were enthusiastically endorsed by government functionaries. When Cecile Clarke expressed concern in 1932—"If I am doing something I should not, I will appreciate it if you will tell me"—about the propriety of her school-based excavations on Indian Island, the curator of the State Indian Museum in Sacramento assuaged her anxieties: "As you are acquiring artifacts for an educational purpose, I can see no plausible reason for criticism concerning your hobby of collecting."[137]

To Cecile Clarke, Doc Stuart, and Tom Hannah, their avocation was not in any way insensitive or ghoulish. Prior to the 1960s, archaeologists—amateur or professional—did not think twice about exhuming and publicly displaying the remains of Native Americans, or describing their finds to the press in vivid detail. "We were like Egyptologists," recalls Hannah, "digging up an old civilization."[138] Collectors had no moral qualms about flaunting the skulls and bones of "docile and harmless peoples," typically characterized by the media as "a people that are no more," disconnected from contemporary humankind.[139] After all, the practice had long been approved by respectable academics, even those who were well aware that their subjects were not extinct.[140]

SIX
Unwelcome Attention

"If not here before, not here now."
—Yurok saying[1]

Testy Relations

Robert Heizer (1915–1979), who studied with Kroeber, joined Berkeley's anthropology department in 1946 and became a core member. He had begun his apprenticeship in archaeology working with the self-taught Jeremiah Lillard in Sacramento in the early 1930s. "On Saturdays we would go dig for Indian relics," recalled Heizer. "Always we dug where we hoped to find some poor old buried Indian whose grave would produce some interesting thing. This was pothunting, pure and simple."[2] For most of his career Heizer would depend on the insights and connections of nonprofessionals who knew the terrain. Until the 1960s, practical necessities made for an uneasy détente between academics and local archaeologists.

Doc Stuart certainly reaped economic benefits and prestige from his collection, but he also imagined himself a serious anthropologist performing a public service by shedding "new light on a mystery tribe of long ago"[3]—an assumption that was reinforced by his academic contacts. The following examples of his cordial exchanges with Berkeley anthropologists give a sense of this apparent rapport:

I was not fortunate in getting complete skeletons but have a dozen or more skulls. All of these are prehistoric or pre-white-man as no metal or glass was found with them. If this material will be any use to you, give me shipping directions. (Stuart to Gifford, 24 November 1930)

In my collecting I run across and save fragments of jaws and teeth of various animals, and while I've studied comparative anatomy, I have no real means of checking the accuracy of my guesses. Have you a man there who could and would identify some of these specimens for me? (Stuart to Gifford 29 January 1931)

This is to acknowledge with many thanks the receipt of the two cartons of skulls together with your valuable notes concerning them. (Gifford to Stuart, 11 June 1931)

Professor Heizer was telling me of the high quality of your collection from the standpoint of accompanying data, an important matter that so many private collectors neglect....When you are next in the Bay Region, I hope that you will call at the museum. Last time you came out with Mr. Miles, whom I have not seen for a long while. (Gifford to Stuart, 15 October 1948)[4]

This is to tell you that I have picked up the steatite slab with the drill marks and hope before long to work up a small descriptive and analytical note on the specimen. When I have finished with it I will take the opportunity to have it returned to you, and in the meanwhile will take good care of it. I appreciate very much your kindness and effort in making it possible to study this extremely interesting specimen. Jim Bennyhoff was very pleased to get the drawings of the harpoon heads which you sent in your letter of November 15th, and wishes me to express his thanks for this kindness...I consider your collection so valuable and important. (Heizer to Stuart, 30 November 1948)[5]

Joint ventures between local and academic archaeologists were reinforced in 1948 when the University of California Archaeological Survey was launched from Berkeley to facilitate "the collection and preservation of prehistoric remains and records concerning them." Heizer, who directed the Archaeological Survey, called for a "friendly, cooperative attack on problems which are the common concern of *all* archaeologists in the state."[6] The interdependence of archaeological projects was underscored in the Archaeological Survey's how-to guide for new practitioners: "Nearly every community contains its local amateur historians and archaeologists and these individuals are the second major source"—after a literature review—"of preparatory information. When their services can be enlisted, they are of invaluable help, not only for what they can tell, but for other local contacts which they can establish."[7]

Whatever disdain academics privately harbored towards locals, they counted on them for inside information. In August 1949, for example, an archaeologist working for Heizer in Trinidad reported that the Yurok site of Tsurai "had been freshly pothunted" and that he had "caught the bastards red-handed." But after he discovered the locals were "loaded with information," they quickly settled their differences and "parted pals."[8] While Berkeley's archaeologists liked to think of themselves as high-minded professionals of "moral responsibility" who refused to "make 'deals' with pothunters or commercial relic collectors," they were "always willing to learn of sites of materials for the purpose of the record."[9]

There are many examples of cooperative efforts and projects, even into the 1960s. Cecile Clarke regularly exchanged ideas with academics, as well as government and museum officials. In 1953 Edward Gifford approached Clarke about the possibility of a joint project with the university on Indian Island. "Our sole purpose," he wrote, "is to salvage what remains of the aboriginal record before the scientific value of the sites is destroyed by private collectors."[10] Similarly, when Tom Hannah conducted his dig and carried out radiocarbon dating tests on Indian Island in the mid-1960s, he exchanged informed views with cultural anthropologist George Phebus at the Smithsonian.[11] In 1969 Hannah alerted San Francisco State University archaeologists that the Yurok village site of Tsahpekw in Stone Lagoon was "being actively and extensively vandalized by pot-hunters and bottle-hunters." As a result salvage operations were soon planned.[12]

But beneath this surface politeness, the relationship was testy and brittle, vacillating between necessary cooperation, begrudging admiration, and outright hostility. Academics typically hedged their appreciation of self-trained anthropologists, even in public documents. The tone was set by Alfred Kroeber's ambivalence towards the pioneering nineteenth-century journalist Stephen Powers, also a commentator on the Yurok. Kroeber acknowledged his "power of observation as keen as it was untrained, and an invariably spirited gift of portrayal that rises at times into the realm of the sheerly fascinating," but could not resist also pointing out the "flimsy texture and slovenly edges" of Powers's work.[13]

In private, academics tended to be scathing in their judgments of local amateurs. Robert Heizer, who flattered Stuart in 1948 for his "valuable and important" collection, a few years later dismissed him as the "notorious pothunter of Eureka" and referred to one of his collecting buddies, Charles Miles, as somebody who "traffics in the bones of the dead."[14] Without such collectors, however, Berkeley would not have had access to important artifacts or been able to amass its collection of crania.

The local archaeologists, not surprisingly, felt slighted and underappreciated by their academic counterparts. Charles Miles, who published a serious book on archaeology and an article about Doc Stuart's work on Indian Island,[15] "repeatedly complained that the University had not recognized him, as though his offers of assistance were such that he should be considered a collaborator," noted Robert Heizer in a confidential memo.[16]

Miles had good reason to think that he had earned the status of collaborator. It was Gifford who approached Miles in 1935, eager to learn about his collection and his knowledge of native sites. And well into the 1940s, the two men exchanged cordial, technical correspondence. "Have you been out to the Concord dig, which has yielded to date eight skeletons with a few artifacts?" Gifford asked Miles in 1946. A couple of years later, after the two men had met, Miles alerted Gifford about a burial area in Shasta County that "would be a good area for archaeological students to visit, I fancy."[17]

When Heizer and Albert Elsasser visited Doc Stuart in the summer of 1948 to look over his Indian Island collection and field notes, they observed that Stuart, "while friendly, treated us with a noticeable measure of reserve."[18] In 1964, when the researchers finally published "Archaeology of HUM-67," which was based on Stuart's "on-the-spot notebook records" about Indian Island,

Stuart was furious. The authors gave him backhanded credit for a "remarkable job," despite his status as "an amateur without a day's training (Stuart did not even know Loud)." Of course, Stuart was well aware of Loud's research.

Moreover, Heizer apparently reneged on his promise to "submit the manuscript for inspection and approval" to Stuart before publication. "I expected a man in his position [Heizer] to be a man of his word," Stuart scrawled over his personal copy of the published report, "not a liar and a thief."[19] A few years later, Albert Elsasser damned Stuart with faint praise as "a slightly above-average private collector. If nothing else, Stuart was zealous."[20]

Heizer quickly went from praising Doc Stuart in June 1949 for his "remarkably complete collection of archaeological material" to denouncing him five years later as a "grave-robber."[21] Similarly, Charles Miles, once a source of valuable information about the location of Native American artifacts, became "persona non grata" for his "commercializing in prehistoric Indian materials." In 1954 Heizer wrote Miles a formal letter accusing him of improperly representing himself "as having affiliation with the University of California, or implying this."[22]

The pecking order was established as the leading locals in turn lorded it over those they considered less qualified than themselves: in his letter to Gifford recommending the Shasta County site for students, Miles reported that it was being "looted" and "rifled."[23] Doc Stuart complained to a local newspaper about "indiscriminate digging by amateurs," who failed to keep "proper records."[24] Similarly, Tom Hannah decried the "unsystematic work of collectors and 'pot hunters.'"[25]

Good Digging

After World War II, university-based archaeology accumulated the personnel and means to carry out excavations a long way from home base. The larger and more resourceful its operations became, the less it needed the services and insights of local collectors and museums. The ensuing split reflected a larger national trend as universities increasingly monopolized scientific knowledge, while local museums lost their "intellectual primacy" and became repositories of diluted information for schools and the public.[26] As a result, the tensions that had simmered for decades erupted into full-scale alienation. And as the academics distanced themselves from local archaeologists, they encountered increasingly organized opposition from local native groups over desecration of graves. And in Humboldt County, they also met unexpected opposition from civic groups over ownership of artifacts removed from graves.

In 1947 Robert Heizer received the go-ahead from the University of California to establish a six-week summer session field course that would combine instructional and archaeological activities.[27] Near the end of the year, he "conducted a reconnaissance along the coast of northwestern California, looking for archaeological sites of sufficient size and depth to offer reasonable prospects of good digging." He settled on the Yurok site of Sumeg in Patrick's Point State Park, a few miles south of Big Lagoon, as the "most likely spot."[28] In January 1948, Heizer's proposal received approval from the California State Park Commission, which was chaired by Joseph R. Knowland, a longtime Republican politician and publisher of the *Oakland Tribune*.[29]

During the summer of 1948, Heizer was in charge of a field party that set up camp at Sumeg. The following year another team moved to excavate Tsurai, in Trinidad, after receiving permission

6.1 Tsurai and Trinidad Bay, c. 1900s.

from the private owners of the site. "Intensive excavation" was done at these two important Yurok sites. In addition, during these two years, the university teams recorded the location of a "large number of additional sites and made surface collections from these." One of these sites was Big Lagoon.[30]

In September 1947, Heizer and A. E. Treganza did a preliminary exploration of the Yurok settlement of Mä'äts, on the eastern side of Big Lagoon, close to Maple Creek. In his field notes, Kroeber identified this place (previously mentioned as the site of a massacre), which he calls Mä'ätsku, as "the chief source of salmon in this vicinity."[31] According to the university's accession records, Heizer and Treganza collected twenty-three utilitarian items, including sinkers, pestles, and a cobble chopper or hammer.[32] About a hundred yards from Mä'äts, on the beach, Heizer and Treganza also collected a few items, including sinkers and notched stones for fishing.[33]

In June 1948 Heizer returned to Mä'äts with his anthropology students. He reported finding several house pits, built into the ground for protection from animals and against the elements. The team collected about 240 utilitarian items, including an arrow straightener, notched pebble sinkers, an obsidian scraper, a deer cannon bone, a jasper scraper, a hammerstone, chert blades, and a sandstone maul for splitting wood. One house pit produced chipped points, blades, mauls, a bone tool, and forty pebble sinkers.[34] According to Heizer's field notes, no graves were excavated during the 1947–1948 field visits to Big Lagoon.

From the beginning of the project, Heizer had made excavations of Yurok cemeteries an important component of his mission to train young archaeologists. In a letter sent to the head of the state's Division of Beaches and Parks early in 1948, Heizer requested permission to keep in Berkeley any "skeletal material" he dug up. A. E. Henning told Heizer that the state insisted on "retaining ownership of the artifacts and skeletal material resulting from the excavation," but it had "no objection" to the university museum displaying "these materials on a loan basis."[35]

During the 1948 Sumeg dig—located in a remote section of the state park, away from residential areas—thousands of artifacts were recovered and six graves excavated.[36] Heizer found signs of deafness in the exhumed bodies and speculated that the disability was congenital.[37] The university's public relations office used this finding to showcase the role of Berkeley's anthropology department in promoting scientific curiosity about the past. But the publicity also pandered to exoticism and reinforced popular misinformation about the inferiority and inevitable extinction of previous civilizations with such improbable statements as: "Evidence of an ancient race of deaf Indians being towed great distances on the open Pacific by sea lions is in possession of the University of California anthropology department." The headline no doubt fueled native resentments against archaeology: "Sea Lions Took Poor Indians for Joy Ride."[38]

"None of the materials uncovered show more than the most primitive life and intelligence," observed a Humboldt newspaper in 1948.[39] A typical account in a San Francisco newspaper summed up the lengthy excavation at Sumeg as follows: "No matter what Californians consider themselves today, early inhabitants of the state were hardly genteel. Their favorite amusement was beating the brains out of dead sea lions, and conversation was limited to sign language about the same sea lions."[40]

Stories about this excavation typically included photographs designed to titillate public interest in archaeology. The *San Francisco Examiner* showed anthropologist John Mills with two skulls, captioned without any sense of irony: "Skull of Indian, left, and head of sea lion."[41] A few years later, a *Humboldt Times* story of a dig near Humboldt Bay carried a photograph of archaeologist James Bennyhoff cradling the cranium of a Wiyot woman with a "demoniacal vision."[42] Even when the press carried a more thoughtful and sympathetic account of Humboldt's first residents, there was no sense that the region was full of living native peoples—anything but extinct—or that they had opinions about their own history.[43] In this way anthropology contributed to the patronizing and racialized images of native peoples that permeated the California Story.

All the publicity about the 1948 expedition caught the attention of the Humboldt County Federation of Women's Clubs. Its leaders were not concerned about the excavation of graves without native permission, but about outsiders from the university making off with what they considered the county's patrimony. At its fall convention, the group called upon the UC Berkeley department of anthropology to "submit an inventory of specimens excavated at Patrick's Point State Park to the chief ranger at Patrick's Point Park within 30 days and to return all specimens so removed within 90 days of the date of the request."[44] And the resolution was publicized in the local press.[45]

"The action of the Federation was unfortunate," Heizer replied to the letter's author, Ruth Smith, with copies to the State Park Commission and university president. "The University of California is a reputable institution, was acting within the framework of a formal agreement with the State Park Commission, and any imputation that the University has perpetrated a theft of the archaeological specimens in question is certainly gratuitous and incorrect. It is my feeling that some sort of public retraction by the Federation may be in order." Heizer suggested that the clubwomen focus their attention instead on the "vandalism" committed by "unauthorized and unscientific excavation of Indian village sites and graves."[46] But he was unable to deflect the brouhaha stirred up by the federation. In deference to "considerable local sentiment" and in response to "unwelcome attention," Heizer agreed to return to Patrick's Point all the artifacts collected at the Sumeg site, except for body parts and funerary artifacts that he quietly retained for the university.[47]

A Lasting Sense of Resentment

"No graves were found or excavated by the University expedition," claimed Robert Heizer and John Mills in their final report on the Tsurai expedition, published in 1952.[48] It was not for want of trying. Sometime in the summer of 1948, when Heizer was checking out Tsurai as a possible site for the 1949 summer session, his crew spent four days there "surreptitiously" digging two test pits and looking for graves—without the permission of the state or local property owners. "Since the site was open, unfenced, and unposted," Heizer later admitted, "we felt we could do our work quietly without advertising it."[49]

Heizer's covert dig did not go unnoticed. Unlike Sumeg, which was not easily accessible, Tsurai was in the middle of the important coastal town of Trinidad. By the time he was preparing for the summer project at Tsurai, Heizer was under pressure to put in writing that he "would specifically not be interested in excavating historic burials in the cemetery away on the upper part of the site."[50] Moreover, as the dig got under way in August 1949, a group of Yurok women which included the formidable Alice Spott and Minnie Shaffer visited the site to check up on Heizer's promise. They lodged protests with Sheriff Charles Raab that the archaeological team was "digging in reservation property."[51] According to a member of the Berkeley team, James Bennyhoff, "the Indians accused the U.C. Field Crew of violating the graves."[52] And to add to the expedition's sense of being under siege, the Federation of Women's Clubs renewed its charges of misappropriation against Berkeley's department of anthropology and "leveled its heaviest artillery" against the Tsurai dig.[53]

As a result of these protests, the dig was suspended and a "widely representative meeting" was convened at the town hall in Trinidad. With input from local Yurok and the state's Department of Indian Affairs, the excavation was allowed to resume on condition that recovered artifacts would be catalogued and eventually returned to Humboldt; that the university would only "explore the ruins of the village and the refuse piles"; that any human remains accidentally exposed would be turned over to county authorities for reburial; and that the sheriff would prosecute anybody caught "pillaging" graves.[54]

The lead archaeologist on the dig, John Mills, assured people who attended the meeting that "no graves would be disturbed" and that his team was primarily interested in "the Indians' garbage."[55] But of course he knew that it was impossible to excavate a Yurok town without uncovering gravesites. After all, it was written in Kroeber's bible that Yurok graves were typically located in the "very heart" of settlements.[56] While the local press reported the meeting as a success—"pipe of peace smoked"—and the dig continued for a few weeks, the protests did not abate.

Back in Berkeley, Robert Heizer heard from J. M. Stewart, the state director of the Bureau of Indian Affairs, that his office had "received several protests from Indians and interested individuals concerning alleged excavation of old Indian burial grounds in the vicinity of Eureka"; and that Stewart had dispatched his assistant to Trinidad to meet with "Indians and other interested parties."[57]

Heizer lobbied state officials to back him up against local

protests. "It was with great regret," the district superintendent of the Division of Beaches and Parks wrote Heizer, "that I learned of the difficulty you had in connection with your research work." E. P. French pledged his future support "in the public relations aspect of research work in our parks."[58] A few weeks later, the politically connected chairman of the State Park Commission offered to help Heizer circumvent local opposition to a proposed dig at Dry Lagoon State Park, just north of Big Lagoon. "There are people who haven't much else to do but cause trouble," Joseph Knowland wrote Heizer. He promised to "see if some plan can be worked out to accomplish what you request."[59]

But such a plan was not worked out. Robert Heizer quickly decided to "abandon our efforts in Humboldt County. It is simply not worth the trouble," he wrote a state commissioner, "to try to discover the prehistory in the face of these disconcerting objections." Privately, Heizer believed that Eureka's Women's Club president Ruth Smith, who had written to him on behalf of the Federation of Women's Clubs, was operating in collusion with "local relic collectors."[60]

It was a few years later, in 1953, that the UC Berkeley department of anthropology wrote to Cecile Clarke proposing a joint excavation with Eureka High School on Indian Island. They were trying to recoup their blotted reputation and to "avoid the antagonisms that have involved the university in the past." Nothing came of the overture.[61]

According to a couple of self-serving accounts written several years after the protest at Tsurai, Berkeley was blameless in the whole affair. The team had only excavated "trenches in refuse deposit." Local collectors were responsible for digging up "historic burials" and "getting out as much as possible before we got here."[62] The main culprits, noted Heizer and Bennyhoff, were Doc Stuart and Charles Miles, who "despoiled a number of recent Indian graves" and "helped plunder the historic cemetery at Trinidad Bay." The academics accused the locals of Machiavellian trickery: "It is quite obvious, since Stuart knew of our intentions to excavate and of our schedule, that the graveyard looting was done so that any blame resulting would attach to the university."[63]

The whole experience at Tsurai, Heizer later recalled, had been "most difficult," but the university extricated themselves from the crisis—so Heizer claimed—when an owner of the land on which the site was located testified that he had witnessed Stuart and Miles "digging and saw them carry off the human bones and grave offerings." The Berkeley team, wrote Bennyhoff in 1954, "was subsequently cleared, and the Indians then cooperated with the project."[64]

But an eyewitness account suggests a more complex and less cut-and-dried account of what happened during and after the 1949 field trip. Axel Lindgren, a fifth-generation descendant of a Swedish seaman and Yurok woman, tells a different story:

> The next tampering with this rich historical landmark
> was a planned scientific study by a group of students
> from the University of California, led by Robert F. Heizer
> and Jack [i.e., John] Mills, in late summer of 1949. This
> study was supposed to be limited to the midden beds,
> but when my Dad and I arrived to monitor the study
> (uninvited), the students were in a six-foot deep trench
> at the foot of "Old Jenny's" grave and my Dad told them
> so. Mills, not a bit happy with our presence, ordered the
> crew out of the trench and directed them to another area.
> After convincing Mills that we came, not to interrupt his
> study, but only to observe, he toned down and explained
> his displeasure with our presence. My mother Georgia,
> her mother Minnie Shaffer, and another family member,
> Olive Frank, were there each day, "raising havoc" over
> this "grave-digging project by the University boys".... The
> oversight by Mills of not "sealing off" the study area led to
> wholesale pillage to the present time [1991].[65]

Despite the confrontation over Tsurai, a Berkeley crew returned to the area in 1953, this time concentrating on a Wiyot settlement on the south spit of the Humboldt Bay that Llewellyn Loud had identified in 1918 as an important village with "many graves."[66] Here Albert Elsasser and James Bennyhoff, finding that seven burials had already been "removed by locals," excavated the remaining burial of an adult woman in a redwood slab coffin. They reported "some reservations among certain townspeople" about their dig.[67]

By the mid-1950s, the relationship of academic archaeologists

6.2 Berkeley archaeologists at Wiyot grave, Humboldt Bay, 1953.

was tense and strained with local Yurok, broken with local collectors, and antagonistic with the Humboldt County clubwomen. "I have now a somewhat jaundiced view of archaeology in Northwestern California," Heizer concluded after experiencing organized opposition on three fronts.[68] Years later, after reviewing his "big accumulation" of California-related archaeological correspondence and notes going back to the early 1930s, Heizer decided to destroy the whole file "so that it will not become 'archival' and subject to the possibility of being pawed through and its contents 'interpreted.'"[69]

Meanwhile, for the first time in the twentieth century, native voices of protest began to receive serious attention in the press, as well as in the political arena. In 1949 a local columnist working in consultation with Robert Spott published a series of articles about Yurok culture, including the observation that:

> Desecration of the graves of their ancestors is, in the
> minds of the Yurok people, the final word in depravity.

Perhaps the greatest cause for the lingering bitterness against the invading whites has been the utter disregard displayed for the sacredness of these family and tribal shrines. The miner, who with his hydraulic devices, sluicing away these memories of the past; the farmer, heedlessly or deliberately plowing up whole village sites and cemeteries; and the stockman turning his cattle upon abandoned village sites; have left a lasting sense of resentment, if not hatred, in the minds of the injured and deeply religious people of other days. Encouragement and aid by the whites in preserving these symbolic evidences of past dignity and glory might well serve as a means of healing the breech between the two races.[70]

It was a breakthrough to have Yurok views taken seriously in a Humboldt newspaper, but it would take at least another twenty years before native protests forced local authorities to protect their cemeteries.

SEVEN
Vigorous Complaint

"Are we not native sons of these United
States?"
— Robert Spott, Yurok, 1926

"I am faithful, I do not give out."
— Walt Whitman, "The Wound-Dresser"

Raising Havoc

Knowing that a native cemetery near his home in Virginia was a
place of "considerable notoriety among the Indians" didn't keep
Thomas Jefferson, later in life, from digging up a thousand human
remains to satisfy his scientific curiosity. Although Captain
George Vancouver, recognizing that even "savage nations" take
seriously their "funeral solemnities," ordered his crew to stay away
from gravesites, other expeditions dug up funerary goods by the
thousands and took them home to European museums—despite
widespread recognition that such actions generated resentment
and resistance. For example, Ernest de Massey, passing by Big
Lagoon in 1850, knew that "anyone who dares defile the graves"
might receive a "deadly arrow" in his back. And Governor Peter
Burnett, notoriously associated with the state's "extermination"
campaign, conceded in 1851 that California's "small and scattered

tribes have some ideas of existence as a separate and independent people, and some conception of their right to the country, acquired by long, uninterrupted, and exclusive possession."[1]

Opposition to excavation of the graves of native peoples follows a familiar historical trajectory that ranges from expressions of sorrow to moral exhortation, to petitioning for redress of grievances, to disruptive militancy, and to organized political action. It was—and continues to be—such a bitter, longstanding grievance that when the Red Power movement exerted its muscle in the late 1960s, the issue of grave desecration was given high priority in political manifestos. At the Second Convocation of American Indian Scholars, held in Aspen in September 1971, there was a lively discussion about "what the great museums were doing with Indian artifacts and sacred objects. Are they mausoleums or are they centers of cultural integrity and cultural awareness?" asked the moderator.[2]

Two decades later, the struggle over repatriation—namely, who has the right to ownership of native artifacts, what constitutes "sacred," and whose authority prevails in determining cultural value—persisted as "the paramount human rights problem for American Indians today," according to Walter Echo-Hawk, an attorney with the Native American Rights Fund.[3]

The first written evidence of opposition to excavation of cemeteries in northern California came from Shasta County in 1874, when a Wintu woman petitioned Livingston Stone, a federal Commissioner of Fish and Fisheries, for help in protecting gravesites. "We were surrounded by Indians, of course, this being an Indian country," wrote Stone in his official report. "Near our camp is the graveyard of their chiefs and magnates, where the good Indians of the McCloud have been buried for centuries. The living members of the tribe are in constant fear lest we should dig up their graves for relics. This fear, caused without doubt by the casual remarks of our party on the subject, is well illustrated by the following unique petition brought to me one day, with great formality and seriousness. The Indian woman who brought it had employed some white friend to draw it up for her." Stone then quoted the letter:

Shasta, September 11, 1874

This is to certify that Mrs. Matilda Charles Empire, one of the old settlers of Shasta County, is now on a pilgrimage to the graves of their ancestors, and she prays Commissioner Stone not to disturb any of her friends and relatives who have gone the way of all flesh, and this they will ever pray.

Signed by
Her husband, Empire Charley
Matilda Charley
Their sister, Kate Charley[4]

Even after the Yurok were burned out and driven from their coastal settlements, they continued to take action to protect abandoned graves and sites of cultural significance. The formation in the 1920s and early 1930s of the Hoopa Valley Indian Tribe and Yurok Tribal Organization provided a political voice for their complaints. "Something has to be done," Robert Spott told a Commonwealth Club audience in 1926. He had served as a "native son of these United States" in the trenches of France during World War I, only to return home to the Klamath to find sickness, despair, and poverty among the Yurok people. "I am here to tell you that we are almost at the end of the road," he told his audience of elite reformers and supporters of eugenics. "I would like to know today if we will ever get our country back."[5] The desire to reclaim original territory was in part motivated by the need to protect graves and other sites of cultural significance.

In 1929, when Humboldt County contracted with the Little River Redwood Company to develop a "public playground and recreational park" in Big Lagoon, the lease included a specific prohibition against "digging for Indian graves or relics"—no doubt an indication of native opinion expressed on the matter.[6] This did not stop Doc Stuart and other local collectors from excavating graves at Big Lagoon. In 1931—the year that Stuart was shipping off human remains exhumed at Big Lagoon to his academic contacts in the Bay Area—the US Indian Service located on the Hoopa reservation reported "some of the Indians are making very vigorous complaint against excavations at Indian burying grounds along the coast." In response, the Little River Redwood Company sent out a letter to Cecile Clarke at Eureka High School revoking its permission to conduct excavations "for scientific purposes" at Big Lagoon and Trinidad. "We now feel," wrote the Little River Redwood Company's vice-president and general manager, "that we must regard the complaint of the Indians; and ask you to consider your permit, to search for Indian relics of any kind on our property, as cancelled. We feel sure you will appreciate the situation, and govern yourself accordingly."[7]

But Cecile Clarke and other diggers did not govern themselves accordingly. The young Axel Lindgren witnessed skeletons "strewn around the gravesites" as he walked with his brothers to school in Trinidad in 1931. Among these human remains were those of "Old Mau, our great-grandfather, the last male leader of Tsurai."[8] Throughout the 1930s and 1940s, Clarke bought and received as donations artifacts collected from graves at Big Lagoon. Stuart's own field notes from the early 1930s put him digging up burials from Tsurai, in Trinidad, and from O-pyúweg—"an ancient site at the south end of the spit" in Big Lagoon—where "50 bodies have been taken out."[9] A credible eyewitness account also reports that during excavations at Big Lagoon in the 1930s and 1940s, Doc Stuart carried out his work surreptitiously "under the cover of a canvas tent, which he set up (as if he was just camping there) and moved gradually as the work progressed across the open field."[10]

In 1964 Robert Heizer and Albert Elsasser recalled that "excavation of graves at Trinidad Bay was strictly avoided in deference to the request of the local Indians."[11] What they neglected to mention was that this deference was only offered in the wake of protests and publicity following the excavation, in the late 1940s, of human remains in Patrick's Point State Park. As we have seen, when a team of Berkeley archaeologists began to excavate burial sites at Tsurai, native organizations complained to the Bureau of Indian Affairs and local Yurok women started "raising havoc" at the digging site.

These early challenges had some success in putting a brake on archaeological excavations, but not stopping them. It took a decade of militant, confrontational activism coast to coast, accompanied by grassroots organizing and political lobbying, before the struggle over patrimony achieved results. "By 1967 there was a radical change in thinking on the part of many of us," recalled Vine Deloria Jr., a leading Native American political and legal activist whose 1969 book *Custer Died for Your Sins: An Indian Manifesto* challenged popular racial stereotypes.[12] In the 1970s, says Russell Means, the first director of the American Indian Movement (AIM), "we lit a fire across Indian country."[13] And inevitably the fire spread across the terrain of anthropology. "It's extremely important for us to realize," said Margaret Mead at the 1970 conference of the American Anthropological Association, "that a shift has taken place."[14]

The activism of the Red Power movement was expressed in a decade of protests, beginning with the formation of AIM in Minneapolis in 1968 and the occupations of Alcatraz from November 1969 to June 1971, the Bureau of Indian Affairs in Washington, D.C. in 1972, and Wounded Knee in 1973. It culminated with the Longest Walk, in 1978.[15] "This is the moment of truth for the American Indian," the keynote speaker announced at the First Convocation of American Indian Scholars, held at Princeton University in March 1970, "a moment when we stand on the threshold of great change."[16]

Issues of cultural patrimony, and the role of anthropologists and archaeologists, were very much on the minds of activists in the movement's early days. In his blistering 1969 polemic, Vine Deloria Jr. compared anthropologists to missionaries—"intolerably certain that they represent ultimate truth."[17] Singer Floyd Red Crow Westerman, whose 1970 album announced "Here Come the Anthros," popularized the message of *Custer Died for Your Sins:*

> And the anthros still keep coming like death and taxes to our lands
>
> To study their feathered freaks with funded money in their hands.
>
> Like a Sunday at the zoo the cameras click away
>
> Taking notes and tape recordings of all the animals at play.[18]

In December 1970, a group of native protesters marched on the Southwest Museum in Los Angeles, carrying signs that called for "Indian Power" and cajoled people to "Dig Up Your Own

Dead." When the protest turned into a sit-in, eleven people were arrested. They were all sentenced to jail for ten days, required to pay a fine of $375 each, and ordered by the judge to write a five-thousand-word essay on civil disobedience.[19]

The manifesto issued by the Indians of All Tribes in 1969 during their occupation of Alcatraz included a proposal that the island be used in part as a museum that would offer a counter-narrative to the prevailing amnesia and representation of native peoples as curiosities and relics:

> Some of the present buildings will be taken over to develop an American Indian Museum, which will depict our native foods and other cultural contributions we have given to all the world. Another part of the Museum will present some of the things the white man has given to the Indians, in return for the land and the life he took: disease, alcohol, poverty, and cultural decimation (as symbolized by old tin cans, barbed wire, rubber tires, plastic containers, etc.). Part of the museum will remain a dungeon, to symbolize both Indian captives who were incarcerated for challenging white authority, and those who were imprisoned on reservations. The Museum will show the noble and the tragic events of Indian history, including the broken treaties, the documentary of the Trail of Tears, the Massacre of Wounded Knee, as well as the victory over Yellow-Hair Custer and his army.[20]

In 1970 the American Indian Student Association at the University of Minnesota satirized the archaeological establishment by submitting a proposal to the National Science Foundation that called for the exhumation and scientific analysis of human remains in a pioneer cemetery. Frederick Dockstader, the Oneida-Navajo director of the Museum of the American Indian (Heye Foundation) in New York, was subjected to sharp questioning from the audience at the Second Convocation of Indian Scholars. "I have very strong feelings about archaeological excavations," said one participant. "Maybe," said another, "we should go and excavate Christ Church Cemetery in Philadelphia or Boston, and check to see how people were doing at the time they were buried." When Dockstader was asked to consider consulting tribes about the appropriateness of displaying or even owning sacred objects, his reply was cautious and defensive: "I'm certainly in the position to ask knowledgeable Indian people about how they feel about it. The return, however, would be up to my trustees."[21] It would take another eighteen years before an act of Congress authorized the transfer of the Heye's collection to the more native-directed National Museum of the American Indian.

The struggles over patrimony and repatriation required leaders willing and able to take on courts and legislatures. The success of the NAACP's Legal Defense Fund in challenging segregation served as a model for judicial activism.[22] In 1967, thanks to a Ford Foundation program, some fifty Native Americans, including Vine Deloria Jr., attended law school at the University of Colorado. The same year, the American Indian Law Center opened at the University of New Mexico, and in 1973 the College of Law at the University of Oklahoma produced the first issue of the *American Indian Law Review*.[23] "It was apparent to me," wrote Deloria, "that the Indian revolution was well under way and that someone had better get a legal education so that we could have our own legal program for defense of Indian treaty rights."[24] The first cohort of native lawyers established an array of organizations, including the Native American Rights Fund, established in Boulder in 1970 to provide advocacy services and coordinate legal strategy nationwide.[25]

Moment of Truth

While the activist wing received a great deal of media attention, the Native American movement itself was highly decentralized, consisting of a variety of independent, regional groups, loosely affiliated with a national social movement.[26] California was the first state in which a grassroots organization was created to specifically halt the desecration and looting of cemeteries. The Northwest Indian Cemetery Protection Association (NICPA), an intertribal nonprofit organization with strong Yurok participation, was officially established in 1970.[27] Its first chairman, Milton Marks, and its second chairman, Walt Lara Sr., were well-known Yurok leaders. In 1988 NICPA gained national prominence for its role as the respondent in the "G-O Road" US Supreme Court case involving Native American religious access to public lands.[28] But long before that case was decided, the association's militancy in California generated widespread recognition and a flurry of results.

The official founding of NICPA in 1970 was the result of a perfect convergence: an accumulation of grievances stretching back at least a hundred years, combined with a receptive political climate, the rise of a new generation of native leaders and strategic activists committed to building organizations for the long run, and the emergence of a cadre of ethically responsible anthropologists willing to play a supporting role in defense of Native American rights. And a triggering incident.

In October 1969, a young assistant professor of anthropology who was working on his doctorate and had just started his first teaching job, at San Francisco State University, received word from Tom Hannah at the Clarke Historical Museum in Eureka that the site of the Yurok settlement of Tsahpekw in the state park at Stone Lagoon (north of Big Lagoon) was being torn apart by collectors. When Michael Moratto checked out the area, it "resembled a battlefield with contiguous potholes and shattered bones from desecrated graves covering about two acres." Moratto

7.1 House pits at Tsahpekw at Stone Lagoon, 1928.

sought and received permission from Francis Riddell, chief archaeologist of the California Department of Parks and Recreation, to initiate a salvage operation.[29] In January and February of 1970, he and two colleagues carried out a reconnaissance of Tsahpekw, refilled potholes, and "made surface collections." With "all the standard permits" in hand, he planned to return in June with twenty students to carry out an excavation of the Yurok site. He felt confident that he had received a go-ahead from "two influential Yurok Indians" who "were fully informed of the proposed excavations and seemed in complete sympathy with our efforts to stabilize the site and to salvage whatever of archaeological value remained, while avoiding cemetery areas."[30]

Moratto must have known—as did archaeologist John Mills during the 1949 excavation of Tsurai—that it would be impossible to carry out an excavation of an important native site without disturbing graves. When an attorney for California Indian Legal Services wrote to him in April 1970 expressing "a strong feeling among the Indians of the North Coast against this constant digging up of Indian burial grounds" and asking, point blank, "whether in fact San Francisco State plans to send a project up there to desecrate this burial ground," Moratto hedged and covered himself on this eventuality: "If we do encounter any burials, it is our intention to re-inter them with proper respect in a part of the site that will not be disturbed by subsequent Stone Lagoon Park developments." The concerns of the attorney for the Yurok were not assuaged by this promise. "It is felt," replied Robert Donovan, "that one of the reasons why there is so much exploration in the North Coast area is that archaeology professors desire to give practical experience to their classes and to do so they must go on a dig. The Indian communities' dignity is constantly infringed upon by these efforts and Indians wish that such efforts would be directed at white cemeteries."[31]

Despite these warning signs, Moratto returned to Stone Lagoon with a crew of eager students who were ready to learn by doing. But by June, NICPA was on the move and the political mood had changed.[32] Now he was facing an organization of "dedicated, self-determined Indians," not just a couple of sympathetic Yurok.[33]

Sometime in 1969, a small group of influential Yurok, Hupa, Karuk, and Wiyot at the core of what would become NICPA

began to discuss "the wanton desecration of Indian family cemeteries by archaeologists, art collectors, hobbyists, necromancers,
and commercial and amateur curio seekers."[34] This was a group of
visionaries who understood that grassroots organizing requires
patience and stamina; and who had a knack for building political
relationships with other organizations and generating publicity
for their campaign. Its leaders also had a toughness and resiliency
hewn from their experiences in working-class jobs and the labor
movement. These qualities served them well in confrontations
with authority, whether in the form of professional archaeologists
or government functionaries or academics.

The founding organizer of NICPA, Milton Marks (1915–
1980), was from a Yurok family whose activism spans four generations.[35] His father, Jimmy Marks, grew up in Morek—according to Thomas Waterman, a "very important" Yurok town on the
Klamath and site of "impressive ceremonies."[36] He was known
as Morek Jimmy until school authorities further Anglicized his
name. "He belonged to an era to be remembered," noted his
obituary.[37] The teachers "couldn't spell Morek, couldn't even
sound it out," recalled Jimmy's daughter in 1990. "Morek, that's
our main name."[38] Her father played a leading role in the community as a dam builder and was "held in high esteem."[39] Later
in his life, when he lived on the coast, he supported the state's
taking over the area around the native site of Espaw from a gold
mining company. He thought the state parks would do a better
job of protecting the settlement and allowing Yurok to gather
berries, roots, ferns, and other traditional materials.[40]

Jimmy's wife, Josephine Brown McDonald Marks (1877–
1965)—known as Josie or Sin-gi-wa—was one of Waterman's
informants about Yurok culture, the "very intelligent woman"
who wouldn't tell the anthropologist her native name. Margaret
and Milton, founding members of NICPA, were two of their
children. Milton's daughter Diane worked with NICPA until her
untimely death at the age of thirty, and his first daughter, Sandy,
was a member of NICPA and went on to develop an innovative Indian education program for Eureka's public schools. Milton's nephew Walt was his right-hand man in the early days of
NICPA. Three of Margaret Marks's children—Frank, Jeanette,
and Walt—became leaders within the Yurok Tribe and are

7.2 Jimmy Marks at Orick, c. 1920s.

currently members of its prestigious Culture Committee. Walt Lara Sr. is married to Callie Lara, who served for several years as the director of the Hupa Language, Culture and Education Center, and their children are emerging as leaders-to-be in their tribal communities.

While the driving force behind the formation of NICPA was Milton Marks, his older sister Margaret Marks Lara (1912–1996) was at his side and more than held her own. Born and died in Ooh-sa-mech, south of Orick, she worked in the sawmills to support her children, was active in her union as well as NICPA, spoke Spanish, and was part of the first cohort of postwar Yurok to emphasize the importance of reclaiming native languages before they died with the elders.[41] As a child she was suspended from school for fighting back when a teacher hit her. And as an adult, she inherited her mother's resiliency and unsentimental

7.3 Josephine Marks with grandchildren Frank and Walt
Lara, c. 1938.

views about anthropologists: "They just talk to us like we're the
most intelligent people in the wide old world, and when we give
them all this information and everything, then they slough us
aside."[42] Margaret, who as a young woman had stayed with the
influential native rights advocate Ruth Roberts in Oakland, had
no trouble operating confidently in the milieu of white, middle-
class professionals. A university-based expert on community
organizing remembers her as a formidable foe in the 1970s: "She
cried, stomped the floor, shook her fist at archaeologists. She
gave archaeologists a hard time."[43]

But within her own community, she was a patient and tireless organizer, serving as chairperson of the Yurok Organization
before it became officially incorporated. Despite "always working," recalls her niece Sandy Burton, "Auntie Margaret pounded
into our heads 'You come from a long line of well-bred Indians

and you must live up to that expectation. Be respectful at all times.' A lot was expected of our family. She would come over to my home on Friday nights and teach me the Yurok language. 'This is your inheritance,' she said. This kind of leadership was also instilled in Milton."[44]

By the time that Milton Marks became the organizational leader and public face of NICPA, he was fifty-four years old and a person of considerable experience, charm, and self-earned knowledge. In the mid-1930s he had received a Bureau of Indian Affairs loan to attend the Sherman Institute in Riverside—a boarding school that no doubt raised his pan-Indian consciousness. After graduation he stayed on in the Los Angeles area, attending junior

7.4 Margaret Marks Lara, c. 1930s.

and business colleges and working various jobs, including a walk-on role as a generic African soldier in a turban in the 1941 Hollywood movie *Sundown*, starring Gene Tierney. After serving in the army from 1944 to 1946, he returned to Humboldt County, where he was employed as a timber faller for the rest of his working life.[45] One of his jobs was with Hammond Lumber, the company that clear-cut the area around Big Lagoon.

7.5 Milton Marks, c. 1950s.

By all accounts, Milton Marks was an extraordinarily effective organizer who combined a steely resolve to keep his eyes on the prize with a capacious patience for diplomacy and education. He was "persistent and amicable," recalls Jim Benson, the first Native American archaeologist to work with NICPA. "I've never met a person who knows more about traditional Yurok culture than Milton. He could go up to anybody and get them to talk. He listened, was very inquisitive....He had his own body of knowledge, told story after story."[46] Dave Fredrickson, one of the first white archaeologists to develop a working relationship with NICPA, remembers Milton Marks as a "charismatic presence...And he always let me know what was going on."[47] He also had a profound impact on Polly Quick, fresh from her doctoral dissertation in anthropology at Harvard. "It was a pivotal moment in my career," she recalled recently. "He took me on as a protégé. He's the one who taught me how to reach out to native communities, how to listen. My relationships with Native Americans have all been patterned on what he taught me: it takes time to build relationships."[48] Other people who worked with NICPA describe Milton Marks as an activist who didn't tread lightly when there was a need to take

7.6 Sandra Burton's framed photograph of her father, Milton Marks.

principled stands, but who understood the importance of tactical alliances with people and organizations that had access to power.

The proposed excavation at Tsahpekw had special meaning for the Marks family: they had relatives buried there. The confrontation with Moratto, recalled Milton, "inspired" the formation of NICPA.[49] "Being raised by my grandparents and a working mother," says Walt Lara Sr., "I can understand the hurt when a site is destroyed. I was there and I saw what it did to my grandparents when these excavations occurred."[50] His experience at Tsahpekw gave him a lifelong suspicion of the motives of academics and a fierce determination to protect Yurok sites. "He didn't like archaeologists," recalls Dave Fredrickson. 'Too much science,' he'd say."[51] And Lara, who to this day exudes a palpable energy, had a reputation for keeping even white supporters of NICPA anxiously on their toes. "He was a very physical person," recalls Tom Parsons, who allowed the association to use his office on the campus of Humboldt State as a mailing address during its formative years. "He was about 80 percent supportive of what I was doing." But Lara's garrulous roughness was as much tactical as it was a reflection of his personality. "You had to be tough," recalls another NICPA activist, "because people were always speaking down to you."[52] As a tag-team, Milton and Walt were a match for any opponents: "I would strong-arm them, then Milton would smooth-talk them," says Lara."[53]

Like his Uncle Miltie and mother, Margaret, Walt Lara worked in the timber industry and was active in its union.[54] By the mid-1960s, some 70 percent of native workers in rural areas and on reservations in California earned less than three thousand dollars annually; and in the Hoopa area, one out of three people was unemployed. The average age of death for Native Americans in the region was forty-two, twenty years younger than the general population; and the Indian infant mortality rate was 70 percent higher. So a job in logging, with an annual income of as much as six thousand dollars, was highly desirable, despite its rigorous physical toll.[55]

When the Lumber and Sawmill Workers union mobilized its membership to oppose the Carter administration's proposed expansion of the Redwood National Park in 1977, Milton Marks and Walt Lara joined a truck convoy and hundreds of angry loggers who traveled to Washington, D.C., and paraded a peanut-shaped redwood log in front of Congress.[56] An Arcata newspaper captured the two of them in hard hats, suspenders, and work shirts on the Capitol steps, with Lara giving an interview to a television crew.[57] And back home

7.7 Milton Marks (on left) and Walt Lara Sr. (center) at the Capitol, Washington, D.C., June 1977, lobbying to stop expansion of Redwood National Park.

in Orick, Margaret Lara buttonholed a sympathetic Senator Sam Hayakawa during a visit to Redwood National Park, telling him that most of her relatives, who worked directly or indirectly in logging, would lose jobs if Phil Burton's legislation passed.[58]

Another early participant in NICPA was Joy Sundberg, a Yurok descendant of Big Lagoon who later chaired the Trinidad Rancheria for twenty-five years. Like Margaret Lara and Milton Marks, she accumulated a great deal of worldly experience early in life—her grandparents visited Kroeber in Berkeley—and whatever her private fears, she thrust herself into "the white man's world." She was, and is, fiercely independent. "I went to school at the college of hard knocks. Look at all these chop marks on my neck," she says, pointing to the back of her head. "Always sticking it out. We fought for things that were right. We didn't do it for ourselves. None of us got rich doing it."

7.8 Joy Sundberg speaking out for Tom Bradley's campaign for governor, Trinidad, 1982.

Sundberg admired women like Jane Fonda, who opposed the war in Vietnam, because "she stood up for what she believed." In Washington, D.C., Sundberg lobbied sympathetic senators, such as Daniel Evans and Daniel Inouye, for native land rights, while locally she supported the campaigns of a white activist, Sara Parsons, the first woman elected to Humboldt's Board of Supervisors, in 1977; and of African American Tom Bradley in his unsuccessful 1982 run for governor of California. In 1974 she led a delegation of California Indians, including a troupe of Tolowa and Yurok dancers, to the Festival of American Folklife in Washington, D.C. She also transported a redwood log provided by Walt Lara for a canoe-building demonstration.

Sundberg brought to NICPA her experience as a member of the Trinidad School Board and many local political and cultural organizations, and as an appointee to the State Historical Resources Commission and United Indian Health Services Board. "There was just a few of us when NICPA started," she recalled recently. "We had to pound on doors, talk to organizations, get up and speak in front of politicians. I didn't give up. It was hard, but we had to do it." She learned that "a ragtag group of folks can defeat the big guys."[59]

By the time that twenty-six-year-old Michael Moratto arrived in Humboldt with his students in June 1970, ready to excavate Tsahpekw, native insistence on the need to protect cemeteries had already caught the attention of local officials and the press. In March 1970, the *Times-Standard* in a moment of rare candor reported that "Indians opposed people digging into the graves of their immediate ancestors."[60] A few weeks later, the Humboldt County Sheriff, Gene Cox, issued a public warning that "every person who mutilates, disinters or removes from the place of interment any human remains without authority of law is guilty of a felony. We sincerely hope that the guilty persons who are committing these acts not only realize the magnitude of the crime they are committing, but also that many bodies they are disturbing have close living relatives in the area."[61] About the same time, the director of the state's Parks and Recreation department added his voice to the growing if belated outcry of indignation by recognizing that "vandals and souvenir hunters" were destroying Tsahpekw. "Evidently, many people aren't aware of the laws protecting these historic sites and, if they are aware of them, they don't understand the serious consequences of their actions."[62]

Meanwhile, Milton Marks was building the foundations of NICPA and looking for political alliances. "He came to me and we talked about a plan to do something to stop grave robbing," recalls Tom Parsons, who came to the Arcata campus in 1965 as de facto director of the university's newly formed Center for Community Development.[63] Parsons arrived with degrees in education from the University of Michigan and experience as a seasoned community organizer in the mold of Saul Alinsky. He was a good match for Marks, his equal in charisma, energy, and determination. Parsons's politics were influenced by the New Left and civil rights movements, with their emphasis on grassroots, cross-racial organizing. Recently married, he and his wife, Sara Mitchell Parsons, were a formidable team. She was a white, upper-middle-class reformer from Georgia who, as a member of the Atlanta Board of Education, had worked with Martin Luther King and civil rights organizations to integrate the public schools. She had divorced her first husband after thirty years of marriage to marry Parsons. "I felt sorry for my first husband," she said, "because he married a sweet southern girl. And I turned out to be this civil rights activist and a flaming feminist."[64]

Under Parsons's leadership, the Center for Community Development received federal and state funds to work with a variety of grassroots groups and to develop field placements for students committed to public service and social justice. "We are community developers, not planners nor technical advisors," explained the center's manifesto. "Our clients, in all cases, do their own program planning in interaction with us. And they must, because the motivation that propels their projects' vigor comes directly and only from their active involvement in planning on their own behalf."[65] Parsons sought out local native leaders and provided resources to support the resurrection of Yurok languages by teaching the basics of vocabulary and grammar through a system of phonetics. "I went to them, won their trust," says Parsons. "Other than a blood transfusion, you couldn't get closer than language." The center is credited with helping to revitalize the Yurok language.[66]

While Moratto's twenty students set up camp at Patrick's Point State Park, he and two colleagues (including the chair of his department at San Francisco State) attended a meeting at Humboldt State, at the Center for Community Development. Moratto naively thought that the meeting would be the beginning of a mutually respectful collaboration. Instead, he recalls, "I listened to a great deal of animosity. I can understand why they felt that way. I caught the brunt of their anger. I paid for the sins of our fathers."[67]

The meeting, which was chaired by Milton Marks and attended by Walt Lara, Margaret Lara, nine other members of NICPA, and their lawyer (with Tom Parsons on hand as an observer), quickly turned tense and argumentative. After Moratto nervously explained that the sheriff's ban on excavations did not apply to state land, and that he hoped to salvage what remained of Tsahpekw and "to avoid cemetery areas," he sat and listened to a lecture of complaints: "Archaeologists have not contributed much beyond what is already known of Yurok history and traditions...

Archaeologists and anthropologists take artifacts and information away from the Indians and their territory without returning
anything of value to the Indians....It is sacrilegious to store the
artifacts and bones of deceased Indians in museums. They should
all be respectfully reinterred."[68]

"I was totally intimidated," recalls Moratto. "A big guy there—
about six feet across his shoulders—spoke up: 'I don't know about
you archaeologists, but you ain't going to dig at Tsahpekw."
Moratto recalls "one particularly irascible Yurok logger"—Walt
Lara—who "spiced the dialogue with periodic threats of actual
violence. Not wishing to jeopardize lives or future Indian-anthro-
pologist relationships, I conceded to leave Tsahpekw and undertake research elsewhere."[69] Moratto was too stunned to turn the
incident into a learning experience for his students. "I was shell-
shocked for several days." Even now, forty years later, he finds it
painful to recall.[70]

The showdown over Tsahpekw quickly became a widely
recounted tale, a cause célèbre in native circles and a topic of
debate and gossip in archaeology. The "unprecedented accord"—in
reality, a victory for NICPA and defeat for the San Francisco State
team—was reported in the press and retold as legend.[71] I've heard
versions of the story that turn what happened into a subversion of
the cowboys-and-Indians narrative by locating the confrontation
in the rugged wilds of Stone Lagoon rather than a sedate university office, with the Yurok running off the archaeological team at
gunpoint, rather than by the ferocity of their words. One outcome,
however, was clear to everybody who was directly involved or
heard about the incident. The rules of engagement had changed:
anybody planning to collect or dig at native sites in Humboldt
County better have the cooperation and authorization of NICPA.

Unprecedented Accord

With momentum created by the Tsahpekw incident, NICPA
quickly recruited members and supporters from a variety of tribal
groups and locales and made a name for itself in the region. In
August 1970, it was formally incorporated as a nonprofit organization, committed to "the protection of Indian cemeteries in the
Northwest California area; the preservation of these cemeteries

as peaceful and final resting places for the relatives and ancestors of Indians of California; the prevention of further desecration of these cemeteries; and the education of the public to the great indignity suffered by Indians whose relatives' graves are interfered with by anthropologists and vandals."[72]

"You had to deal with NICPA. There was nobody else to deal with," says Polly Quick about political relations with native organizations in northwest California in the 1970s, long before tribes developed formal organizations to deal with cultural resources.[73] With the participation of Jimmy Moon from the Hupa, Velma Carlson from the Wiyot, Josephine Peters from the Karuk, as well as inland and coastal Yurok, NICPA was intertribal and intergenerational, and hospitable to strong women.

In March 1971, the association had its first major political success when Humboldt's board of supervisors, in response to NICPA lobbying, unanimously pledged to "vigorously enforce those laws which protect Indian burial grounds, cemeteries, and ceremonial sites." The board also ordered the county to "conscientiously attempt to consult and reach agreement with representatives of the Northwest Indian Cemetery Protective Association" during the planning stage of "any project or operation" involving "activities which may adversely affect Indian graves, cemeteries, burial grounds, or ceremonial sites."[74] At about the same time, the state legislature, under pressure from NICPA and other groups, imposed a statewide moratorium on the disturbance of any native burial sites abandoned for less than two hundred years.

Building upon these accomplishments, NICPA quickly moved to sever its dependency on the university, which had provided public credibility and infrastructure for the new organization. With its own federal funding through the Comprehensive Employment and Training Act of 1973, support from the Inter-Tribal Council of California, and contracts with local governments, the association opened an office in McKinleyville and hired its own staff. By 1976, NICPA matters constituted only 2 percent of the work of the Center for Community Development.[75] While the center was committed to a policy of "disengaging constructively" when its community projects became self-sufficient,[76] some NICPA members regarded Tom Parsons as over-controlling and self-promoting.[77] It didn't help to alleviate suspicions of paternalism when he was depicted in the press as a "definite influence" on the "Indian people's thinking."[78] Whatever the validity of allegations about Parsons's role, the tensions between native and white activists in the early 1970s paralleled similar developments in the civil rights movement; as the politics of nationalism and self-determination prevailed, many biracial organizations collapsed.

Meanwhile, NICPA's influence significantly expanded. Its agreement with Humboldt County became the model for legislation in other counties. By 1976 the association had consulted with government officials and native groups to protect burial sites and resources in San Diego, San Luis Obispo, Marin, Tehama, Mendocino, and San Jose. Whenever issues relating to burial sites surfaced in northern California, NICPA representatives were there to voice their opinions.[79]

In January 1973, nine members of NICPA met with representatives of the county and Army Corps of Engineers to express opposition to the proposed Butler Valley Dam Project because the project would flood native burial sites. "I don't want the graves disturbed," said Velma Carlson on behalf of NICPA. "My father doesn't want them disturbed, my children don't want them disturbed."[80] By December, the Corps of Engineers had given up the project. In 1975 NICPA successfully lobbied the Trinidad city council to establish policies for the protection of Tsurai from looting and vandalism. "We have to have feelings and respect for what is buried there," said a representative of the association.[81]

NICPA sustained its reputation for militancy by participating in a land takeover in Watsonville in March 1975, protesting the desecration of Ohlone burials by a private contractor.[82] After a tense standoff with sixty native activists, some of whom were armed, the dispute was resolved when the landowner agreed to sell the land to an Ohlone group.[83] NICPA's grassroots organizing also achieved results in 1981 when Yurok activists compelled the state's Parks and Recreation department to return exhumed human remains for reburial in an unmarked plot in Patrick's Point State Park. State archaeologist Francis Riddell—a former student of Robert Heizer's—reluctantly complied with the demand: "We're giving back what I spent twenty-five years excavating and preserving," he told *Time* magazine. Walt Lara Sr. responded: "We're not property, and neither are our ancestors."[84]

Despite the lingering antagonisms following the showdown at Tsahpekw, NICPA was not opposed to working with archaeologists. They hired Jim Benson, a South Fork Hupa (Tsnungwe) with training in archaeology and environmental studies. "I was very different from most archaeologists," he says. "My native background was an important part of my identity. I was a local guy, knew the landscape and the people. My work with NICPA allowed access to and engendered trust with many Native Americans. Because of this association, I was able to gather solid ethnohistorical information to support archaeological investigations. Self-awareness and self-determination of Indians was at a critical point when I was in NICPA."[85] Benson's involvement also opened the door to joint work with other archaeologists. Even Mike Moratto returned, in 1978, to participate in a collaborative study of cultural resources in Redwood National Park.[86]

NICPA also took on the much less glamorous, behind-the-scenes work of writing technical reports and drafting policies, consulting the district attorney's office in Ukiah in 1976 about the wording of a county ordinance protecting Native American archaeological sites; and working with the Humboldt Bay Wastewater Authority in 1977 on an "Archaeological Resources Analysis," the California Coastal Commission in 1977 to assess archaeological resources at Shelter Cove, and CalTrans in 1979 regarding construction of the Redwood National Park Bypass on Highway 101.

At the statewide level, NICPA and other organizations lobbied Governor Jerry Brown and the legislature to create a government agency, directed and staffed by tribal representatives, that would be devoted to the "preservation of areas of religious or ceremonial importance" to Native Americans. The initiative was opposed by the Association of California Water Agencies and the Municipal Utilities Association on the grounds that such legislation would interfere with and delay public projects. Despite reservations expressed by some of his staff about the involvement of the state in protecting a specific religious interest, the governor supported the creation in 1976 of the Native American Heritage Commission, whose responsibilities include identifying, cataloguing, and safeguarding native cultural resources.[87] NICPA's Milton Marks was appointed to the commission and served as its chairman, later to be succeeded by Walt Lara Sr.[88] Today, the commission's work includes providing "protection to Native American human burials and skeletal remains from vandalism and inadvertent destruction."[89]

During the 1970s, relations between native communities and archaeologists in California were, according to one participant, in a "state of extreme polarization." And anthropologists themselves were fiercely divided against each other, with some defending the scientific importance of retaining and studying human remains, and others dismissing the practice as useless, as well as culturally insensitive. As Polly Quick observed in 1982, "some Native Americans have fundamental beliefs about the sanctity of interred human remains and inappropriateness of disturbing them. Some archaeologists have basic beliefs about the sanctity of scientific data, and the inappropriateness of destroying it, or destroying potential access to it."[90] The name-calling got nasty, with archaeologist Frank Norick referring to his colleagues who sought contracts with native groups as "mercenaries," who were "quite prepared to sacrifice future legitimate scientific study of skeletal remains on the altar of financial expediency."[91]

NICPA's relationship with government and university-based archaeologists went through a baptism of cantankerous distrust. When state park officials came from Sacramento to Humboldt to meet with NICPA in 1973, the "local Indian leaders found other things to do," as one participant noted. Eventually, Milton Marks "returned from an early morning buck hunt" and the meeting took place in his home.[92] Another archaeologist recalls attending a meeting with NICPA in 1976 at which he was required to listen uneasily while Milton Marks lectured him about the history of massacres in northern California and how anthropologists had "entered into the homes of local Native Americans, asking numerous questions, and then publishing information, available to all, of a sensitive nature."[93]

This kind of testing was common in the early days of the association, but at times the hard line softened, offering a glimpse of the future. A confessional voice in academia, for instance, acknowledged that "probably few museums or universities in the United States have completely clean hands."[94] Beginning in the

1970s, activism within as well as against anthropology mobilized a new generation of archaeologists for whom collaboration and consultation with Native Americans regarding excavations and surveys became a matter of not only legal compliance but also moral obligation.[95] When asked in 1969 to make a list of "useful anthropologists," Deloria replied, "It would be very short."[96] By the mid-1970s, the list was a little longer.

The spirit of socially responsible anthropology was exemplified in the career of Dave Fredrickson, who received his doctoral degree from UC Davis in 1973 and spent most of his career in the anthropology department at Sonoma State University building its archaeology program. Fredrickson had reluctantly entered a doctoral program at Berkeley in the 1950s but dropped out, feeling uncomfortable around the class pretensions of the faculty and the assumptions of academic anthropology. "I constantly felt my uninvited intrusion into the lives of other peoples." For several years, he drove a taxi and a truck, worked as a landscaper and art school model, sang folk songs, and gave guitar lessons. Before he became known for his work as an archaeologist, he had already made his mark nationally as a folksinger.[97] His rural background and working-class jobs put him at odds with academia but prepared him well for his midlife work with native groups. He too knew what it was like to be an outsider, patronized and not taken seriously. Even at the height of his career, he did not want his sense of himself to be consumed by his professional credentials. "Certainly I have done archaeology," he wrote to a colleague in the mid-1980s, "have argued archaeology, have been defined by others as an archaeologist, and have done a number of things over the years that I have felt to be in the best interests of archaeology, but my personal identity has always been—and remains—elsewhere."[98]

Early in his career, Fredrickson was "well aware that there was widespread distrust of archaeologists, one of the most serious [issues] being the archaeological treatment of the dead." He thought that archaeology did not have to be a "culturally destructive undertaking," that relations with native people could be based on dialogue rather than condescension, and that "a new, collaborative, mutually reinforcing archaeology was indeed possible." When he started teaching at Sonoma State, he taught

7.9 Dave Fredrickson (rear) and Lowell Damon backfilling at Stone Lagoon with NICPA's permission, July 1976.

his students to "always take notes when Indians speak at digs, be alert to cultural differences, and show respect. Don't complain, keep your mouths shut, be friendly, and things will eventually happen the way they should. A lot of my success," he reflected recently, "was due to me listening."[99] Fredrickson's attitude and consciousness were widely appreciated. "He was a person of exceptional integrity, generosity, and good will," says Jim Benson. "I never met anyone who would disagree."[100]

By 1976, the site at Tsahpekw was in bad shape, the result of erosion, neglect, and looting that had taken place since Moratto began his ill-fated efforts at salvage six years earlier. Milton Marks invited Fredrickson to a meeting that he approached with trepidation, knowing about NICPA's reputation for humiliating archaeologists. "I have to say I was somewhat paranoid and anxious, wondering if somehow one of the goals of the meeting was to get me." But he was pleasantly surprised to find that NICPA wanted to hire him to work on the stabilization of Tsahpekw as part of a grant from the state's Parks and Recreation department. From that moment on, whenever meetings took place with state officials, "I sat with the Indians," says Fredrickson. "I don't remember being asked, it just happened."[101]

A two-year "cooperative effort" (1976–1978) between Sonoma State's Anthropological Laboratory—led by Fredrickson and his colleagues, working with Jim Benson—and NICPA made it possible to stabilize and temporarily protect the site of Tsahpekw at Stone Lagoon. NICPA also permitted Fredrickson to remove the remains of nine people and take them to the university for preservation and study.[102] Margaret Lara led seminars at the site on "Yurok life, ways, and values" for the field crew. Milton Marks hosted salmon feasts, made his boat available to the archaeological team, and organized a special dinner for everybody involved. He appreciated that Fredrickson had donated much of his time and expertise to the project.[103] The final report, submitted to the California Department of Parks and Recreation, was dedicated to Milton Marks and Margaret Lara.[104] The experience convinced Fredrickson that "I need not withdraw from the profession."[105] As a result of this joint project, he developed a bond of trust with Milton Marks, from whom he learned a great deal. "It was one of those magic moments that made me into a different person. I felt he was my better. I would have done anything for him."[106] When his friend died in 1980, Fredrickson was invited to give a tribute at his funeral.

What happened at Tsahpekw laid the foundations for other collaborative projects. In 1978 NICPA worked with archaeologists from San Francisco State and Sonoma State universities to survey cultural resources in Redwood National Park. Milton Marks provided "invaluable advice," and NICPA was hired as an independent contractor. For two days in May, some forty native experts and representatives joined academics, researchers, and government officials in a conference that issued a joint resolution establishing a permanent role for Native Americans in the development and implementation of park policies. In particular, the conference advocated "the right for Indians to use at no cost traditional site areas within the park to obtain materials necessary for the continuation of religious activities and other cultural needs"; and "an appropriate management plan for Indian burials within the park system."[107]

In the early 1980s, when the California Department of Parks and Recreation revisited a longtime proposal to reconstruct a Yurok village on public land, state officials gave high priority to "cooperation with and involvement of the local Native Americans" and agreed that the final outcome "should be undertaken 'in concert' with NICPA." Eight out of the twelve criteria for selecting a site for the village—eventually built at Patrick's Point State Park—involved the needs and requirements of Native Americans, which were taken seriously. "The present leadership of NICPA," reported archaeologist Jim Woodward in 1982, "is not opposed to archaeology per se, but would strongly oppose any disturbance to Indian burials or cemeteries."[108]

Activism of the 1970s also led to significant changes in the law over the next two decades in California. "Malicious disturbance" of a Native American cemetery became a felony in

7.10 Reunion, March 2011, of NICPA veterans (left to right) Jim Benson, Joy Sundberg, and Walt Lara Sr.

1976; a 1987 law made it a felony to remove "Native American artifacts or human remains with an intent to sell or dissect"; in 1991 the legislature passed a law authorizing the repatriation of human remains and grave artifacts; and in 2004 a law was passed preventing the public disclosure of the location of Native American prehistoric cemeteries.[109]

After the death of Milton Marks in 1980, NICPA began to decline.[110] Native communities faced a daunting array of economic and social issues that put huge demands on a small cadre of leaders. Also, it was difficult to find a successor with Marks's ability to represent the public face of the association while handling intra-organizational tensions over such issues as the hiring of white employees, charges of sexism, and complaints about styles of leadership—struggles that were pervasive in civil rights organizations in the 1970s.[111] More importantly, the demise of NICPA was accelerated by its own success, namely that the major demands the association had fought for—consideration for native cultural sites, respectful partnerships between anthropologists and tribal communities, and public condemnation of looting—were beginning to receive recognition in law and legislation, and to be practiced in the emerging field of "compliance archaeology."

EIGHT
An Argument about the Past

"History is an argument about the past,
as well as the record of it, and its terms
are forever changing."
— Raphael Samuel, 1994

Regime Change

The last forty years have seen some extraordinary developments
in efforts to protect and regulate native gravesites and their
contents: a slew of federal, state, and local laws; debates within
anthropology and archaeology about the ethics of repatriation;
and the emergence of revisionist histories of the California Story.

In 2009 the Senate's unanimous apology to "native peoples of
the United States" for "ill-conceived policies," "the breaking of
covenants," and "the many instances of violence, maltreatment,
and neglect" was a significant symbolic gesture, as was President
Obama's decision a few weeks later to meet with the representatives
of 564 federally recognized tribes. "I get it," said Obama. "I'm on
your side. I understand what it means to be an outsider."[1] This shift
in the legal and political ambiance represents a significant break
with the past, but as in the case of the twentieth-century civil
rights movement, it remains unfinished and subject to reversals,
and it poses new contradictions. And there are no guarantees that

there will be a steady march forward down the road to cultural justice.

What happened in California was paralleled in several other states, and eventually in federal legislation. The NICPA model of grassroots organizing and in-your-face militancy persisted for a few years. American Indians Against Desecration was organized in 1980 under the auspices of the International Indian Treaty Council after its founding members, visiting museums and universities during the Longest Walk, discovered "bodies of our ancestors stored in cardboard boxes, plastic bags and paper sacks."[2] In 1985 Rosemary Cambra, tribal chair of the Muwekma Ohlone, protested the unearthing of human remains at a construction site in downtown San Jose. "A turning point came," she recalled, "when an archaeologist provoked me and I hit him with a shovel, creating a lot of publicity."[3] She spent a year's weekends in jail for assault.[4]

By the mid-1980s, the struggle to preserve graves and their contents shifted primarily to the legal and legislative arenas. There have been laws on the books protecting archaeological sites since 1906, when the Act for the Preservation of American Antiquities made it illegal at the federal level to excavate or do damage to any "historic and prehistoric ruin or monument, or any object of antiquity on Government lands." But the act was rarely enforced, it was constitutionality vague, and it privileged scientific over native authority regarding definitions of "objects of antiquity."[5] The Antiquities Act, observes anthropologist Randall McGuire, made "the archaeologist the hero of the story and either split Indian peoples from their past or treated them as artifacts of that past. Rarely have our public presentations given an Indian view of the past or treated that past as part of an ongoing native cultural tradition."[6] Prior to the 1980s, the courts were equally unhelpful in protecting unmarked native graves, recognizing native people's desire to stay closely connected with their "ancient dead," or guarding cemeteries on land from which tribes had been forcefully removed.[7]

While state legislatures—especially in California, Oklahoma, Colorado, New Mexico, and Arizona—passed laws to protect native patrimony in the 1970s, the most significant and far-reaching legislation occurred in Congress. The 1978 American

Indian Religious Freedom Act emphasized the importance of access to "sacred sites," including cemeteries, to Native Americans exercising their "inherent right" to "believe, express, and exercise [their] traditional religions." The 1979 Archaeological Resources Protection Act recognized "archaeological resources on public and Indian lands" as an "irreplaceable part of the Nation's heritage" and provided criminal penalties for unauthorized excavations of graves and "human skeletal remains."[8] Both acts had limited practical consequences for native communities, but raised questions about the ethics of prevailing practices in museums and fueled public interest in the politics of patrimony.

In 1988 the US Supreme Court decided a case in which the Forest Service appealed the ruling of a lower court that had sided with the Northwest Indian Cemetery Protection Association to ban the building of a fifty-five-mile road from Gasquet to Orleans (the G-O Road) through the Chimney Rock area of the Six Rivers National Forest, a place of longtime cultural significance to the Yurok, Karuk, and Tolowa tribes.[9] In *Lyng v. NICPA*, the respondents lost the battle but won the war. The court, in a five-to-three split, decided in favor of the Forest Service despite having recognized that "the logging and road-building projects at issue in this case could have devastating effects on traditional Indian religious practices." In a powerful dissenting opinion, joined by Justices Marshall and Blackmun, Justice William Brennan argued that spiritual beliefs should trump property rights. "Ceremonies are communal efforts undertaken for specific purposes in accordance with instructions handed down from generation to generation." In 1990 NICPA appealed the Court's decision to the Inter-American Commission on Human Rights of the Organization of American States but withdrew the case when the unbuilt part of the road was incorporated into the Siskiyou Wilderness and the Forest Service—presumably concerned about damage to its public reputation—abandoned its plans to build the G-O Road.[10]

This case, despite its legal outcome, provided momentum for passage of the National Museum of the American Indian Act, which in 1989 authorized the creation of a museum "about Indians run by Indians."[11] The revelation in 1986 that some 18,500 human remains were warehoused in the Smithsonian propelled

Native American organizations and their allies in Congress to campaign to create a political entity that would facilitate the repatriation of "skeletal remains, cultural artifacts, and other items of religious or cultural significance."[12] The National Museum of the American Indian opened in 2004 to house the government's native holdings, which at the time were spread throughout the Smithsonian's museums and the Heye Foundation in New York. The law explicitly acknowledged that the human remains in the government's cache "have long been a matter of concern for many Indian tribes" and that "identification of the origins of such human remains is essential to addressing that concern." It required the Smithsonian to carry out an inventory of its "Indian human remains and Indian funerary objects" with a view to "expeditiously" returning them to tribes that could demonstrate a biological or cultural connection.[13] In 1996 the law was amended to make "unassociated funerary objects, sacred objects, or objects of cultural patrimony" also subject to the repatriation process.[14]

In 1990 a panel of Native Americans, museum representatives, and scientists issued a report that called for "the development of judicially-enforceable standards for repatriation of Native American human remains and objects."[15] This call culminated in passage in November 1990 of the Native American Graves Protection and Repatriation Act (NAGPRA), far-reaching legislation designed, in the words of Senator Daniel Inouye, to restore the "civil rights of America's first citizens."[16] Together, the National Museum of the American Indian Act and NAGPRA fundamentally changed relations between governments, museums, universities, and tribes by requiring federal agencies and recipients of federal funds to publish an inventory of human remains and "funerary objects" in their collections; and to repatriate these items to lineal descendants and tribes that claim a biological or cultural affiliation to them. Results were immediate. In 1991 the Smithsonian repatriated about one thousand human remains and hundreds of funerary items to the Kodiak Area Native Association in Alaska. Two years later, some 539 institutions that receive federal funds submitted inventories taking up thirty feet of shelf space in the offices of the NAGPRA Committee in the National Park Service; and in 1994 Congress appropriated $2.3 million to enable tribes to develop proposals for repatriation.[17] The obligatory reporting revealed that federal agencies all over the country—including the departments of Defense, Navy and Marine Corps, Air Force, Agriculture, and Energy—had amassed some twenty-eight thousand native body parts.[18]

While the implementation of NAGPRA over the last twenty years has been uneven, slow, and at times tempestuous, it is "unique legislation," claim Jack Trope and Walter Echo-Hawk, "because it is the first time that the federal government and non-Indian institutions must consider what is *sacred* from an Indian perspective."[19] Occasionally, there are moving ceremonies to mark the process of repatriation, such as the one held in 2008 at the American Museum of Natural History in New York, when the remains of fifty-five ancestors were returned to the Tseycum First Nation for reburial some three thousand miles away, on Vancouver Island.[20]

Understandably, the shift in political, legal, and public opinion set off a firestorm of debate within anthropology and profoundly changed the practice and relations of archaeology.[21] "The reburial issue has been costly for anthropology," notes Larry Zimmerman. "It has turned colleague against colleague."[22] In 1970 a symposium on "Anthropology and the American Indian," organized by the Bureau of Indian Affairs, was held during the annual meeting of the American Anthropological Association (AAA) in San Diego. Despite the chairman's call for "monumental patience and a high tolerance for ambiguity," it was a lively, partisan, and contentious event. "Where in the hell did you get your information?" one of the participants asked the anthropologists present. "It seems to us that anthropology today," observed a representative of the American Indian Historical Society, "is becoming a sterile discipline."[23]

The confrontation made Margaret Mead nervous. "I don't know whether I should say [Indian] 'people' or 'peoples,'" she began awkwardly. "I feel a little happier still saying 'peoples.'" She acknowledged her tendency to get "very angry" when "the younger anthropologists tell those of my generation that we were exploiting, frightful people." She attributed this attack to a generation gap and the mood of the 1960s that made it "fashionable" to oppose authority: "In the present-day world, one of the major rebellions is against anybody who ever wanted to do anything good....We are being scolded primarily because we did care about Indian culture." Mead defended her profession's "well-intentioned" efforts "to preserve the record of the ancient cultures." She triggered a round of acrimony when she ingenuously argued that anthropologists did not need to get the informed consent of native peoples for their research "because we had no *subjects*. We do not treat human beings as subjects; we treat them as informants, which means colleagues and collaborators"—an unfortunate use of terms—"and we work with their understanding and permission."[24]

"I do not believe that *you* maliciously harm Indians," Vine Deloria replied to "Miss Mead." The problem, he continued, is structural, not personal: "The anthropologist has unconsciously occupied a role of authoritative interpreter standing between the American Indian community and other segments of society, so that issues flowing from the American Indian community to the rest of American society filter through a person who is unconsciously an interpreter rather than a reporter of what he is passing on, and, in the interpretation, a new orientation of issues comes about—the results of which in many instances are detrimental to the things that Indian communities are doing." As for the allegedly collegial relationship between Indians and anthropologists, Deloria wondered, where were you "when we were under severe pressure that you as colleagues could have come in and given us assistance ....Why did no social scientist, particularly anthropologist, raise his voice on our behalf...when the government of the United States [was trying] to liquidate Indian property rights?"[25]

The 1970 symposium resembled, in the words of Roger Buffalohead, "a rite of purification, both for Indians and for anthropologists," and some common ground was uneasily reached. Despite being made to feel "aggrieved and uptight" by the anger of native "subjects" and New Left anthropologists, Margaret Mead recognized that change was inevitable. "We no longer live in a world," she acknowledged, "where we want those with authority and power to be running things. We want whoever is *involved* in any enterprise to be part of it....We are going to have to develop a dialogue between Indian people and anthropologists who are interested in this field. We need new forms of cooperation. We must realize they *are* new." Deloria concurred, saying it was "time for Indian organizations and the American Anthropological Association to sit down and discuss what issues are relevant in the Indian community; what studies you have that are relevant to the things we are doing; what needs we have that would be relevant to future research that you might want to undertake on a professional basis." Another participant, Jeannette Henry Costo, called upon anthropologists to establish a code of ethics regarding projects in and with native communities. "I think it's needed."[26]

The following year, the AAA adopted a code of ethics that did not speak to specific issues but cautiously urged anthropologists to "do everything in their power to protect the physical, social and psychological welfare and to honor the dignity and privacy of those studied."[27] It would take several years before concrete measures were adopted. In 1986 the International Council of Museums resolved that "collections of human remains and material of sacred significance should be acquired only if they can be housed securely and cared for respectfully." Their display should take into account "the interests and beliefs of members of the community, ethnic or religious groups from whom the objects originated....Requests for removal from public display of human remains or material of sacred significance from the originating communities must be addressed expeditiously with respect and sensitivity. Requests for the return of such material should be addressed similarly."[28]

In 1989 the World Archaeological Congress called for "respect for the mortal remains of the dead," instructing its members that "agreement on the disposition of fossil, skeletal, mummified and other remains shall be reached by negotiation on the basis of mutual respect for the legitimate concerns of communities for the proper disposition of their ancestors, as well as the legitimate concerns of science and education."[29] In 1996 the Society for American Archaeology, after considerable debate, called for its members to practice their craft "for the benefit of all people" and develop a "working relationship" with "affected groups."[30]

Speaking the Unspeakable

In addition to significant changes on the legal and political fronts, narratives of the past ("lies agreed upon," in W. E. B. Du Bois' caustic phrase) were subject to scrutiny and revision. California figured prominently in the debate among historians and anthropologists about what happened in the nineteenth century to tribes and native communities. In the first half of the twentieth century, most scholars considered biological-cultural factors as partial determinants of the demise of native peoples, so that responsibility for extermination was mitigated and shared, and ultimately forgotten. The language of "genocide" changed the discourse.

In the wake of efforts by the Nazi regime to physically exterminate a whole category of people on the basis of their alleged racial characteristics, in 1948 the United Nations passed a Convention on the Prevention and Punishment of Genocide. The convention defined genocide as the commission of acts "with intent to destroy, wholly or in part, a national, ethnic, racial or religious group." These acts include killing, infliction of serious bodily or mental harm, and "deliberately inflicting on the group conditions of life calculated to bring about its physical destruction in whole or in part," such as preventing reproduction or forced transfer of a group's children to another group.[31]

The new critical histories that emerged in the 1970s to discuss the fate of California's native peoples in the language of "genocide" were not without precedent. A handful of writers had previously challenged amnesic and saccharine versions of the state's bloody origins. In 1940 a textbook by John Caughey, one of California's most progressive historians, gave unusual attention to "a sordid and disgraceful chapter, never stressed in local histories," namely "the heartless liquidation of the Californian Indian."[32] In 1943 demographer Sherburne Cook, who subscribed to prevailing attitudes about the biological deficiencies of "vanishing" tribes, nevertheless exposed "the shock and impact" of the Gold Rush on California's native inhabitants, describing the effect as "precisely the same as if they had been bodily removed and set down in a strange region. They were subjected not to invasion but to inundation." There was "no place for the Indian." The new settlers, wrote Cook, "brought with them an implacable hatred of the red race, which made no discrimination between tribes or individuals. All Indians were vermin, to be treated as such." The result was "social homicide."[33]

In the mid-1940s, journalist Carey McWilliams searched for

"skeletons in the closet [of] American democracy" and found "deep-seated and ingrained" patterns of racism rooted in the earliest days of the republic. "The Indian problem is central to the whole question. It represents not only the point of departure, but the point to which any discussion of the larger problem must return." It is critical, said McWilliams, to break through mythological and romantic portraits of native peoples: "with race attitudes in America, one must begin at the beginning."[34]

But these voices of outrage were rare prior to the 1970s. The post–World War II paradigm of genocide, the public presence of the Red Power movement, and the rise of a new generation of socially responsible historians combined to unsettle the California Story and for the first time make the state's history a topic of serious argument.

In his 1969 book *Custer Died for Your Sins*, Vine Deloria Jr. did not use the term "genocide" but nevertheless located American policies towards tribes within a tradition of "militantly imperialistic" nationalism, from war against the Sioux to Vietnam.[35] The experiences of Nazism and the United Nations convention were very much on the minds of Theodora Kroeber and Robert Heizer when *Almost Ancestors*, their popular Sierra Club book of photographs, was published in 1968. "No one troubled to name what was happening in California a hundred years ago genocide. It was only with the Second World War, after a Lidice, a Coventry, the almost successful attempt to wipe out a whole culture and religion in places like Auschwitz and Buchenwald, that the true meaning of the word, of the act, and of its inhumanity bore in upon the collective conscience."[36]

Prior to the publication of Kroeber and Heizer's book, popular accounts of the Gold Rush had tended to be coy about the bloodshed. Tourist brochures routinely referred—and still do— to how miners "displaced local Native American bands," how the Gold Rush "signaled an end to the way of life Indians had known for thousands of years," and how "local Native American cultures experienced serious disruption."[37] And such euphemistic accounts could point for justification to the contents of serious academic works, such as Alfred Kroeber's observation, phrased so passively, that "the native of low civilization in many parts of the world passes away.[38]

A typically sunny version of California history, written in 1962, described Spain's mission policies as designed to keep the Indians "contented with food and with cloth for clothes or else they would go off to live as they pleased."[39] And as late as 1984, an elementary school textbook transformed the bloody horrors of the 1850s into a mild case of culture conflict: "The people who came to look for gold and to settle in California did not understand the Indians. They made fun of the way the Indians dressed and acted."[40]

There are no such niceties in *Almost Ancestors:* compared to Spain's domination of the region, "the Anglo-Saxon phase of invasion... and conquest took on new and more ruthless aspects....It was experientially and imaginatively unprepared to find a place within it for the Indian." A policy of "kill them, exterminate them" was carried out by "conquerors," who were not only "brave and adventurous" but "racist as well." What is important about Theodora Kroeber and Robert Heizer's analysis is not only its uncompromising expression of moral outrage, but also its break with the longstanding tendency to blame the excesses of the Gold Rush on a marginalized riffraff of hoodlums unmoored from the restraints of civilization, a view popularized by Bancroft's view of California as a "paradise for wild men."[41] Among those "responsible for the genocide of Californians," wrote Kroeber and Heizer, were "those who were not ignorant, not benighted, but who were humane, knowledgeable, and perceptive of the exotic, the beautiful, the tragic."[42]

The first Native Americans to write on the topic in the late 1970s left no doubt as to their views on the past. In *Our Home Forever,* Byron Nelson Jr. described in great detail how the Hupa experienced "a kind of violence the area had never known" as the post–Gold Rush settlers "came to consider themselves the owners of the valleys and rivers and mountains filled with grass, minerals, fish, timber, and fertile soil." By the mid-1860s, "many Hupa children could not remember the time when the valley had been a peaceful place."[43] Jack Norton titled his book *Genocide in Northwestern California* and included in his appendices the full text of the United Nations Genocide Convention.[44] As Thomas Buckley has observed, Nelson and Norton broke traditional constraints on "rehearsing the bad" and public discomfort associated with bringing the genocidal past into

Humboldt's story of progress. They made it "safer to speak the once unspeakable."[45]

But some writers of popular books are not convinced that what happened in California amounted to a crime against humanity. "Wherever Indians were in the way, they were removed," noted W. H. Hutchinson's *California* in 1969. "Despite allegations to the contrary from modern observers conditioned by the horrors of Buchenwald and Auschwitz," it did not constitute "genocide" because it wasn't "organized."[46] Another illustrated history of California, published in 1983, makes a similar argument:

> In an excess of delayed reaction, some historians and anthropologists have applied the word "genocide" to what happened to the California Indians. It is a poor use of the term.... Whatever else may be said of California's Indian-killing, it was neither particularly systematic nor planned, and certainly the extinction of the entire race of California Indians was at no time the official policy of the government—if it had been, there would have been *no* Indians left within a few years.[47]

Meanwhile, many scholars have accepted the framing of white-native relations in nineteenth-century California as genocide or its equivalent. In his encyclopedic survey of genocide worldwide, Ben Kiernan includes northwest California as one of several examples in the United States.[48] Laurence Hauptman cites the "rapid destruction" of northern California's native population as one of only two examples of genocide in the country.[49] And Buckley subscribes to the view that what happened in northern California—"the particular evil of state-sanctioned attempts to exterminate outright all Indian people"—was perhaps the most definitive example of "the great North American colonial tragedy."[50]

James Rawls's important 1984 study, *Indians of California*, reminds us that the effectiveness of genocide as a popular project necessitates the mobilization of a broad swath of participants and construction of a code of morality. Implementing the killing, dispossession, removal, neglect, and humiliation of thousands of native people required the support, tacit and active, of state agencies, the participation of many good Californians—the humane and the knowledgeable—and a sense of righteousness or, at least, inevitability that enabled perpetrators to sleep at night. "The reduction of the Indians of California to the level of beasts," observed Rawls, "was a necessary precondition of their extermination."[51]

Tomás Almaguer's *Racial Fault Lines* summarizes what had become a widely held point of view among California historians by the mid-1990s. "Indians were ruthlessly segregated onto reservations, marginalized in the new Anglo economy, and subjected to violent pogroms no other racialized ethnic groups experienced."[52] In 1989 Karl Kroeber, the son of Alfred and Theodora, wrote that "no state in the Union surpassed the Golden State in systematically and shamelessly harassing, murdering, and stealing from its native inhabitants."[53] A detailed study of massacres in Humboldt County concluded that "fear and racism, when combined with acquisitiveness, led in the end to policies intended to subdue, remove, or kill indigenous people."[54] Or as the novelist Larry McMurtry put it more bluntly, "Men who believed that the only good Indian was a dead Indian overwhelmingly prevailed. During the Gold Rush particularly, exterminationists were thick on the ground. Indians were killed as casually as rabbits."[55]

While some writers prefer to stay away from the term "genocide" because it appears loaded up with moral baggage and detracts from a cool-headed assessment,[56] others argue that morality and analysis are not necessarily incompatible. In my view, the use of "genocide" shakes up the complacent belief in history as a march of progress, makes us pay attention to the magnitude of a decade of butchery, and invites us to consider "family resemblances" between California in the 1850s and 1860s, Turkey in 1915, Germany in the 1930s, and Rwanda in 1994.[57] Naming what happened "genocide" is important because of its moral and legal connotations, and because it enables us to locate the California Story within a broad array of human-made tragedies. It makes a difference whether we understand a historical event as rooted in accident or malice, as unfortunate or systemic, or as the result of culture conflict or conquest. A comparative analysis also helps us to contextualize the mass violence of the 1850s and 1860s in California as an example of the "violent process of nation-making" that occurred worldwide in the nineteenth century.[58] What happened to the native populations of California was similar to what happened to other self-sufficient, pre-capitalist rural communities, but worse. "Their story," observes Albert Hurtado, "shows clearly the human costs of bringing California into the ambit of the modern world economic system. That so few Indians survived is stark evidence of the prodigious upheavals of a remarkable time."[59]

The tone for introspection within anthropology was set in 1974 by Robert Heizer, who, no doubt influenced by the stand taken by his colleague Theodora Kroeber, decided after giving the matter thought "for a long time" and "without discussing it with any Native Americans" to issue a public mea culpa for the practices of his profession. The now fifty-nine-year-old Heizer (a few years away from his death) did not revisit his excavation of six graves in Patrick's Point or his "most difficult" experiences in Trinidad in 1948, when the combined protests of the Yurok and local women's clubs sent him packing; nor his personal role in surreptitiously searching for gravesites at Tsurai. Nevertheless, Heizer's public statement was surprisingly reflective and honest:

> It is time now for American archaeologists to listen to the survivors of the people they profess to be so interested in....California Indians have become, for me, more than a population which could be objectively and dispassionately studied, as though they were objects, and have become in my thinking a people who have been mistreated and ignored and whose mistrust and dislike of being so considered I not only understand, but have full sympathy with....We, as a "Berkeley group," excavated many sites—probably a hundred in all....We were serious about our work, thought that we were helping to recover one segment, however provincial, of the human past....Thus far archaeologists in the United States have not discussed in their meetings or in their writings on professional ethics the matter of whether Indian sensitivity over the continued digging up of the graves of their ancestors can be condoned in the face of the objections which Native Americans express over this activity. I believe that we must consider this as a human ethical question rather than one of professional ethics and that when we do, we will decide that this should no longer be done.[60]

Unlike most professors of his generation, Heizer welcomed the campus activism of the New Left, appreciated the "exciting days of the Free Speech Movement," and found his students now "more intellectually alive." It gave him "hope for the future" that "the new generation is not simply accepting the values of the one which produced it."[61] And like his students, he too began to see historical connections that he had previously failed to see. The war in Vietnam became "analogous" to the war against California Indians a century earlier. Both wars treated the enemy as "non-persons" and made combatants "so accustomed to the killing of others" that they would become "brutalized [and] abrogate their humanity."[62] The "pious dissimulations" of Woodrow Wilson in 1913—when the president praised the nation's treatment of "the red man" as "wise, just, and beneficent"—reminded Heizer of Nixon's hypocrisy as revealed by the Watergate tapes.[63] And when he wrote about the history of white-native relations in California, his analysis was forthright, his tone uncompromising: "Indians were rejected, alienated, and dehumanized, and they were continually faced with the risk that anything they did would be interpreted as a challenge. So long as they stayed out of sight, and allowed anything to be done to them without protest, Indians were permitted to live."[64]

In 1974 Heizer anticipated the 1990 passage of NAGPRA when he addressed the issue of reburial of human remains held by museums and universities. While he recognized that skeletons are important to scientists seeking clues about health and diet, as well as to "living Indians as a source of information about their own past," he argued that "it would be difficult for any museum to insist, in the face of a demand by living descendants, that its human bone collection was the museum's legal property and that the Indians were simply being emotional about the whole thing."[65]

Berkeley's anthropology department revisited its past again in 1999 when Art Angle, a Maidu activist, asked the university to support the return of Ishi's brain (preserved in a jar in the Smithsonian) and his ashes (buried in a Bay Area cemetery) to his cultural descendants for reburial near Mt. Lassen. The request set off a heated debate within the university, in large part because it triggered a reexamination of the reputation of Alfred Kroeber, Ishi's "guardian" and the department's founding father. Some anthropologists, embarrassed by the university's initial denial that

Ishi's brain had been "maintained as a scientific specimen," called for an outright apology: "We are sorry for our department's role, however unintentional, in the final betrayal of Ishi, a man who had already lost all that was dear to him at the hands of Western colonizers and we recognize that the exploitation and betrayal of Native Americans is still commonplace in American society."

After much discussion and acrimony, the faculty issued a unanimous, more cautiously worded statement that recognized Ishi as a survivor of "genocide"; acknowledged Alfred Kroeber's failure "to honor Ishi's wishes not to be autopsied" and his inexplicable decision to send Ishi's brain to Washington, D.C.; and regretted "our department's role in what happened to Ishi, a man who had already lost all that was dear to him." The department voted to support repatriation of Ishi's remains and called, rather vaguely, for "a new era in the relationship between indigenous peoples, anthropologists, and the public."[66]

A New Era

In Humboldt County, a region that in Germany today would be known as an "authentic site" of genocide, it took one hundred years and the activism of the Northwest Indian Cemetery Protection Association before a public reckoning of the area's troubled history was begun. Though NICPA receded in the 1980s—its work absorbed by other organizations—its legacies are evident everywhere in northwest California.[67] For one, NICPA successfully battled the state's Parks and Recreation department to repatriate and rebury human remains nine years before passage of NAGPRA.[68]

In 1990 the University of California began the process of publishing inventories of and repatriating human remains and grave goods. Two years later, it acknowledged possession of the human remains of one person which had been dug up by Robert Heizer's crew at Patrick's Point in 1948. It is not known what happened to the other five skeletons that prompted Berkeley's anthropologists to speculate about "an ancient race of deaf Indians." In 2000 Sonoma State University repatriated the remains of one person to the Yurok.[69] In 2002 UC Berkeley returned to the Yurok the remains of six people: one dug up by Alfred Kroeber in 1924 and five excavated by Doc Stuart—two from Tsurai in the 1920s and three from Big Lagoon in 1931.[70] The university has no record of what happened to the rest of the "31 skulls and various human bones" that Stuart shipped to Berkeley in 1931. Berkeley also repatriated to the Wiyot Tribe the remains of twenty-four people and hundreds of funerary objects excavated by Llewellyn Loud on Indian Island in 1913; and seven of the hundreds of human remains dug up on the island by Doc Stuart in the 1920s and 1930s.[71]

In 2004 the Yurok Tribe successfully repatriated several artifacts—including War Dance and Brush Dance items—that the Brooklyn Museum of Art had bought in 1905. "If you don't use these things, they cry," says Walt Lara. "We need to get them out of the museums so they can live and breathe again."[72] Recently, the Smithsonian returned some 217 sacred items—including eagle and condor feathers and white deerskins—to the tribe. "It's a big thing with our people," said Thomas O'Rourke, chairman of the Yurok Tribe. "These are our prayer items. They are not only symbols, but their spirit stays with them. They are alive. Bringing them home is like bringing home prisoners of war."[73]

In Eureka in 2009, as the first stage of repatriation, the Clarke Historical Museum completed an inventory of hundreds of artifacts taken from Wiyot and Yurok cemeteries. It undertook this responsibility voluntarily; as a private institution without federal funds, it is not required to comply with NAGPRA. The decision to deaccession many unique and priceless items generated a vigorous debate within the organization and was opposed by some old-timers, including Tom Hannah. The Clarke, to its credit, no longer displays any items that may have been dug up from gravesites. "We understand the desire of native peoples to have items that are associated with the burial of their ancestors receive appropriately respectful treatment," says Pam Service, the Clarke's director. "At the time that many of these artifacts were collected, it was considered not only legal, but also scientifically valuable to have these items excavated, preserved, and studied. But times and social values have changed....It will be of great satisfaction to the Clarke when we can eventually see these items, for which we have served as caretakers for many decades, finally returned to their appropriate homes."[74]

NICPA and its supporters have also been active in efforts to resuscitate Yurok languages and traditions. Some important ceremonies had not been practiced at traditional Yurok villages since 1939. In 1971 and 1972, revivals of the Brush Dance at Weitchpec and Requa initiated an era of extraordinary cultural revitalization, with Jump Dances, War Dances, and White Deerskin Dances, as well as Brush Dance ceremonies, becoming regular events in the region.[75] In September 1990 the state, in consultation with NICPA and other native leaders, opened to the public the Yurok redwood plank village of Sumeg in Patrick's Point State Park. It had taken twenty-seven years to implement a proposal first made by the legislature in 1963. The park now regularly hosts educational and ceremonial events, including the Brush Dance.[76]

In 1992 an annual ecumenical vigil in memory of the 1860 Indian Island massacre was instituted in Eureka; it continues to be held each year, on the last Saturday of February. In 2001 grassroots fundraising enabled the Wiyot to purchase one and a half acres of Indian Island, and on May 18, 2006, the Eureka city council made history when it returned sixty acres of Indian Island to the Wiyot Tribe as a gesture of reparations.[77] In September 2008, for the first time the tribe allowed archaeologists back on the island to begin the process of "restoring history."[78]

Efforts to protect and commemorate Yurok cultural legacies at Big Lagoon finally achieved some success in 2009 after at least forty years of "scrupulous forgetting."[79] Since 1920, when Thomas Waterman published in *Yurok Geography* a meticulous map of Yurok settlements and sites at O-pyúweg, the cultural significance of the area has been publicly known. For many decades, the looting of Big Lagoon has been common knowledge. And at least since 1969, county and state agencies have had official knowledge about the importance of Big Lagoon as a cultural resource and about the history of its unprotected cemeteries.

In 1969, when the California Department of Parks and Recreation commissioned a survey of Big Lagoon, archaeologists not only reported that "pot hunting is going on now," but also included a map to show precisely where it was taking place.[80] When I visited the site in 2008 with archaeologist Janet Eidsness, the midden was still exposed and unprotected, with an obsidian projectile point used by the Yurok visible on the surface.

An environmental report prepared for Humboldt County in

1973—regarding the proposed construction of a parking lot, boat dock, road, and campsite—noted that "Big Lagoon contained several Yurok Indian villages along its shoreline. The project site contains an Indian burial ground and a village site. Several Indian burial sites and other Indian cultural and sacred sites exist throughout the park area. Most of these sites were disturbed by construction and curious people from 1929 to 1962."[81] When ground near the lagoon was dug up for a new boat ramp in 1973, there were rumors of burials found during construction. "We were informed," reported state archaeologist Jim Woodward, that O-pyúweg "was a cemetery site."[82] Nothing was done to protect or commemorate the area.

In 1981 the state acquired part of Big Lagoon from Louisiana-Pacific and incorporated it into the newly named Harry A. Merlo State Recreation Area.[83] An official inventory of the new park's resources included cultural legacies and called for the "protection of archaeological resources."[84] Woodward met with Walt Lara and Joy Sundberg as representatives of NICPA to discuss the survey.[85] A few weeks later, another state report noted that the nearby site of Keixhem "has been badly vandalized, but has some remaining intact midden which should be protected."[86] The state park's 1983 General Plan called for stabilizing Keixhem and protecting it from vandalism, but four years later the Big Lagoon site was still being looted. Woodward documented "numerous small vandal pits."[87] Nothing was done to protect or commemorate the area.

In 1982 California's Department of Parks and Recreation considered Big Lagoon as a possible site for the reconstructed Yurok village that was eventually built at Patrick's Point. The Big Lagoon Rancheria expressed an interest in working with the state on this project. Also, local Indian leaders proposed that "a monument be erected at Mä'äts to commemorate this historically tragic clash of cultures," where a massacre took place in the mid-nineteenth century. Walt Lara, chairman of NICPA, told Woodward that the area around O-pyúweg and Pi'npa was the site of "many Indian burials." Nothing was done to protect or commemorate the area.[88]

In November 2007, the Yurok Tribe passed a resolution calling for protection of O-pyúweg, a "place of ceremonial renown." Soon afterwards, a report commissioned by the Big Lagoon Park

Company supported the development and implementation of a comprehensive cultural management plan to protect a "significant Yurok village and ceremonial site." Similarly, a state archaeologist recommended "the development of an inter-agency resource management plan for the area."[89] It was in response to this flurry of activity that in March 2009 the Coalition to Protect Yurok Cultural Legacies at O-pyúweg was formed. As Walt Lara pointed out at the coalition's first meeting, in March 2009, it had been "a mistake to end NICPA in the 1980s." Though it is a far cry from the purposeful, native-led militancy of the 1970s, the coalition echoes the spirit and concerns of NICPA.

The coalition—consisting of representatives of the Yurok Tribe, Big Lagoon Rancheria, Yurok descendants of Big Lagoon, county and state officials, and a cabin owners association (Big Lagoon Park Company)—was organized to "protect, preserve, and ensure respectful management of Yurok cultural legacies and traditional practices at O-pyúweg (Big Lagoon) for the benefit of California's diverse populations and future generations; and to promote understanding and appreciation of Yurok cultural resources." A first in Humboldt County, this coalition represents a cooperative partnership between groups that have typically pursued their own competing agendas—the defense of private property rights versus the public preservation of cultural patrimony; the expansion of state and county parks' facilities versus recognition of longstanding human legacies; and the proposed development of a Vegas-style "gaming facility" as an economic resource on rancheria land versus the protection of Big Lagoon's unique ecological habitat.

Understandably, these conflicting agendas generate tensions that could derail the coalition at any time. Some of my neighbors in Big Lagoon's private estate have been reluctant to allow native artisans from local communities access to a spruce forest and worry that the assertion of Yurok cultural rights might segue into proprietary claims. And my own roles as both a historian working with the coalition and as a cabin owner at Big Lagoon have at times raised concerns about where my true loyalty lies. Given the long history of distrust and competing interests embedded in Big Lagoon, it will take an enormous effort of good faith for all the parties to find common ground. Yet there has been slow and encouraging progress: the Big Lagoon Park Company's recent disclosure to prospective cabin buyers that the private community includes "part of the ancient Yurok village, O-pyúweg, that existed up until Euro-American contact" and that "Yurok burial sites may exist which will restrict uses that would disturb the ground at these sites"; signage installed to discourage cars parking on O-pyúweg; cooperative patrols instituted by the sheriff, park rangers, and tribal police to deter looting; cabin owners keeping a lookout for pothunters; and an ongoing conversation about how to reconcile this wondrous place of beauty with its violent past. Hopefully, the coalition will become a model of cultural management and public remembrance for communities that are dealing with issues of reparative justice.

In December 2010, the Humboldt County Board of Supervisors unanimously approved the coalition's proposal to protect Yurok legacies at O-pyúweg. "Thirty years ago we weren't allowed to give an opinion because we weren't professional people and we didn't have a degree," said Joy Sundberg, whose great-great-grandfather lived at Big Lagoon. Sundberg, a veteran of NICPA, and other members of the coalition were on hand to give testimony to the board.[90]

Crossroads

These accomplishments, the result in part of NICPA's activism in the 1970s, should not be underestimated. But radical efforts to break with the past, once institutionalized, have a tendency to lose momentum, and old relations of power find ways to reassert themselves. Hopefulness and disappointment are first cousins.

In contrast to the Clarke Historical Museum in Eureka, many private museums and collectors have not declared their holdings nor complied with the spirit of NAGPRA. The Favell Museum in Klamath Falls, Oregon, for example, continues to exhibit artifacts taken from gravesites, including many of the most precious items that Doc Stuart excavated from Yurok and Wiyot graves. The "End of the Trail Museum" in the kitschy tourist attraction Trees of Mystery, in Klamath, proudly displays ceremonial regalia and funerary artifacts, including two zoomorphs "found" by Doc Stuart on Indian Island.

The pace of repatriating human remains, grave goods, and

sacred objects at the national level is glacially slow. By 2006, sixteen years after passage of NAGPRA, the National Park Service had identified only 31,383 "culturally identifiable" human remains held by federally funded institutions. Assuming very conservatively that half a million bodies were dug up in the nineteenth and twentieth centuries, this is about 6 percent of the total. By September 2009, some three years later, 124,301 human remains had been inventoried, with 8,200 identified and repatriated: less than 2 percent of the bodies exhumed. And of the millions of artifacts taken from graves, fewer than one million have been inventoried.[91]

The situation in northern California mirrors the national trend. Only a handful of the six hundred skeletons dug up by Doc Stuart have been recovered. The University of California is now engaged in the repatriation process, but for many years a deep wedge of animosity between Berkeley and California's tribes stalled the process.[92] The university, claimed Vine Deloria in 1997, "considers the reburial issue simply a minor political squabble that has nothing to do with religious and cultural beliefs."[93]

As of summer 2010, Berkeley had repatriated only 179 human remains; another 10,000 remain unclaimed, with 70 percent unidentifiable as to origins or tribal affiliation, according to the university's repatriation coordinator. "Many boxes of remains were delivered to the university without identification." Moreover, a "very miniscule number" of the university's 134,000 funerary objects have been repatriated.[94]

The human remains at Berkeley are stacked in metal containers in the temperature-controlled basement of the Hearst Gym. "There are rows and rows and rows and rows of bodies," says a staff member who works for the Hearst Museum. "It's hard for me to go in there, but I have to do it when native groups want to see the remains of their people. It's very depressing," he says somberly, shaking his head. The Hearst's small repatriation staff is overworked and beleaguered. "We get requests almost every week from tribal representatives wanting to look at collections." The staff has no power over decisions. All they can do is submit detailed, legalistic recommendations that make their ponderous way through faculty, campus, and university committees.

The reasons for this near-impasse are complicated, and not

simply the result of recalcitrant government agencies and federally funded agencies blocking righteous native demands.[95] First, repatriation is a legal and bureaucratic process that is expensive and time-consuming, requiring considerable cultural capital. This privileges the small number of wealthy tribes over the majority of impoverished tribes. It cost the Tseycum First Nation, for example, $150,000 to send a delegation to New York to reclaim the remains of its ancestors. It takes expertise and staff to write NAGPRA proposals, and federal funding has been drastically reduced in the current economic crisis.[96] For those tribes wishing to preserve repatriated artifacts, special storage facilities are necessary.

Moreover, tribes have to negotiate three separate procedures and applications: NAGPRA for institutions that have received federal funds; the National Museum of the American Indian for items in their collection, mostly inherited from the Heye Foundation/ Museum of the American Indian in New York; and the National Museum of Natural History in Washington, D.C., which houses most of the Smithsonian's huge collection. Consequently, "most human remains and funerary items are unclaimed," says Bambi Kraus, president of the National Association of Tribal Historic Preservation Officers. "The onus is on the tribe to make the claim and provide proof. It should be the other way around. I'd say we are only about 10 percent down the road towards completing repatriation."[97]

Second, federal law excludes the many native groups that the US does not officially recognize as tribes from the repatriation process. Most of Berkeley's collection, for example, was derived from such groups. "We follow NAGPRA, which binds and limits us," says a historian who works for the Hearst Museum.[98]

Third, most museums and universities possess thousands of items that are poorly, inadequately, and incorrectly documented. Some bones identified as human turn out to be faunal, and body parts of different individuals may be mixed together.

During a visit to the National Museum of the American Indian's Cultural Resource Center in 2010, I viewed drawer after drawer of material vaguely categorized as "northern Californian," and some items labeled "Hupa" only because they were bought from a trading post on the Hoopa Reservation. Even when there is a genuine effort to reconnect people with artifacts of historical and cultural significance, this good will is often undermined by the failure of many collectors—from pothunters to academics—to carefully document provenience; and the failure of curators—from local museum volunteers to nationally renowned philanthropists—to demand and preserve documentation.

Finally, there are major differences in policies and attitudes towards repatriation among and within native organizations. Some tribes are reluctant to repatriate human remains and grave goods on the grounds that they have been polluted, figuratively or literally. Ceremonial items recovered by the Yurok Tribe from the Brooklyn Museum in 2004, for example, require special handling because they have been contaminated with toxic preservatives—and this is not unusual.[99] Some tribes are discouraged by the bureaucratic and expensive application process.

When there is more than one organization representing a tribe, it is sometimes unclear whose authority prevails. In the case of Geronimo's remains, for example, some of his descendants not only want Yale's Order of Skull and Bones to disclose whether or not they possess his skull. They also want the rest of his remains to be exhumed from a granite tomb in the Apache Indian Prisoner of War Cemetery at Fort Sill, Oklahoma, and repatriated to a gravesite at the headwaters of the Gila River in New Mexico, where Geronimo was born. The Fort Sill Apache Tribe opposes this demand on the grounds that "there is nothing to be gained by digging up the dead."[100] Whether Geronimo should be interred where he was born or where he died should be resolved by the tribes, and not by the courts, unless Judge Solomon is available.

Some organizations, such as the Yurok Tribe, take the position that artifacts associated in any way with graves or funerary practices—no matter how culturally or economically valuable—should be reburied, while others wish to retrieve artifacts for preservation or display in a tribal museum. Some descendants of the Yurok of Tsurai, for example, are glad to have their relatives' artifacts on display in the recently opened Trinidad Museum. For the moment, the retrieval of funerary artifacts is not a priority for the Yurok Tribe. Their emphasis is on reclaiming artifacts for ceremonial purposes that were once traded or stolen, or sold by native individuals without community permission. The tribe envisions building a "destination resort, gaming facility, and cultural center"[101] in which Yurok history, traditions, and ceremonies will be told through stories, videos, and interactive displays. "We don't want an object-driven center," says the tribe's repatriation and cultural collections manager. "We don't want to repatriate artifacts just to put them on a shelf or in storage. We'll only display objects if there is a story to be told."[102]

Many tribes face the dilemma of how to juggle material and cultural needs during a time of recession and cutbacks. In Humboldt County, native people face deep economic hardships and struggle to meet the basic needs of food, health care, and education. Since the late 1980s, when the Supreme Court and Congress cleared the way for gaming on native lands, tribes throughout the US have negotiated agreements (or "compacts") with state governments, borrowed money from investors, and built hundreds of casinos. Northern California currently has about eighteen native "gaming facilities," including casinos run by the Trinidad Rancheria, Blue Lake Rancheria, Rohnerville Rancheria, and Hoopa Tribe—all concentrated within a small region of northwest California. In addition, there is the casino/resort complex envisioned by the Yurok Tribe; the Wiyot Tribe's Table Bluff Reservation has plans to open a casino near Yosemite; and the Big Lagoon Rancheria has been trying for many years to develop a casino project.

A few of these casinos have definitely improved the living conditions for some tribal members (and reaped considerable profits for outside investors), but their long-term economic benefits are unclear. And how many casinos can be sustained in impoverished rural counties such as Humboldt and Del Norte? A small casino on the coast near the Yurok Tribe's headquarters, run by the Resighini Rancheria, recently closed. Given the generally depressed nature of the regional economy, local tribes and rancherias cannot match the four successful gaming tribes in southern California that are among the top ten political donors in the United States; or hope to sell twelve million cartons of cigarettes annually, as the Senecas do in western New York; or aspire to build a $200 million heritage museum, as the Pequots have done in Connecticut with profits from the largest casino in the Americas.[103] The Yurok Tribe looks beyond gaming as a solution to chronic unemployment, envisioning the reclamation of ancestral lands through either purchase or co-management with local government, and the development of ecotourism and cultural resources.

Meanwhile, the looting of graves and illegal trading in native artifacts for profit continue, despite an array of local, state, and federal laws. In 1989 relic hunters again desecrated graves at Tsurai;[104] some twenty years later, local authorities are still discussing how best to preserve the area.[105] In 2007 a collector was convicted of excavating a burial site at Stone Lagoon—the site that the Northwest Indian Cemetery Protection Association tried to protect in the 1970s.[106] In 2008 a looter was arrested for stealing artifacts from a Yurok site at Patrick's Point State Park, but only after he bragged about his accomplishment on YouTube.[107] He was sentenced to only thirty days in county jail and sixty hours of community service,[108] despite an editorial in the local newspaper condemning "so-called collectors" who plunder "sacred sites" in order to "adorn their mantles" with relics.[109] Recently, according to tribal officials, "an alarming number" of native burial sites "have been targeted by looters."[110] There have been several cases of attempted looting of O-pyúweg and extensive looting of a Tolowa site at Point St. George.[111] In April 2010, grave robbers searching for artifacts dug up Tolowa human remains in the Yontocket Cemetery near Crescent City.[112]

Nationwide, about 840 federal looting cases are reported each year, but only a small percentage of looters are prosecuted, and of those convicted, very few end up in prison.[113] In 2009 a federal judge in Salt Lake City rejected a prosecutor's request to imprison a looter who had stolen enough artifacts from tribal and federal lands to fill 812 boxes.[114] Of twenty-four people indicted in 2010 in Utah for trading in artifacts worth millions of dollars, two related to the scandal have committed suicide, as has the federal government's key witness, Ted Gardiner, who witnessed the time "diggers dug up a human skull and just tossed it aside." According to his son, Gardiner "saw a lot of things that disgusted him."[115]

Scrupulous Forgetting

Whether you live in Humboldt or visit as a tourist or pass through on your way to somewhere else, there are few visible reminders in the landscape or in guides to the area of a history much longer than that of the state of California or of a tragic past buried in shallow ground. The debate among historians about the region's genocidal legacy has not touched the public space. The travel literature understandably promotes the best of Humboldt's attractions: redwoods, pristine lakes, and picturesque small towns.[116] But you can find dabs of history within the relentless focus on the present. The Victorian era figures prominently in the region's selective, nostalgic history. The Humboldt County Convention and Visitors Bureau describes Eureka as a "Victorian seaport," once the site of "gracious living, grand mansions, arts and fine dining." Another guide recommends the "Victorian village of Ferndale." Trinidad is a "quaint fishing village," while Willow Creek offers a museum displaying vintage tools and the "world's largest collection of Bigfoot curios." According to Fodor's guide to northern California, Trinidad's history began with "Spanish mariners" in 1775.

Native peoples occasionally show up in the travel literature as sidebars or historical curiosities. Humboldt Bay is said to have a "fascinating past," including the Wiyot who "considered the bay the center of their world." But there is no mention of the 1860 massacre that dispersed the survivors to the periphery. The Clarke Historical Museum offers a "strong focus on Native American basketry and ceremonial regalia," but what of the people who made the baskets and wore the regalia? Trinidad was home to "first inhabitants" who "fished the waters from dugout canoes." Where did they go? An informational plaque invites us to "step back in time at Sumeg Village" at Patrick's Point State Park, but it does not connect the past with the present, the dispersed and decimated ancestors with thousands of flesh-and-blood living people.

A *Times-Standard* guide to the North Coast informs tourists that Yurok Indians lived in Trinidad from at least 800 A.D. and that the Hoopa Valley Indian Reservation, "home to the Hupa people for centuries," is close to Willow Creek. But there is no mention of Yurok in Weitchpec, a "fishing paradise," and not even a whiff of genocide in the region: "In 1828, white settlers arrived in the area and in 1864 a Peace and Friendship Treaty was ratified between the Hupa people and the United States." On the Klamath, a fort was established in 1857 "to keep peace between the Yurok Indians and settlers," suggesting that state and local governments were neutral when in fact they were deeply implicated in massacres and policies of extermination and apartheid.[117] *Coastal California,* published recently, does a better job of including information about the 1860 massacre on Indian Island and commends Eureka for returning part of the island to the Wiyot. But inclusion doesn't necessarily mean accuracy or complexity: echoing one of Kroeber's early anthropological observations, the author bizarrely depicts the Yurok as a "very private people" with a "warlike nature and natural reticence.... Their villages are off-limits to visitors."[118] Nobody told me this when I visited Yurok families or was graciously invited to present my research to the Yurok Tribe's Culture Committee.

Humboldt is not atypical when it comes to airbrushing the past. On a trip to Washington, D.C., in April 2010, I was interested in how the Smithsonian deals with a foundational event in American history: the destruction by disease, warfare, massacres, starvation, and humiliation of three-quarters of the indigenous peoples of the continent. How much did I learn as I made my way through the nation's most prestigious museums? Not much.

At the National Museum of the American Indian, the focus is on the humanity and diversity of native peoples. This approach is understandable given the longstanding portrayal of Native Americans as indolent and brutish, predestined to extinction by their inherent degeneracy. But the museum does not require visitors to work through their own assumptions or confront the country's troubling past. Its exhibitions are for the most part informative and uplifting, but there's nothing to rattle our sleep at night.[119]

This would not be a problem if you could confront history's sorrowful weight at the National Museum of American History. "Where can I find information about the history of American policies towards native peoples?" I ingenuously asked a guide at the museum in 2010. She paused, brow furrowed. "There's not much here," she replied. That's an understatement. You have to search purposefully to find references to this decisive component of the nation's origin story in the national history museum. The overall ambience is heroic and jingoistic, the nation's story told as a relentless trek to democracy. The "Hall of Military History" includes a few token cases on the settling of the West and "Indian removal," highlighting the Trail of Tears as "among the most tragic episodes in American history." But that's it, folks, as you quickly move on through the country's penchant for warfare, inexorably framed as "The Price of Freedom."

It's a pleasant surprise, though, to find that a special exhibition on American maritime history, "On the Water," includes two cases on "The Salmon Coast," with a particular focus on the importance of the ocean and rivers for the Hupa and Yurok in California's northwest. But this effort at inclusion is undermined by a text that rewrites the unremitting violence against native peoples during the Gold Rush as "a series of threats" to tribal communities by gold prospectors, settlers, and dams. Again, there's nothing here to make us catch our breath or question the price of freedom.

As I was leaving the National Museum of American History, Cecilia encouraged me to look more closely at Horatio Greenough's iconic 1841 statue of George Washington that, together with a dramatically huge exhibition on the Star-Spangled Banner, smothers visitors to the museum in a fog of patriotism. "Where's the Native American?" she challenged me. I slowly walked around the massive marble sculpture, in which a toga-draped Washington offers his sword to the people. "Here he is," I said eventually, when I spied the familiar image of a miniature noble Indian, head down in defeat, tucked away behind the back of the nation's great white father.

8.1 Hidden from history: the statue of George Washington in the National Museum of American History, Washington, D.C., March 27, 2010.

NINE
Never Too Late

"It's never too late to honor the dead."
—Toni Morrison, 2008

Present Absences

The tendency to forget is understandable, and sometimes preferable or necessary.[1] Few people want to relive tormented pain and suffering. Witnesses to and survivors of atrocities typically do not voice their opinions about their experiences in the immediate aftermath of these human-made catastrophes. And some remain silent for a lifetime. Governments have their own reasons to forget. In the case of post–World War II Germany, the politics of the Cold War justified a "move-on mentality." Similarly, after the death of the Spanish dictator Franco in 1975, the government promoted a "collective pact of forgetting" in the name of forging a united nation. Guilt, sorrow, and denial all play their parts in the aftermath of atrocities.

It makes sense that people want to look forward, not back; that they want to protect the next generation from the horrors of memory; and that political leaders emphasize the future over the past. Not surprisingly, governments have a tendency to either bury catastrophic events that interfere with glorious stories of national or regional origins, or reinvent a past that is suitably heroic and inspirational. As Joan Didion famously observed about California, "the future always looks good in the golden state because no one remembers the past."[2]

But revealing and complicating the underside of history is a matter of decency and respect for unrecognized victims, as well as a way to integrate diverse experiences into our narratives of the past. Also, coming to terms with this country's long record of social injustices helps us to chip away at chauvinist notions of the United States as destined by providence and militarism to lead the world, and of California as a citadel of Progress. Addressing our common history in all its contradictions helps us to be on guard against hubris and to recognize our modest place in an interdependent world.[3]

Organized efforts to protect and commemorate native legacies throughout northwest California have been going on for more than forty years. Still, there are no public memorials in the region that ask us to reflect on the human history of the redwood coast; or public cultural programs that encourage introspection about how the development of California into one of the world's largest economies involved policies of extermination against native peoples, as well as the transformation of Latinos into strangers in their own land, ethnic cleansing of Chinese communities, racist segregation in education and housing between the world wars, and the disenfranchisement and unlawful imprisonment of Japanese Americans during World War II.

California can hold its own with other regions of the world with regards to a history of atrocities and suffering. Yet amnesia trumps remembrance. We have not set aside prominent public places, such as Berlin's centrally located Memorial to the Murdered Jews of Europe, to commemorate victims of genocide. In Paris, the Shoah Memorial fills a city block that is impossible to avoid as you stroll from the fashionable Marais district to Notre Dame. Here you come face-to-face with the names, engraved in stone, of seventy-six thousand Jews who the Vichy government deported to concentration camps between 1942 and 1944. In Berlin, as you walk around the city, you inevitably stumble over plaques in the ground outside cafes, stores, and homes that provide information about the Jews who lived there prior to deportation to death camps. Right outside the Berlin

Philharmonic's celebrated concert hall is a reminder that nearby the Nazi government engineered the murder of two hundred thousand mentally disabled people and "social misfits" in the guise of euthanasia. Here on the northwest coast, you have to travel to Tacoma, Washington, for an equivalent civic commitment to exhuming the worst of the past: a large public garden dedicated to remembrance of the forced expulsion of Chinese immigrants from this Puget Sound city in 1885.[4]

But giving victims of systemic injustice a human face is only a first step. We also need public educational programs and exhibitions that probe issues relating to the people who knowingly and thoughtlessly participated in genocidal policies, who approved secretly or turned a blind eye to what they knew was wrong, who robbed graves and traded in artifacts. How was it possible, we must ask, for so many of California's finest—politicians, civic leaders, the well-educated, intellectuals, economic pioneers, professionals, and reformers—to participate in or permit in the first place such widespread slaughter and degradation, and then the pillage of so many graves in the name of enlightenment? California needs an institution like Berlin's Topography of Terror Documentation Center, where you can learn about the history, values, and bureaucracy of perpetrators in the exact location where the Nazis planned and administered their crimes against humanity.[5]

It requires influence, resources, political clout, and stamina, as well as some good luck, to institutionalize into everyday life a particular memory that challenges and disrupts celebratory narratives of national and regional exceptionalism. Without the economic and political ascendancy of the Jewish middle class, there would be no Holocaust Museum in Washington, D.C., nor the dozens of holocaust memorials around the country. Without the generous donations and fund raising of a handful of wealthy Native American tribes, there would be no National Museum of the American Indian. It has taken almost 150 years since the abolition of slavery to break ground for the Smithsonian's African American Museum and, still to this day, there is no official celebration of the Emancipation Proclamation, one of the most significant events in American history.

Remembrance of the dead is also a selective political project. Some of our collective dead are memorialized more than others.

In the second half of the nineteenth century—while collectors and scientists raided native cemeteries in the name of science, and medical schools exhumed black bodies in the name of education—the nation mourned those killed during the Civil War and established new policies and rituals to honor those who die in war. Between 1861 and 1865, an estimated 620,000 soldiers, or about 2 percent of the population, died in battle or from their wounds. Most were buried anonymously and "unknown" in mass graves. After the war, the nation made amends. "Death created the modern American union," observes historian Drew Gilpin Faust, "not just by ensuring national survival, but by shaping enduring national structures and commitments."[6] Native body parts, however, were exempt from this redemptive ritual, and fair game for collectors and scientists.[7]

Out of the slaughter of the Civil War and a postwar, grassroots movement organized by survivors came an extensive pension system for veterans and their families; the creation of national cemeteries; a system for preserving the names and identities of those killed; and "a commitment to identify and return every soldier killed in the line of duty."[8] Today the federal government takes seriously its responsibility to locate the eighty-four thousand American soldiers missing from wars stretching back to World War II. A four-hundred-person unit in the Defense Department with an annual budget of $55 million searches all over the world for missing remains in order to "bring everyone home," either literally or metaphorically. "What's important," says an anthropologist on staff, "is that the stories of all these people get remembered."[9]

But there have been no comparable efforts to establish national rituals acknowledging the hundreds of thousands of native dead wrenched from their graves. Federal policies of repatriation are a step in the right direction. But most human remains are unclaimed or unknown. What should be a national ritual of remembrance and mourning has become a technical, bureaucratic process. In addition to tribal claims for the return of their dead, there is also a need for public commemoration that speaks to our common tragedy. The federal and state governments could work with native organizations, for example, to create regional and local cemeteries for the burial, symbolic and actual, of the unclaimed dead. They could also become places for monuments, reflection, storytelling, histories, and rituals.

"Everyone knew, but no one said," confesses novelist John Banville about the cruelties unleashed on thousands of children in Irish state institutions for most of the twentieth century.[10] The same can be said about the people who remained silent during and after the Armenian genocide, the Nazi reign of terror, and bloody horrors of Rwanda. What happened in California, after unspeakable policies of extermination, neglect, and humiliation, was a century of widely endorsed grave looting and desecration of cultural sites that not only denied the dead the right to rest in peace but tormented the living.

Coming to terms with this history is for native people comparable to the painful legacy of lynching in African American communities. Acknowledgment, apology, repatriation, and solemn ceremonies will help to heal a festering wound. It will be a mark of real progress, however, when ancient cemeteries are publicly recognized and appreciated, when the native dead of Big Lagoon receive the same kind of intimate rituals that I am able to practice for my son; when we can pay our respects to the ancestors of Pete Peters, for whom O-púyweg was at the center of the world. At the moment and for the foreseeable future though, the Yurok are hesitant, with good reason, to publicly acknowledge the location of their burial grounds for fear of looting and relic hunting. Sometimes, as I have discovered in the course of writing this book, there is a fine line between respecting the need for confidentiality and making public what has been buried for too long.

Throughout much of the twentieth century, while the government built memorials to the victims of World War I and World War II buried in mass graves, and now, as it continues to make efforts to account for every person missing from the Vietnam War, hundreds of thousands of native remains have been stored anonymously in basements and boxes and displayed as mementos of a "vanishing race" or as freak show curiosities. However much we have tried to assiduously forget this sorrowful history, the landscape's tectonic layers continue to send shudders through the here and now. And they will continue to do so until we face the past in all its troubling discomfort.

9.1 and 9.2:
Descendants of Big Lagoon Yurok, carrying a 1928 photograph of
Pete Peters, gather at O-pyúweg in April 2011 to commemorate their
ancestors.

Bertha Peters with (left to right) great-nephews William Peters and Damien Scott and
great-niece Jesselyn Peters.

Back row, left to right: Zack Brown, Terrance Brown, Pliny Jackson. Front, left to
right: Rachel Sundberg, Joy Sundberg, Linnea Jackson, Betty Jackson, Jacqueline Winter, Troy Simon Fletcher Jr.

Facing the Past

While on a trip to New York early in 2010, I get the news from Big Lagoon that small-time looters have been digging in O-pyúweg, hoping to strike it rich. This information is on my mind as I check out a new memorial in Manhattan.[11]

The Negros Buriel Ground, as it was called in colonial New Amsterdam in the seventeenth and eighteenth centuries, was located outside the city's palisades in a few acres of marshy, godforsaken land. Here, before sundown, Africans and their descendants were allowed to bury their dead—perhaps as many as fifteen thousand. By 1991 this same piece of land was prime real estate in Lower Manhattan, surrounded by corporate offices and city hall, close to Ground Zero, the perfect site for the new federal building at 290 Broadway. The huge thirty-story building was opened in 1994, but its original conception was significantly changed following the unearthing of human remains during the early phase of construction.

Today the federal building is symbolically overshadowed by its relatively small neighbor, the African Burial Ground National Monument, which was officially opened to the public on October 5, 2007. It's possible to visit the federal building without walking past the monument or seeing it. But with the recent opening, on February 27, 2010, of the monument's companion visitor center on the ground floor of the federal building, it's almost impossible to ignore the presence of a cemetery of slaves in the heartland of capitalism.

In memorials to large-scale tragedies, it's very difficult to integrate heart and head. Typically, as is the case with the Vietnam Memorial in Washington, D.C., or the Memorial to the Murdered Jews of Europe in Berlin, they churn up emotions and provide an opportunity for sorrowful reflection. When museums try to make us feel *and* think, as in the Holocaust Museum in the nation's capital, they typically fail: the flood of feelings crowds out thoughtful engagement.

The African Burial Ground in New York manages to integrate our senses and straddle the usual divide between affect and cognition. You can pay your respects to the dead by entering the memorial, marked by a hefty, tomblike granite structure, then walk into a memorial circle, or stand next to seven raised grassy mounds and seven newly planted trees where the remains of 419 bodies have been reinterred. President Bush conferred upon the memorial the status of a National Monument in February 2006. This means that it's taken seriously: on the day that I visited the memorial, a National Parks ranger was on duty and a Homeland Security van was parked out front.

The nearby visitor center is geared up for teaching a steady stream of schoolchildren, community groups, and tourists. Here, we learn—as we did in 2009 at the New York Historical Society's revelatory exhibitions—about the importance of slavery to New York's economic development and that trading in human beings was a national, not just Southern, tragedy. There is also detailed information about the daily lives of Africans living in New York hundreds of years ago, the result of scientific analysis of human remains made by anthropologist Michael Blakey and colleagues at Howard University. Despite deep suspicions among African Americans about the impartiality of science—based on a long history of racist misuse, such as the Tuskegee experiment—a collaborative and mutually respectful relationship was forged in this case. There's hope, then, for partnerships between Native Americans and anthropologists, despite the calcified residue of distrust.

The visitor center includes considerable information about the history of the memorial, in particular the role played by protest in shaping its development and outcome: how community organizations forced Congress to put a halt to excavations; how Mayor Dinkins established a blue-ribbon committee to propose models of remembrance; how hundreds of community volunteers were trained to teach visitors about the site's history; how the design of the memorial was a public process; and how the transportation of human remains from Washington, D.C., and their reinterment in New York were marked by ceremonies of formal dignity. "You may bury me in the bottom of Manhattan," said Maya Angelou at one such ceremony. "I will rise. My people will get me out. I will rise out of the huts of history's shame."

This visit to the African Burial Ground National Monument in New York leaves me hopeful that it's possible to create memorials that are dignified and educational, and that science can enhance the humanity of history. But as I head back to California to work with a coalition to protect Yurok cultural legacies on the northwest coast, I'm also well aware that it takes struggle, determination, organizing, and the persistence of a long-distance runner to do justice to the past.

NOTES

One: Between the Lines

1. Shaunna Oteka McCovey, *The Smokehouse Boys*, 8.

2. The phrase comes from Walter Benjamin, *Berlin Childhood around 1900*, 129.

3. Twyla Tharp, *The Creative Habit: Learn It and Use It for Life*, 119.

4. Unless noted, information about the Yurok Tribe comes from the Yurok Tribe's website, www.yuroktribe.org; Yurok Tribal Council, *Yurok Tribe* (2007); and *Constitution of the Yurok Tribe* (22 October 1993).

5. The Madison Grant Forest and Elk Refuge was named in 1948 to commemorate the author of *Passing of the Great Race* (1921).

6. Yurok Tribal Council, Resolution no. 07–84, 29 November 2007. See, also, letter from Marian Tripp, chair of Yurok Tribe, to Don Tuttle, president of Big Lagoon Park Company (29 November 2007).

Two: Present and Alive

1. Bob Lorentzen, *The Hiker's Hip Pocket Guide to the Humboldt Coast*, 109.

2. Ibid., 108–112. On the ecological significance of Big Lagoon, see Office of the Governor, "Governor Schwarzenegger Announces Indian Gaming Agreements," 9 September 2005, www.cgcc.ca.gov/Press/BigLagoon.htm.

3. J. Michael Fay, "The Redwoods Point the Way," *National Geographic* 216, no. 4 (October 2009), 60.

4. "California: 36 Best Campgrounds," *Sunset Magazine* (May 2009).

5. Allison White, "Families in Need Pick up Food and Toys during Salvation Army Event," *Times-Standard* 23 December 2009, 1.

6. By January 2010, employment in Humboldt reached a record low, while unemployment increased to 12.2 percent. Information about Humboldt's economy comes from "Humboldt Economic Index," ed. Erick Eschker, Humboldt State University website, www.humboldt.edu/econindex.

7. Jonathan B. Tourtellot, "Destination Scorecard: 115 Places Rated," *National Geographic*, March 2004, 60–67.

8. John S. Hittell, *A History of San Francisco and Incidentally of the State of California*, 9.

9. Golden State Museum, Sacramento, California, press release, 19 August 1998.

10. M. Kat Anderson, Michael G. Barbour, and Valerie Whitworth, "A World of Balance and Plenty: Land, Plants, Animals, and Humans in a Pre-European California," in *Contested Eden: California before the Gold Rush*, ed. Ramón A. Gutiérrez and Richard J. Orsi, 14.

11. McArthur-Burney Interpretive Association, "McArthur-Burney Falls Memorial State Park 2008 Visitors Guide," Burney, California; Stephen Dow Beckham, *Requiem for a People: The Rogue Indians and the Frontiersmen*, 5.

12. Rebecca Solnit, *Savage Dreams: A Journey into the Landscape Wars of the American West*, 275.

13. On the evidence and debates about how and when the Yurok settled in northwestern California, see Thomas Buckley, *Standing Ground: Yurok Indian Spirituality, 1850–1990*; and Ray Raphael and Freeman House, *Two Peoples, One Place*.

14. On the legal and political history of the Yurok and Hoopa tribes, see James J. Rawls, *Indians of California: The Changing Image*, 205–217.

15. Buckley, *Standing Ground*, 6.

16. The Indians of the Big Lagoon Rancheria formally organized themselves in 1985 when they adopted a constitution. See "Constitution of the Big Lagoon Rancheria," http://www.narf.org/nill/Constitutions/lagoonconst/biglagoonconst.htm, accessed 28 August 2009.

17. See www.bluelakerancheria-nsn.gov and www.trinidad-rancheria.org.

18. Shaunna Oteka McCovey, "Measurements," *The Smokehouse Boys*, 25.

19. Donna Tam, "Enrollment Requirements Change for Hoopa Valley Indian Tribe," *Times-Standard*, 13 April 2008, 1, 7.

20. Shaunna Oteka McCovey, "Resilience and Responsibility: Surviving the New Genocide," in *Eating Fire, Tasting Blood: An Anthology of the American Indian Holocaust*, ed. Marijo Moore, 287.

21. "Yurok Tribe Sponsors Gathering to Fight Methamphetamine," *Times-Standard*, 22 March 2009.

22. Axel R. Lindgren, Introduction to *The Four Ages of Tsurai: A Documentary History of the Indian Village on Trinidad Bay*, ed. Robert F. Heizer and John E. Mills.

23. From the journal of Don Bruno de Hezeta, translated and reprinted in Heizer and Mills, *The Four Ages of Tsurai*, 33.

24. During his fieldwork in Yurok territory in 1909, anthropologist Thomas Waterman identified Oket'o as a "center of population" with "numerous Indian towns." See Thomas T. Waterman, *Yurok Geography*, University of California Publications in American Archaeology and Ethnology (hereafter UCPAAE) 16, no. 5 (31 May 1920), 264–266. Waterman recorded evidence of six inhabited Yurok settlements at Big Lagoon. A. L. Kroeber's informant suggested there had been eight towns at Big Lagoon. See A. L. Kroeber Papers, 1869–1972, Bancroft Library, University of California, Berkeley (hereafter cited as Kroeber Papers), Banc film 1022, reel 31, frame 54. According to a recent study, there may have been as many as nine settlements at Big Lagoon. See Jerry Rohde, "Big Lagoon Rancheria Cultural Assessment: Ethnogeographical and Historical Review," unpublished manuscript (September 2008).

25. Albert B. Elsasser and Robert F. Heizer, "Speculations on the Prehistory of Northwestern California," in *The California Indians: A Source Book*, ed. R. F. Heizer and M. A. Whipple, 229. This essay was originally published in 1966.

26. Waterman, *Yurok Geography*, 205. Waterman's landmark study was reprinted by the Trinidad Museum Society in 1993.

27. Kat Anderson, *Tending the Wild: Native American Knowledge and the Management of California's Natural Resources*, 327–328.

28. Waterman, *Yurok Geography*, 205; Kroeber Papers, Field Notes (23 July 1918), Banc film 1022, reel 31.

29. Ernest de Massey, *A Frenchman in the Gold Rush: The Journal of Ernest de Massey, Argonaut of 1849*, trans. Marguerite Eyer Wilbur, 62.

30. On the effectiveness of the Yurok and other riverine groups in preserving their food supply, see Arthur F. McEvoy, *The Fisherman's Problem: Ecology and Law in the California Fisheries, 1850–1980*, 19–40.

31. Anderson et al., "A World of Balance and Plenty," 18.

32. McCovey, "Resilience and Responsibility," 293.

33. A. L. Kroeber and E. W. Gifford, *World Renewal: A Cult System of Native Northwest California*, Anthropological Records 13, no. 1, 102.

34. Jim Woodward, "A Preliminary Report on Plans to Reconstruct a Yurok Indian Village as Part of the Dry Lagoon State Park General Plan," 18.

35. Kroeber and Gifford, *World Renewal*, 101–103.

36. Center for Community Development, *The Yurok Language, Literature and Culture Textbook*, 3rd ed., 31. The Yurok teachers and translators who worked on this project were Frank Douglas, Jessie Exline, Milton Marks, and Aileen Figueroa.

37. As told to Pliny Earle Goddard, *Hupa Texts*, UCPAAE 1, no. 2 (1904), 132.

38. Buckley, *Standing Ground*, 7.

39. Waterman, *Yurok Geography*, 186.

40. A. L. Kroeber, "Yurok National Character," in *The California Indians: A Source Book*, 2d ed., ed. R. F. Heizer and M. A. Whipple, 387.

41. A. L. Kroeber, *Handbook of the Indians of California*, 13.

42. A. L. Kroeber, "At the Bedrock of History," *Sunset* 25, no. 3 (September 1910), 255–260.

43. Thomas M. Gates, "Along the Ridgelines: A History of the Yurok Trail System" (Ph.D. dissertation, University of North Carolina at Chapel Hill, 1995), 461.

44. Waterman, *Yurok Geography*, 184, 186.

45. Arnold R. Pilling, "Yurok," in *Handbook of North American Indians*, vol. 8, "California," ed. Robert F. Heizer, 137, 141.

46. Mavis McCovey and John F. Salter, *Medicine Trails: A Life in Many Worlds*, 36.

47. From the journal of Don Juan Francisco de la Bodega y Quadra, translated and reprinted in Heizer and Mills, *The Four Ages of Tsurai*, 24.

48. George Vancouver, *A Voyage of Discovery to the North Pacific Ocean and Round the World*, vol. 2, 241–242, 247.

49. "Contrary to the idea of mini-systems (self-reproducing autarchic societies), the peoples of Northern California interacted intensively with their immediate neighbors, even across huge linguistic boundaries." Christopher Chase-Dunn and Helly M. Mann, *The Wintu and Their Neighbors: A Very Small-World System in Northern California*, 73–74.

50. Joshua Paddison, ed, *A World Transformed: Firsthand Accounts of California before the Gold Rush*, 64–65.

51. "An Act of Possession of the Spanish Crown at Trinidad Bay, June 11, 1775," reprinted in Heizer and Mills, *The Four Ages of Tsurai*, 57–60.

52. Vancouver, *A Voyage of Discovery*, 245; "Visit of the Brig *Columbia* to Trinidad Bay, July 24, 1817, from the Journal of the First Officer, Peter Corney," Heizer and Mills, *The Four Ages of Tsurai*, 101.

53. Quoted in E. W. Giesecke, "Unlikely Partners: Bostonians, Russians, and Kodiaks Sail the Pacific Coast Together, 1800–1810," *Mains'l Haul* 43 (Summer-Fall 2007), 34–69. See also E. W. Giesecke, "Discovery of Humboldt Bay, California, in 1806 from the Ship *O'Cain*, Jonathan Winship, Commander," *Terrae Incognitae* 29 (1997), 1–24.

54. Thomas Bender, *A Nation among Nations: America's Place in World History*, 21.

55. Anderson et al., "A World of Balance and Plenty," 18; Kroeber, *Handbook*, 883.

56. Mariana Ferreira, "Sweet Tears and Bitter Pills: The Politics of Health among Yuroks of Northern California" (Ph.D. dissertation, University of California, Berkeley, 1996), 20.

57. McCovey, "Resilience and Responsibility," 289.

58. On the case for genocide, see Laurence M. Hauptman, *Tribes and Tribulations: Misconceptions about American Indians and Their Histories*, 3–14.

59. Preface to Robert Spott and A. L. Kroeber, *Yurok Narratives*, v.

60. Rohde, "Big Lagoon Rancheria," 20.

61. Typewritten memo from A. L. Kroeber to T. T. Waterman, c. 1909, Kroeber Papers, Banc film 1022, reel 130, frames 88–89.

62. Kroeber and Gifford, *World Renewal*, 103. Waterman's 1909 survey of Big Lagoon similarly noted that the Yurok sites had been "abandoned since the villages there were in the midst of agricultural land, which was settled at an early date by the whites." See Thomas Waterman, "Yurok Marriages."

63. McCovey, "Resilience and Responsibility," 289.

64. "Memorial of the Northern California Indian Association" (1904) in *Federal Concern about Conditions of California Indians, 1853–1913: Eight Documents*, ed. Robert F. Heizer, 101.

65. Susie Van Kirk, personal communication to author, Jan.-Feb. 2010. See also Janet Eidsness, "Initial Cultural Resources Study for Proposed Hazard Tree Removal and Water Tank Replacement Project, Big Lagoon Park Company," 28–30.

66. Susan Bernardin, "Capturing and Recapturing Culture: Trailing Grace Nicholson's Legacy in Northwestern California," in *Trading Gazes: Euro-American Women Photographers and Native North Americans, 1880–1940*, ed. Susan Bernardin et al., 151–185.

67. *Arcata Union*, 16 September 1893, as quoted in introduction to Ericson Photograph Collection, Humboldt State University Library, Arcata, California.

68. Letter from Alfred Kroeber to Llewellyn Loud (12 August 1913), in *An Anthropological Expedition of 1913 or Get It Through Your Head or Yours for the Revolution*, ed. Robert F. Heizer, 12.

69. A member of the expedition, Lewis Keysor Wood, was mauled by bears, and another member, Josiah Gregg, later starved to death near Clear Lake. Clarence E. Pearsall et al., eds., *The Quest for Qual-A-Wa-Loo*, 131–133. This account is based on the diaries of L. K. Wood.

70. Georgia Willis Read and Ruth Gaines, eds., *Gold Rush: The Journals, Drawings, and Other Papers of J. Goldsborough Bruff*, 2, 944–946.

71. On the expulsion of the Chinese from Humboldt, see Jean Pfaelzer, *Driven Out: The Forgotten War against Chinese Americans*.

72. Thomas Gihon, "An Incident of the Gold Bluff Excitement," *Overland Monthly* 18, no. 108 (December 1891), 649.

73. De Massey, *A Frenchman in the Gold Rush*, 58.

74. Carl Meyer, *Bound for Sacramento*, trans. Ruth Frey Axe, 187.

75. Handwritten journal of Greenleaf Curtis, 15 May 1862, Del Norte Historical Society, Crescent City, Calif., 35.

76. For reports on death and danger on the coast at Big Lagoon, see Susie Baker Fountain Papers, vol. 23, 350, 367; and vol. 69, 34, 37, Humboldt Room, Humboldt State University, California.

77. Shirley M. Hannah, "Country School Teacher Reminisces," *The Humboldt Historian* XVII, no. 4 (July-August 1969), 1.

78. Susie Baker Fountain Papers, vol. 23, 367.

79. Henry Gannett, "The Redwood Forest of the Pacific Coast," *National Geographic* 10, no. 5 (May 1898), 154, 159.

80. Joel Bourne Jr., "Redwoods: The Super Trees," *National Geographic* 216, no. 4 (October 2009), 38.

81. Commissioner Livingston Stone, quoted in McEvoy, *The Fisherman's Problem*, 50.

82. Jim Woodward and George R. Stammerjohan, "A Cultural Resource Inventory of Harry A. Merlo State Recreation Area," California Department of Parks and Recreation (December 1987), 6. This report is on file at the State Park Archaeology Lab, Sacramento, Calif., R_136_64.pdf.

83. Chet Schwarzkopf, "Crannel–Big Lagoon, Modern Logging," *Humboldt Times*, 16 January 1949.

84. Bill and Phyllis Hill, personal communication to the author, 9 August 2004.

85. Lynwood Carranco and John T. Labbe, *Logging the Redwoods*.

86. This history of Big Lagoon draws upon research by Susie Van Kirk and Don Tuttle, cited in Eidsness, "Initial Cultural Resources Study."

87. "Humboldt Bay—Its Destiny," *Daily Alta California*, 12 August 1850.

88. "The New North Coast Settlements," *Daily Alta California*, 5 August 1850.

89. Meyer, *Bound for Sacramento*, 189, 192.

90. Spott and Kroeber, *Yurok Narratives*, 251.

91. J. M. Eddy, *In the Redwood's Realm: By-Ways of Wild Nature and Highways of Industry, as Found under the Forest Shades and amidst Clover Blossoms in Humboldt County*, 22. See also Peter Palmquist, *Fine California Views: The Photographs of A. W. Ericson*, 55.

92. *Arcata Union*, 15 November 1902.

93. Waterman, *Yurok Geography*, 263.

94. A reproduction of the map can be found at the front of Pamela F. Service and Raymond W. Hillman, *Eureka and Humboldt County*, 2001.

95. Reed F. Noss, ed., *The Redwood Forest: History, Ecology, and Conservation of the Coast Redwoods*, 10.

96. David Glassberg, *Sense of History: The Place of the Past in American Life*, 195–197.

97. "Search for Indian Relics," *Arcata Union*, 17 May 1928.

98. *Arcata Union*, 24 October 1929.

99. According to a 1999 investigation by the Army Corps of Engineers, Big Lagoon was used as a site of a "rocket training program" in 1944–1945. "The target area should be screened for potential ordnance," concluded the report. United States Army Corps of Engineers, Sacramento District, Formerly Used Defense Sites (FUDS) Program, "Big Lagoon Bombing Target," April 2006, http://www.corpsfuds.org/reports/INPR/J09CA7466inpr.pdf.

100. David Lowenthal, *The Past Is a Foreign Country*.

101. See, for example, Gabrielle Tayac, ed., *IndiVisible: African–Native American Lives in the Americas*.

102. Unnamed Yurok informants as told to Waterman, *Yurok Geography*, 190–192, 266–267.

103. Eidsness, "Initial Cultural Resources Study."

104. By contrast, it's hard to imagine visiting memorials in Germany that commemorate pre–World War II Jewish culture but skip the Holocaust. On the proliferation of a memorial culture in Germany, see Karen E. Till, *The New Berlin: Memory, Politics, Place.*

105. The photograph was taken on the Klamath River, not Big Lagoon, in 1918, when it was mostly tourists, not Yurok, who fished Big Lagoon. Information about Alice Spott comes from Buckley, *Standing Ground*, 284.

Three: It Is Not Gone Into Here

1. From transcript of interview by Judith Dides, California Department of Parks and Recreation, with Margaret Lara, Walt Lara, and Joy Sundberg, 8 January 1990. Thanks to Janet Eidsness for making this available to me.

2. Letter from Harry Roberts to George Roether, US Forest Service (18 October 1973). Thanks to Ned Simmons for making this available to me.

3. It was through his initiative that the University of California Botanical Garden in Berkeley developed an extensive collection of native flora. See University of California Botanical Garden Newsletter 28, nos. 2, 3 (Spring-Summer 2003).

4. For correspondence between Kroeber and Ruth Roberts, see Department of Anthropology, University of California, Berkeley, Archives, CU-23, Box 126 (hereafter cited as UCB Anthropology Archives).

5. Thomas Buckley, *Standing Ground: Yurok Indian Spirituality, 1850–1990*, 58.

6. Harry K. Roberts, "Walking in Beauty: Reflections of a Yurok Education," ed. Thomas Buckley, unpublished manuscript, August 1980, Trinidad Museum Society.

7. Lucy Thompson, *To the American Indian: Reminiscences of a Yurok Woman*, 197. Thompson's book was first published by Cummins Print Shop in Eureka, 1916.

8. Letter from Kroeber to Vierling Kersey, California Superintendent of Public Instruction (6 February 1934), UCB Anthropology Archives, CU-23, Box 126.

9. For a brief summary of his research, see T. T. Waterman and A. L. Kroeber, *Yurok Marriages*, UCPAAE 35, no. 1 (1934), 1–14.

10. Thomas Waterman, "Yurok Marriages," unpublished typed and handwritten manuscript, c. 1909–1928.

11. There are several exceptions, such as Thomas Buckley, author of *Standing Ground* (2002). His "adoptive uncle and teacher" was Harry Roberts.

12. Julian H. Steward, "Alfred Kroeber, 1876–1960: A Biographical Memoir," *American Anthropologist* 63, no. 5 (October 1961), 1038–1060.

13. For examples of work produced in this period, see A. L Kroeber, *The Languages of the Coast of California North of San Francisco*, UCPAAE 9, no. 3 (29 April 1911), 273–345; A. L. Kroeber, *Handbook of the Indians of California* (1925); Thomas T. Waterman, *Yurok Geography*, UCPAAE 16, no. 5 (1920); Llewellyn L. Loud, *Ethnogeography and Archaeology of the Wiyot Territory*,

UCPAAE 14, no. 3 (23 December 1918), 221–436; Edward Winslow Gifford, *Californian Anthropometry*, UCPAAE 22, no. 2 (19 March 1926), 217–390; Robert Spott and A. L. Kroeber, *Yurok Narratives* (1942); and R. F. Heizer and M. A. Whipple, *The California Indians: A Source Book* (1960).

14. See Robert F. Heizer's introduction to Stephen Powers, *Tribes of California*, 1–5.

15. National Museum of Natural History, Smithsonian Institution Archives, Record Unit 305, Accession no. 4856.

16. Quoted by Barbara A. Davis in *Edward S. Curtis: The Life and Times of a Shadow Catcher*, 15. Curtis's photographs of the Yurok appeared in vol. 13 of *The North American Indian* (Norwood, Conn.: Plimpton Press, 1924).

17. Erik Homburger Erikson, *Observations on the Yurok: Childhood and World Image*, UCPAAE 35, no. 10 (1943), 283.

18. "Here Come the Anthros," from a recording by Floyd Red Crow Westerman, *Custer Died for Your Sins* (Red Crow Enterprises, Inc., 1970).

19. Orin Starn, *Ishi's Brain: In Search of America's Last "Wild" Indian*, 139.

20. Steward, "Alfred Kroeber," 207.

21. For information about Kroeber's career, I draw upon Theodora Kroeber, *Alfred Kroeber: A Personal Configuration*; Douglas Cazaux Sackman, *Wild Men: Ishi and Kroeber in the Wilderness of Modern America*; Ira Jacknis, "The First Boasian: Alfred Kroeber and Franz Boas, 1896–1905," *American Anthropologist* 104, no. 2 (2002), 520–532; Ira Jacknis, "Alfred Kroeber as Museum Anthropologist," *Museum Anthropology* 17, no. 2 (1993), 27–33; Ira Jacknis, "A Museum Prehistory: Phoebe Hearst and the Founding of the Museum of Anthropology, 1891–1901," *Chronicle of the University of California* 4 (2000), 47–77; and Ira Jacknis, personal communication to author, 1 April 2010.

22. Quoted in Jacknis, "Alfred Kroeber as Museum Anthropologist," 29.

23. Theodora Kroeber, *Alfred Kroeber*, 2.

24. Kroeber bought an acre of land for $31 in 1923 ("Real Estate Transcript," *Humboldt Standard*, 21 July 1924, 4). The site of Kroeber's cabin was later turned by the State Highway Commission into a turnabout and viewpoint. Timothy H. H. Thoresen, "Kroeber and the Yurok, 1900–1908," in A. L. Kroeber, *Yurok Myths*, xix; Kroeber, *Yurok Myths*, 181.

25. Theodora Kroeber, *Alfred Kroeber*, 158.

26. A. L. Kroeber, "Thomas Talbot Waterman," *American Anthropologist* 39, no. 3 (July–September 1937), 527.

27. Theodora Kroeber, *Alfred Kroeber*, 57.

28. *An Anthropological Expedition of 1913 or Get It through Your Head or Yours for the Revolution*, ed. Robert F. Heizer, 24, 33.

29. Ibid., 12.

30. Sackman, *Wild Men*, 112, 166.

31. Ibid., 144.

32. A later generation would learn about Ishi through the enormously popular book by Theodora Kroeber, *Ishi in Two Worlds: A Biography of the Last Wild Indian in North America*.

33. Thoresen, "Kroeber and the Yurok, 1900–1908," xxvi.

34. Foreword to Kroeber, *Yurok Myths*, xiii.

35. Kroeber, *Handbook*, 1.

36. Foreword, *Yurok Myths*, xiii.

37. Theodora Kroeber, *Alfred Kroeber*, 54–56.

38. According to Kroeber, between 1900 and 1907 he "visited the Yurok repeatedly, working with their old men." Spott and Kroeber, *Yurok Narratives*, v.

39. See letters from Kroeber to Ruth Roberts (14 January 1933); Roberts to Kroeber (16 January 1933); and Kroeber to Roberts (27 January 1933) about paying Robert Spott $2 per day to teach graduate students in Berkeley about "ethnological field work." UCB Anthropology Archives, CU-23, Box 126.

40. Letters from Kroeber to Alice Woodcock (20 January 1921) and from Woodcock to Kroeber (25 January 1921), UCB Anthropology Archives, CU-23, Box 182.

41. Letter from W. Frank to Kroeber (5 November 1920), UCB Anthropology Archives, CU-23, Box 57.

42. See, for example, letters from Kroeber to Ruth Roberts (19 October 1933) and Roberts to Kroeber (15 November 1933), UCB Anthropology Archives, CU-23, Box 126.

43. Information about Ruth Roberts draws upon an introduction to the Roberts Photograph Collection, especially a summary of newspaper references to the Roberts family, by Susie Van Kirk, Humboldt State University Library, Arcata, Calif.

44. Letters from Margaret Marks to Kroeber (6 May 1930) and from Kroeber to Marks (15 May 1930), UCB Anthropology Archives, CU-23, Box 99.

45. A. L. Kroeber, "The Indians of California," *Transactions of the Commonwealth Club of California* 4 (December 1909), 437.

46. Karl Kroeber, *"Ishi in Two Worlds:* Forty Years Later," in Theodora Kroeber, *Ishi in Two Worlds* (2002), x.

47. Arthur J. Ray, "Kroeber and the California Claims: Historical Particularism and Cultural Ecology in Court," in *Central Sites, Peripheral Visions: Cultural and Institutional Crossings in the History of Anthropology,* ed. Richard Handler, 248–274.

48. Mary Gist Dornback, "Anthropologist, Educator—UC's Alfred Kroeber Dies," Council of California Indians Newsletter (15 December 1960).

49 Spott and Kroeber, *Yurok Narratives,* vi.

50. Foreword, *Yurok Myths,* xiv.

51. Ibid., xvi.

52. Judith Dides interview (8 January 1990).

53. Quoted by Buckley, *Standing Ground,* 16.

54. Alan Dundes, "Folkloristic Commentary," in Kroeber, *Yurok Myths,* xxxvi.

55. Richard Keeling, "Kroeber's *Yurok Myths*: A Comparative Re-evaluation," *American Indian Culture and Research Journal* 6, no. 3 (1982), 72.

56. Introduction to Thompson, *To the American Indian,* xx.

57. Arthur F. McEvoy, *The Fisherman's Problem: Ecology and Law in the California Fisheries, 1850–1980,* 55.

58. Bruce G. Trigger, *A History of Archaeological Thought,* 122.

59. A. L. Kroeber, "Yurok National Character," in *The California Indians: A Source Book,* 2d ed., ed. R. F. Heizer and M. A. Whipple, 385–390. Kroeber also uses this essay to debate his friend Erik Erikson as to whether the "infantile attitude" of the Yurok is shaped by an anal or oral temperament. "Each is presumably true on its own level and degree."

60. A. L. Kroeber, *Anthropology,* 59, 85.

61. Kroeber, "The Indians of California," 434.

62. A. L. Kroeber, "It's All Too Much for Ishi, Says the Scientist," *San Francisco Call* (8 October 1911).

63. Erna Gunther, *Indian Life on the Northwest Coast of North America: As Seen by the Early Explorers and Fur Traders during the Last Decades of the Eighteenth Century,* xi.

64. Kroeber, "Yurok National Character," 387; and *Handbook,* 5.

65. Quoted by Steward, "Alfred Kroeber," 207.

66. A. L. Kroeber, "Two Papers on the Aboriginal Ethnography of California," *Reports of the University of California Archaeological Survey* 56 (1 March 1962), 58. One of these papers, "The Nature of Land-Holding Groups in Aboriginal California," prepared for the California Indian Claims hearings, was written in 1954.

67. Margaret Mead, "The American Indian as a Significant Determinant of Anthropological Style," in *Anthropology and the American Indian,* ed. James E. Officer and Francis McKinley, 70–71.

68. Heizer, Introduction to Powers, *Tribes of California*, 4.

69. Judith Dides interview.

70. Buckley, *Standing Ground*, 13.

71. Kroeber, "The Indians of California," 432.

72. Kroeber, *Handbook*, 883, 886. These numbers for the Yurok are accepted by subsequent writers. See Buckley, *Standing Ground*, 9–10.

73. Kroeber, *Handbook*, 880–891.

74. Carl Meyer, *Bound for Sacramento*, 175.

75. *Northern Californian*, 29 February 1860, quoted in Ray Raphael and Freeman House, *Two Peoples, One Place*, 165.

76. Powers, *Tribes of California*, 404.

77. Josiah Royce, *California: From the Conquest in 1846 to the Second Vigilance Committee in San Francisco: A Study of American Character*, 2, 222.

78. Helen Hunt Jackson, *A Century of Dishonor: A Sketch of the United States Government's Dealings with Some of the Indian Tribes*, 29.

79. Hubert Howe Bancroft, *History of California, 1860–1890*, vol. 7, 474.

80. Loud, *Ethnogeography and Archaeology*, 305.

81. Quoted by Barbara Davis, *Edward S. Curtis*, 70.

82. Rockwell D. Hunt, *California and Californians*, vol. II, 347.

83. "I am not aware that my father wrote anything of the kind you are seeking on the topic of genocide," writes anthropologist Karl Kroeber, personal communication to the author, 7 March 2009.

84. Kroeber, "Two Papers," 58.

85. Kroeber, "Yurok National Character," 385.

86. Theodora Kroeber and Robert F. Heizer, *Almost Ancestors: The First Californians*, 19.

87. See 1913 correspondence between Loud and Kroeber in Heizer, *An Anthropological Expedition of 1913*.

88. Albert L. Hurtado, *Indian Survival on the California Frontier*, 1. Over the years there has been considerable debate about the size of the precontact population in California. Hurtado and others accept the estimates of Sherburne F. Cook, *The Population of the California Indians, 1769–1970*.

89. Governor Peter H. Burnett, "Governor's Annual Message to the Legislature." 7 January 1851, *Journals of the Senate and Assembly of the State of California, 1851–1852*, 15.

90. Raphael and House, *Two Peoples*, 172–178. During the same period, there was one massacre of settlers. "Massacre" is defined here as a "conflict in which one side attacks the other unawares, leading to five or more deaths among those who were attacked..."

91. Blue Lake Rancheria, "History," http://www.bluelakerancheria-nsn.gov, accessed 29 September 2009. See also, Jerry Rohde, "Genocide and Extortion," *North Coast Journal* (25 February 2010), 10–17.

92. Thomas Gihon, "An Incident of the Gold Bluff Excitement," *Overland Monthly* 18, no. 108, 648, 649, 661.

93. Reported in Janet Eidsness, "Initial Cultural Resources Study for Proposed Hazard Tree Removal and Water Tank Replacement Project, Big Lagoon Park Company," 17. There is also a reference to the Mä'äts massacre in Jim Woodward, "A Preliminary Report on Plans to Reconstruct a Yurok Indian Village as Part of the Dry Lagoon State Park General Plan," 20.

94. "Another Indian War! Six Euro-American Men Killed, Two Ferry Boats Cut Away, the Indians Well Armed," *Crescent City Herald*, 31 January 1855; J, "Correspondence," *Crescent City Herald*, 14 February 1855. Thanks to Jerry Rohde (personal communication, 22 November 2008) for providing this information.

95. "Latest Indian News," *Humboldt Times*, 16 August 1862.

96. Ernest de Massey, *A Frenchman in the Gold Rush: The Journal of Ernest de Massey, Argonaut of 1849*, trans. Marguerite Eyer Wilbur, 60–64.

97. Meyer, *Bound for Sacramento*, 197.

98. See, generally, on the complexities of Indian-white relations, Richard White, *The Middle Ground: Indians, Empires, and Republics in the Great Lakes Region, 1650–1815*.

99. *Daily Alta California*, 6 August 1850.

100. John Carr, *Pioneer Days in California*; de Massey, *A Frenchman in the Gold Rush*, 56; Meyer, *Bound for Sacramento*, 146.

101. Walter Van Dyke, "Early Days in Klamath," *The Overland Monthly* 18, no. 104 (August 1891), 174–181.

102. "Amalgamation of Gold by Mercury," *Daily Alta California*, 28 August 1850.

103. Meyer, *Bound for Sacramento*, 212.

104. Clyde A. Milner II, "National Initiatives," in *The Oxford History of the American West*, ed. Clyde A. Milner II, Carol A. O'Connor, and Martha A. Sandweiss, 183.

105. James J. Rawls, *Indians of California: The Changing Image*, 81–133. "Nowhere in North America was the labor of Native Americans more important than in California, first to the European settlers and then to the Yankees," notes Daniel Cornford, ed., *Working People of California*, 29.

106. Quoted in Heizer and Whipple, *The California Indians*, 270.

107. Blue Lake Rancheria, "History," http://www.bluelakerancheria-nsn.gov, accessed 29 September 2009.

108. Rawls, *Indians of California*, 149.

109. Ibid., 151–153.

110. David Wallace Adams, *Education for Extinction: American Indians and the Boarding School Experience, 1875–1928*.

111. Shaunna Oteka McCovey, "Resilience and Responsibility: Surviving the New Genocide," in *Eating Fire, Tasting Blood: An Anthology of the American Indian Holocaust*, ed. Marijo Moore, 289.

112. Adams, *Education for Extinction*, 336.

113. Royce, *California*, 500.

114. Davis, *Edward S. Curtis*, 39.

115. R. H. Pratt, "The Advantages of Mingling Indians with Whites," *Proceedings of the National Conference of Charities and Correction* (1892), 46.

116. Richard White, *"It's Your Misfortune and None of My Own": A New History of the American West*, 103.

117. Powers, *Tribes of California*, 44, 47.

118. A. J. Bledsoe, *History of Del Norte County, California, with a Business Directory and Traveler's Guide*, 106, 108.

119. Hubert Howe Bancroft, *California Inter Pocula*, 254.

120. Hubert Howe Bancroft, *The Wild Tribes*, vol. 1 of *The Native Races*, 301.

121. C. E. Kelsey, "Report of Special Agent for California Indians" (1906), reprinted in *Federal Concern about Conditions of California Indians, 1853–1913: Eight Documents*, ed. Robert F. Heizer, 130.

122. Raphael Samuel, *Theatres of Memory: Past and Present in Contemporary Culture*; Phoebe S. Kropp, "'There Is a Little Sermon in That': Constructing the Native Southwest at the San Diego Panama-California Exposition of 1915," in *The Great Southwest of the Fred Harvey Company and the Santa Fe Railway*, ed. Marta Weigle and Barbara A. Babcock, 36–46.

123. Academic historians in California did not have an impact until after World War I. Herbert Bolton was hired at UC Berkeley in 1911; the first, one-volume history of California was published in 1921; and the first college-level text was not written until 1929. See Gerald D. Nash, "California and Its Historians: An Appraisal of Histories of the State," *Pacific Historical Review* 50, no. 4 (November 1981), 387–413.

124. Carey McWilliams, *California: The Great Exception*, 58–59.

125. See, for example, John S. Hittell, *Hittell's Hand-Book of Pacific Coast Travel*; D. L. Thornbury, *California's Redwood Wonderland: Humboldt County*; and Hero Eugene Rensch and Ethel Grace Rensch, *Historical Spots in California*.

126. See, for example, Herbert E. Bolton and Ephraim D. Adams, *California's Story*; Rockwell Hunt, *New California The Golden*; and Robert Glass Cleland, *California Pageant: The Story of Four Centuries*.

127. Later, movies, television, and large-format pictorial books—such as Lucius Beebe and Charles Clegg, *The American West: The Pictorial Epic of a Continent*—would supplant this genre.

128. As Carey McWilliams noted, the creation of this legend was tied to the development of California as a tourist destination and to utopian images of Southern California as a real estate paradise. McWilliams's insights in *Southern California: An Island on the Land* are still relevant and form the basis for all subsequent cultural analyses. See, for example, David M. Wrobel and Michael C. Steiner, eds., *Many Wests: Place, Culture, and Regional Identity*; and William Deverell, *Whitewashed Adobe: The Rise of Los Angeles and the Remaking of Its Mexican Past*.

129. Theodore H. Hittell, *History of California*, vol. 1, 729.

130. C. D. Willard, "The Padres and the Indians," *Land of Sunshine* (September 1894), 73.

131. Burnett, "Governor's Annual Message," 14–15.

132. Ibid., 14.

133. Henry K. Norton, *The Story of California: From the Earliest Days to the Present*, 10.

134. Enola Flower, *A Child's History of California*, 22.

135. Robert Glass Cleland, *California Pageant: The Story of Four Centuries*, 33. Cleland taught for many years at Occidental College before joining the Huntington Library in 1943 to develop its Western collections and shape the contours of California history.

136. Lucia Norman (aka Louise Heaven), *A Youth's History of California*, 21.

137. Arthur W. Dunn, *Civics: The Community and the Citizen*, 43.

138. John S. Hittell, *A History of San Francisco and Incidentally of the State of California*, 9, 20. This view prevailed well into the twentieth century among respectable academics.

139. Hunt, *New California*, 20.

140. Cornford, *Working People*, 29.

141. Harry Ellington Brook, "Olden Times in Southern California," *Land of Sunshine* (July 1894), 29–31.

142. Helen Elliott Bandini, *History of California*, 89.

143. John McGroarty, *California: Its History and Romance*, 42, 48.

144. Gertrude Atherton, *California: An Intimate History*, 25, 78.

145. Herbert E. Bolton and Ephraim D. Adams, *California's Story*, 80–81.

146. Harr Wagner and Mark Keppel, *California History*, 6, 66, 69, 70.

147. Rockwell D. Hunt and Nellie Van De Grift Sánchez, *A Short History of California*, 73, 84.

148. A. A. Gray, *History of California from 1542*, 338.

149. Hittell, *A History of San Francisco*, 60.

150. Phil Hanna, *California through Four Centuries: A Handbook of Memorable Historical Dates*, viii.

151. Sherburne F. Cook, *The Conflict between the California Indian and White Civilization*, 34.

152. Robert Glass Cleland, *From Wilderness to Empire: A History of California, 1542–1900*, 287–288.

153. John A. Crow, *California as a Place to Live*, 13, 14.

154. Maynard Dixon, "The Singing of the West," *Sunset* (December 1906), 98.

155. Clifford Trembly, "The Irrigated Land," *Sunset* (September 1905), 4.

156. Gray, *History of California*, iii.

157. Grace S. Dawson, *California: The Story of Our Southwest Corner*, 169.

158. Robert Cleland, *A History of California: The American Period*, 466.

159. Royce, *California*, 277.

160. For background and the philosophy of the museum, see Duane Blue Spruce, ed., *Spirit of a Native Place: Building the National Museum of the American Indian.*

Four: Unpleasant Work

1. See, for example, exhibitions at the Museum of Natural History in New York City and National Museum of Natural History, Washington, D.C. On an important 2010 exhibition at the NMNH that includes Neanderthal and Cro-Magnon skulls, see Richard Potts and Christopher Sloan, *What Does It Mean to Be Human?*

2. This "cabinet of curiosities" is displayed without critique in a room devoted to "origins of the museum." Author's field visit to Museo Nacional de Antropologia, 16 September 2010.

3. On the shift in museums from historical to aesthetic display of native artifacts, see Steven Conn, *Museums and American Intellectual Life, 1876–1926.*

4. The following analysis is based on email correspondence with Jim Hamill and research at The Centre for Anthropology, Department of Africa, Oceania and the Americas, British Museum, London, 25 June 2009.

5. George Vancouver, *A Voyage of Discovery to the North Pacific Ocean and Round the World*, 404, 414.

6. Erna Gunther, *Indian Life on the Northwest Coast of North America: As Seen by the Early Explorers and Fur Traders during the Last Decades of the Eighteenth Century*, ix, 203.

7. Peter Bolz, "Origins and History of the Collection," in *Native American Art: The Collections of the Ethnological Museum Berlin*, ed. Peter Bolz and Hans-Ulrich Sanner, 23–49.

8. Douglas Cole, *Captured Heritage: The Scramble for Northwest Artifacts*, 2.

9. J. C. H. King, "Vancouver's Ethnography," *Journal of the History of Collections* 6, no. 1 (1994), 35–58.

10. Ibid., 43.

11. George Goodman Hewett, "Inventory of Vancouver Expedition Collection," c. 1800, manuscript no. 1126, Centre for Anthropology, British Museum, London.

12. Charles H. Read, "An Account of a Collection of Ethnographical Specimens Formed During Vancouver's Voyage in the Pacific Ocean, 1790–1795," *The Journal of the Anthropological Institute of Great Britain and Ireland* 21 (1892), 100. The bone box and spoon are in the British Museum collection, AM1985,Q.36 and Am1987,Q.27.

13. The original correspondence relating to the British Museum's acquisition of the Hewett Collection in 1891 is in the archives of the British Museum's Centre for Anthropology.

14. "Sir Augustus Wollaston Franks," *Encyclopaedia Britannica Online*, www.britannica.com; "Augustus Wollaston Franks," *Wikipedia*, accessed 10 October 2009, http://en.wikipedia.org/wiki/augustus_wollaston_franks.

15. This description can be found in the British Museum's database, AN330699001.

16. Read, "An Account," 107. The bow is in the British Museum collection, Am1891C25.5.

17. The purse is in the British Museum collection, Am1891C25.169.

18. Thomas C. Blackburn and Travis Hudson, *Time's Flotsam: Overseas Collections of California Material Culture*, 120–128.

19. The tendency of museums to lose track of borrowed skulls or see their collections diminished by mildew is noted by Ann Fabian, *The Skull Collectors: Race, Science, and America's Unburied Dead*, 44.

20. Hans-Ulrich Sanner, "California," in Bolz and Sanner, *Native American Art*, 131–145.

21. Paul Schumacher, 1876, quoted ibid., 135.

22. Fabian, *The Skull Collectors*, 195–196.

23. Cole, *Captured Heritage*, 286–287.

24. King, "Vancouver's Ethnography," 56.

25. Blackburn and Hudson, *Time's Flotsam*, 33–38.

26. Quoted ibid., 28.

27. Lee Davis, review of *Time's Flotsam: Overseas Collections of California Indian Material Culture*, *Journal of California and Great Basin Anthropology* 17, no. 1 (1995), 141; Thomas Blackburn, personal communication to author, 12 August 2009.

28. Sanner, "California," 142; Blackburn and Hudson, *Time's Flotsam*, 97–98.

29. Sanner, "California." This is based on a survey done by Travis Hudson in the 1980s.

30. Ibid., 14.

31. Robert E. Bieder, *A Brief Historical Survey of the Expropriation of American Indian Remains*, 12.

32. Douglas J. Preston, "Skeletons in Our Museums' Closets," *Harper's* (February 1989), 67; Suzanne J. Crawford, "(Re)Constructing Bodies: Semiotic Sovereignty and the Debate over Kenniwick Man," in *Repatriation Reader: Who Owns American Remains?*, ed. Devon A. Mihesuah, 214.

33. Cole, *Captured Heritage*, 2–5.

34. George Vancouver, *A Voyage of Discovery to the North Pacific Ocean and Round the World, 1791–1795*, ed. W. Kaye Lamb, vol. 1, 40; King, "Vancouver's Ethnography," 37. According to King, "the Admiralty emphasized the importance of good relations with everyone encountered....Transactions between the crew and native peoples were strictly controlled: no inflationary over-payment for curiosities was permitted, and trading could begin only with the captain's permission."

35. Vancouver, *A Voyage of Discovery*, ed. Lamb, vol. 2, 538–539.

36. Ibid., vol. 3, 1021–1022.

37. Ibid., vol. 2, 539.

38. Thomas Jefferson, "Notes on the State of Virginia" (1787), *Writings*, 226.

39. Ibid., 223–225.

40. Harriet A. Washington, *Medical Apartheid: The Dark History of Medical Experimentation on Black Americans from Colonial Times to the Present*, 115–142.

41. Fabian, *The Skull Collectors*. See also, Ronald Niezen, *Spirit Wars: Native North American Religions in the Age of Nation Building*, 163.

42. Bruce G. Trigger, *A History of Archaeological Thought*, 122, 195.

43. Ibid., 110–147.

44. Ibid., 117–118.

45. Quoted in Bieder, *A Brief Historical Survey*, 11.

46. Robert E. Bieder, *Science Encounters the Indian: The Early Years of American Ethnology*, 79.

47. Ibid., 55–103. For an in-depth assessment of Morton's ideas and his role in the development of "scientific racism," see Fabian, *The Skull Collectors*.

48. Ibid., 67; letter from Zina Pitcher to Morton (4 March 1837), quoted in Bieder, *A Brief Historical Survey*, 8.

49. Preston, "Skeletons," 69.

50. Ernest de Massey, *A Frenchman in the Gold Rush: The Journal of Ernest de Massey, Argonaut of 1849*, 60.

51. Carl Meyer, *Bound for Sacramento*, trans. Ruth Frey Axe, 200.

52. Quoted in Bieder, *Science Encounters the Indian*, 67.

53. Fabian, *The Skull Collectors*, 189.

54. Ira Jacknis, "The First Boasian: Alfred Kroeber and Franz Boas, 1896–1905," *American Anthropologist* 104, no. 2 (2002), 520–532. Jacknis suggests that Kroeber "undoubtedly did what he was told to do by his mentor and superiors and may not have been aware of the details."

55. Douglas Cazaux Sackman, *Wild Men: Ishi and Kroeber in the Wilderness of Modern America*, 71–72.

56. Theodora Kroeber, *Ishi in Two Worlds: A Biography of the Last Wild Indian in North America*.

57. Letter from Kroeber to Gifford (24 March 1916); and from Gifford to Kroeber (30 March 1916), quoted ibid., 234–235.

58. Quoted in Orin Starn, *Ishi's Brain: In Search of America's Last "Wild" Indian*, 159. For a fascinating account of the journey of Ishi's brain from autopsy to repatriation, see Starn's book. A few more details are added to the story in Sackman, *Wild Men*, 248–285. And both books suggest that Theodora Kroeber's account in *Ishi in Two Worlds* tends to sugarcoat her husband's role in the matter.

59. Crawford, "(Re)Constructing Bodies," 214.

60. Fabian, *The Skull Collectors*, 208.

61. Robert W. Rydell, *All the World's a Fair: Visions of Empire at American International Expositions, 1876–1916*.

62. Bieder, *A Brief Historical Survey*, 26–27.

63. Sackman, *Wild Men*, 70–71, 105–106.

64. Rydell, *All the World's a Fair*, 221–223.

65. Aleš Hrdlička, *Directions for Collecting Information and Specimens for Physical Anthropology*, 8, 10, 11, 23.

66. Ibid., 4, 5, 7, 15, 16, 17.

67. Conn, *Museums and American Intellectual Life*, 99.

68. Bieder, *A Brief Historical Survey*, 24–25.

69. Quoted by Mary Jane Lenz in "George Gustav Heye," in *Spirit of a Native Place: Building the National Museum of the American Indian*, ed. Duane Blue Spruce, 89.

70. Bieder, *A Brief Historical Survey*, 42–43.

71. For reporting on the case and its history, see *Geronimo vs. Obama* (17 February 2009), case # 1:09-cv-00303, US District Court, District of Columbia; James C. McKinley Jr., "Geronimo's Heirs Sue Secret Yale Society over His Skull," *New York Times*, 20 February 2009; Cary O'Reilly, "Yale, Skull and Bones Sued over Remains of Geronimo," *Bloomberg.com*, 18 February 2009; Kathrin Day Lassila and Mark Alden Branch, "Whose Skull and Bones?", *Yale Alumni Magazine* (May–June, 2006); Robert Tomsho, "Dig through Archives Reopens the Issue of Geronimo's Skull," *Wall Street Journal*, 8 May 2006.

72. Ibid.

73. Personal communication to author, 29 April 2009.

74. Curtis M. Hinsley Jr., "Digging for Identity: Reflections on the Cultural Background of Collecting," in Mihesuah, *Repatriation Reader*, 45.

75. Cole, *Captured Heritage*.

76. Theodora Kroeber, *Alfred Kroeber: A Personal Configuration*, 56–57.

77. The exact provenience of these materials is unclear, though they are listed as Yurok. American Museum of Natural History, Department of Anthropology, Ethnographic Collection, accession numbers 50–3482 to 50/3833.

78. Quoted in Jacknis, "The First Boasian," 524–525.

79. Letter from Kroeber to K. T. Preuss (16 March 1911), quoted in Sanner, "California," 143.

80. Quoted in Ira Jacknis, "Alfred Kroeber as Museum Anthropologist," *Museum Anthropology* 17, no. 2 (1993), 27–32.

81. A. L. Kroeber, "Specimens," memo from Kroeber to Waterman, c. 1909, Kroeber Papers, microfilm 2635, reel no. 130.

82. Letter from Thomas Waterman to Kittie Goodwin (19 August 1915), UCB Anthropology Archives, CU-23, Box 64.

83. Letter from Ruth Roberts to Kroeber (4 October 1919), UCB Anthropology Archives, CU-23, Box 126.

84. Letters from Rev. Eugene Williams to Kroeber (24 November 1944) and from Kroeber to Williams (8 December 1944), UCB Anthropology Archives, CU-23, Box 181.

85. Retrieved from *artifacthound.com* on 14 April 2008. Another site—*westernartifacts.com*—offered eleven abalone artifacts from Big Lagoon for prices ranging from $12 to $40.

86. Donna Tam, "Wiyot Tribe: Return Burial Artifacts," *Times-Standard*, 26 April 2008.

87. According to historian Ann Fabian (*The Skull Collectors*, 186), the violence of the Gold Rush and subsequent epidemics made California the largest source of native skulls for museums and scientists.

Five: Joint Ventures

1. Quoted by Frederic Golden, "Some Bones of Contention," *Time* (21 December 1981).

2. Philippe Ariès, *Western Attitudes toward Death from the Middle Ages to the Present*, 13, 25.

3. A. L. Kroeber, *Yurok Myths*, 228.

4. Ariès, *Western Attitudes*, 96. On the shift in funerals from meaningful events of "community theater" to "thinned-out ceremonies" that diminish "the reality and meaning of mortality," see Thomas G. Long, "Chronicle of a Death We Can't Accept," *New York Times* (1 November 2009), Sunday Opinion 10.

5. Lucy Thompson, *To the American Indian: Reminiscences of a Yurok Woman*, 104.

6. Ibid., 103–105.

7. Stephen Powers, *Tribes of California*, 33.

8. Ibid., 440.

9. Ernest de Massey, *A Frenchman in the Gold Rush: The Journal of Ernest de Massey, Argonaut of 1849*, trans. Marguerite Eyer Wilbur, 58.

10. A. L. Kroeber, *Handbook of the Indians of California*, 46–47. Similar descriptions of local native burials can be found in Austen D. Warburton and Joseph F. Endert, *Indian Lore of the North California Coast*, 123, 169; and Virginia M. Fields and Peter E. Palmquist, *100 Years of Humboldt County Culture and Artistry: 1850 to 1950*, 23–25. See also "The Indians of Humboldt," *Daily Alta California*, December 1850, for a description of how "the dead are buried after the manner of Christian burials....the grave filled with earth, heaped up and rounded off after our manner, leaving the boards at the head and feet, like two grave stones."

11. Kroeber, *Handbook*, 46; Arnold R. Pilling, "Yurok," in *Handbook of North American Indians*, vol. 8, "California," ed. Robert F. Heizer, 150.

12. Thomas T. Waterman, *Yurok Geography*, UCPAAE 16, no. 5, 192.

13. Kroeber, *Handbook*, 47.

14. Ariès, *Western Attitudes*, 14.

15. Pilling, "Yurok," 150.

16. Theodora Kroeber, *The Inland Whale*, 37.

17. Kroeber, *Handbook*, 47.

18. As told to Kroeber, *Yurok Myths*, 382–384.

19. Robert Spott and A. L. Kroeber, *Yurok Narratives*, 207.

20. Waterman, *Yurok Geography*, 193. There was an "absolute taboo laid on the names of the dead," also notes Kroeber, *Handbook*, 48.

21. Albert E. Ward, "Navajo Graves: An Archaeological Reflection of Ethnographic Reality," *Ethnohistorical Report Series* 2, 49.

22. Theodora Kroeber, *Ishi in Two Worlds: A Biography of the Last Wild Indian in North America*, 237.

23. C. E. Kelsey, quoted in Robert Heizer, *Federal Concern about Conditions of California Indians, 1853–1913: Eight Documents*, 137.

24. Spott and Kroeber, *Yurok Narratives*, 170. And some Yurok are still hesitant today to name their ancestors. See Thomas Buckley, Introduction to Harry K. Roberts, "Walking in Beauty: Reflections of a Yurok Education," ed. Thomas Buckley, 7.

25. Waterman, *Yurok Geography*, 267.

26. Thomas Waterman, "Yurok Marriages," unpublished typed and handwritten manuscript, c. 1909–1928, 58.

27. Julian Lang, Introduction to Thompson, *To the American Indian*, xviii.

28. Walt Lara Sr., "Respect for the Dead," *News from Native California* 9, no. 4 (Summer 2006), 21.

29. Thompson, *To the American Indian*, 104.

30. Robert McConnell, personal communication to author, 3 November 2009.

31. Robert F. Heizer and Albert B. Elsasser, "Archaeology of HUM-67, The Gunther Island Site in Humboldt Bay, Northwestern California," *Reports of the University of California Archaeological Survey* 62 (1964), 5–122.

32. de Massey, *A Frenchman in the Gold Rush*, 58.

33. Thomas Gihon, "An Incident of the Gold Bluff Excitement," *Overland Monthly* 18, no. 108.

34. "Doing at Trinity City," *Daily Alta California*, 10 July 1850.

35. Sue Silver, "History of California Cemetery Laws," USGenNet website, accessed December 2008, www.usgennet.org/usa/ca/county/eldorado/history_law.htm.

36. Here I draw upon Raphael Samuel's observations about the discipline of history in "Unofficial Knowledge" and "Hybrids," in his *Theatres of Memory: Past and Present in Contemporary Culture*.

37. Mary Jane Lenz, "George Gustav Heye," in *Spirit of a Native Place: Building the National Museum of the American Indian*, ed. Duane Blue Spruce, 87–115.

38. The inventory of Deisher's Pacific Coast Collection and information about Deisher and Reverend Meredith are available in the Cultural Resources Center, National Museum of the American Indian. Thanks to Patricia Nietfeld for making this available to me.

39. According to a *New Yorker* profile quoted by Lenz in "George Gustav Heye," 114.

40. Theodora Kroeber, *Alfred Kroeber: A Personal Configuration*, 144.

41. Ira Jacknis, personal communication to author, 1 April 2010.

42. Garry J. Tee, "The Elusive C. D. Voy," *Journal of the Historical Studies Group* 39 (Sept. 2010), 17–50.

43. Kroeber, *Yurok Myths*, 178, fn 1.

44. National Park Service, National NAGPRA, "Notice of Inventory Completion," *Federal Register* 67, no. 8 (11 January 2002).

45. Phoebe A. Hearst Museum of Anthropology, University of California, Berkeley (hereafter PAHMA), "Notice of Inventory Completion," National NAGPRA, *Federal Register* 70, no. 132 (12 July 2005), 40056–40057.

46. See, for example, Gifford's *Californian Anthropometry*, UCPAAE 22, no. 2 (19 March 1926).

47. See, for example, letter from Gifford to F. M. Parcher (15 October 1928), UCB Anthropology Archives, CU-23, Box 108.

48. Cable from Grace Thoburn to Department of Archaeology (sic) (27 July 1939), UCB Anthropology Archives, CU-23, Box 146.

49. Letter from William G. Huff to Robert Heizer (10 December 1959), UCB Anthropology Archives, CU-23, Box 73.

50. Letter from Dr. H. G. Chappel to Kroeber (18 December 1911), UCB Anthropology Archives, CU-23, Box 211.

51. The Indian Island massacre, which also included the murder of about another 100 Indians, mostly Wiyot, at two other sites in coordinated attacks within twenty-four hours, is discussed in chapter three and in Ray Raphael and Freeman House, *Two Peoples, One Place*, 165, 174–175.

52. Letters from Kroeber to Loud (30 August 1913) and from Loud to Kroeber (3 September 1913), in *An Anthropological Expedition of 1913 or Get It through Your Head or Yours for the Revolution*, ed. Robert F. Heizer, 16, 18.

53. Letter from Kroeber to Loud (30 August 1913), ibid., 16–17.

54. Llewellyn L. Loud, *Ethnogeography and Archaeology of the Wiyot Territory*, UCPAAE 14, no. 3 (23 December 1918), 329–330.

55. Letters from Loud to Kroeber (24 August 1913); Kroeber to Loud (6 September 1913); and Loud to Kroeber (13 September 1913), in Heizer, *An Anthropological Expedition*, 14, 22, 25.

56. Loud, *Ethnogeography*. According to an inventory carried out by the University of California in 2004, Loud returned to Berkeley with the remains of 24 people and 366 funerary objects. The university also reported possession of the remains of one individual that it had received prior to 1902 from the owner of Indian Island. National Park Service, National NAGPRA, "Notice of Completion of Inventory," *Federal Register* 69, no. 196 (12 October 2004), 60662–60663.

57. Letter from H. H. Stuart to Lila M. O'Neale, Acting Curator, Museum of Anthropology, University of California, San Francisco (c. 15 February 1931), Archaeological Archives, Manuscripts Division, Phoebe A. Hearst Museum of Anthropology, University of California, Berkeley (hereafter cited as MD-PAHMA). See also H. H. Stuart, "Zoomorphs," typed manuscript (10 December 1956), 1, in "Archaeology and Geology" file, Humboldt County Historical Society, Eureka, Calif.

58. Letter from J. E. Depue to Kroeber (13 October 1921), UCB Anthropology Archives, CU-23, Box 48.

59. Letters from A. P. Ousdal to Kroeber (16 December 1927); from Kroeber to Ousdal (27 December 1927); AP, "Santa Barbara Skull Nearest Missing Link," *San Francisco Chronicle* (11 December 1927), UCB Anthropology Archives, CU-23, Box 117.

60. Letters from O. W. Shattuck to University of California, Berkeley (23 October 1931); and from Kroeber to Shattuck (28 October 1931), UCB Anthropology Archives, CU-23, Box 134.

61. Letters from Harry Sanford to Kroeber (23 August 1932); from Kroeber to Sanford (27 August 1932), UCB Anthropology Archives, CU-23, Box 129. Kroeber's instructions to Olson are handwritten on the letter to him from Sanford.

62. Letters from Charles Wetherbee to Kroeber (22 April 1934); and Kroeber to Wetherbee (30 April 1934), UCB Anthropology Archives, CU-23, Box 179.

63. Letter from Gifford to John Comstock (15 January 1923), UCB Anthropology Archives, CU-23, Box 108.

64. Letters from Gifford to G. S. Millberry (14 February 1924); from Millberry to Gifford (15 February 1924); from Millberry to Gifford (14 February 1928); from Gifford to Millberry (15 February 1928), UCB Anthropology Archives, CU-23, Box 103.

65. Letters from Golda Williams to Department of Anthropology (22 October 1925 and 9 November 1925); Gifford to Williams (27 October 1925 and 12 November 1925), UCB Anthropology Archives, CU-23, Box 181.

66. Letters from George Shattuck to Gifford (7 December 1931); and from Gifford to Shattuck (20 December 1931), UCB Anthropology Archives, CU-23, Box 134.

67. Letters from Fritz Kuffer Jr. to Gifford (16 February 1934) and from Gifford to Kuffer (23 February 1934), UCB Anthropology Archives, CU-23, Box 87.

68. See, for example, letter from Gifford to H. Kirby Jr. (26 August 1936), UCB Anthropology Archives, CU-23, Box 83.

69. On the role of "paraprofessional diggers" in the development of archaeology in central California, see Arlean Towne, "History of Central Californian Archaeology, 1880–1940," M.A. thesis, California State University, Sacramento, 1976.

70. Thomas R. Hester, "Robert Fleming Heizer, 1915–1979," National Academy of Sciences, accessed 27 April 2011, http://www.nap.edu/openbook.php?record_id=5406&page=157.

71. Between 8,000 and 12,000 according to various sources. The 12,000 figure is noted in Richard C. Paddock, "UC Berkeley's Bones of Contention," *Los Angeles Times*, 13 January 2008; the 8,000 figure was provided to me by Natasha Johnson, Collections Manager, NAGPRA Unit, PAHMA, 22 April 2008; and Anthony Garcia, Berkeley's Repatriation Coordinator, estimates 10,000 (personal communication to author, 29 March 2010).

72. Elmer Hodgkinson, "Dr. Stuart Rediscovered a Lost People," *Times Standard*, 8 March 1970.

73. Thomas S. Hannah, "Gone Hunting," *The Humboldt Historian* (May–June 1976).

74. According to an informational text at the Favell Museum in Klamath Falls, Oregon.

75. Stuart, "Zoomorphs," 1.

76. Heizer and Elsasser, who had access to Stuart's field notes, report in "Archaeology of HUM-67" that Stuart excavated 382 graves. Another archaeologist puts the number of graves at 390. See John E. Mills, "Recent Developments in the Study of Northwestern California Archaeology," *Reports of the California Archaeological Survey* 1 (1950).

77. Heizer and Elsasser, "Archaeology of HUM-67."

78. "Find Indian Relics at Big Lagoon," *Arcata Union*, 29 April 1926.

79. *Arcata Union*, 26 August 1926.

80. Waterman, *Yurok Geography*, 266.

81. Tom Hannah, personal communication to author, 16 April 2008.

82. The original handwritten map is included in a letter from H. H. Stuart to Lila M. O'Neale, Acting Curator, University of California Museum of Anthropology (c. February 1931), Accession no. 655, MD-PAHMA.

83. I have found two sets of Stuart's notes on Big Lagoon. One, which is in the archives at MD-PAHMA (accession no. 655), reports on his excavations between 1926 and 1931. The other, which was acquired by archaeologist James Roscoe in 1989, includes a sketch map and reports on Stuart's excavations between 1930 and 1949. Roscoe's report on Stuart's notes has been entered into the official site record at the North Coastal Information Center, Klamath, California.

84. Information from accession cards, dated "Big Lagoon 1926," Cecile Clarke Papers, Clarke Historical Museum, Eureka, California (hereafter cited as CCP). One card refers to an "agreement" between Stuart and School Superintendent George B. Albee, who turned over the knives to Cecile Clarke at Eureka High School.

85. See, for example, letter from Stuart to Gifford (20 October 1948), MD-PAHMA.

86. This zoomorph was in the Lillard Collection (L-16127, PAHMA) as of 22 April 2008 when I visited PAHMA. Edward Gifford acknowledged acquisition of this "slave-killer"— "fragment with restored head and legs from Big Lagoon"—in a letter to Cecile Clarke (12 November 1953), CCP.

87. According to museum records, Stuart sold the two zoomorphs, which displayed "indications of cremation," to Harry Hines Woodring, who in turn sold them to Erich Kohlberg. National Museum of the American Indian, "Humboldt County Archaeological Collections," Accession nos. 231874.000 and 231875.000.

88. Accession no. 655, MD-PAHMA.

89. Mel Lavine, "Weird Objects Throw Light on Mystery Tribe of Long Ago," *Humboldt Times*, 10 February 1952.

90. Letter from Gifford to Stuart (26 November 1930); and Gifford to Robert G. Sproul (7 April 1931), MD-PAHMA.

91. Gifford, *Californian Anthropometry*.

92. Alexandra Minna Stern, *Eugenic Nation: Faults and Frontiers of Better Breeding in Modern America*.

93. NAGPRA requires, inter alia, institutions receiving federal funding to publish an inventory of human remains and associated funerary objects with a view to their repatriation. See, generally, Kathleen S. Fine-Dare, *Grave Injustice: The American Indian Repatriation Movement and NAGPRA*.

94. Joan Knudsen, Registrar, PAHMA, personal communication to author, 4 June 2008.

95. Natasha Johnson, Collections Manager, PAHMA NAGPRA Unit, personal communication to author, 22 April 2008.

96. Many of Stuart's most valuable artifacts can be seen at the Favell Museum in Klamath Falls, Oregon. As of October 2008, Stuart's collection at the Favell had not been professionally identified or catalogued.

97. Stuart, "Zoomorphs."

98. Lavine, "Weird Objects."

99. Today, "excavation of human remains is a slow, delicate task." For a thoughtful discussion of ethical and technical issues involved in excavation, see William R. Hildebrandt and Michael J. Darcangelo, *Life on the River: The Archaeology of an Ancient Native American Culture*, 84–86.

100. Pat McMillan, Director, Favell Museum, Klamath Falls, Oregon, personal communication to author, 16 June 2008.

101. On NAGPRA and its regulations, see US Department of Interior, "Native American Graves Protection and Repatriation Act Regulations," *Federal Register* 60, no. 232 (4 December 1995), 62134–62169.

102. Letter from Kroeber to Gifford (24 March 1916), quoted in Orin Starn, *Ishi's Brain: In Search of America's Last "Wild" Indian*, 47.

103. Letter from John Comstock to Gifford (24 January 1923), UCB Anthropology Archives, CU-23, Box 108.

104. Ann Fabian, *The Skull Collectors: Race, Science, and America's Unburied Dead*, 45, 210.

105. Lenz, "George Gustav Heye," 113.

106. Pat McMillan, personal communication to author, 16 June 2008.

107. Quoted in Ira Jacknis, "Alfred Kroeber as Museum Anthropologist," *Museum Anthropology* 17, no. 2 (1993), 29.

108. Cecile Clarke, diary entries for 12 October and 7 December 1967, CCP. Biographical information about Cecile Clarke was provided by the Clarke Historical Museum, Eureka. I have also drawn upon entries in her personal diaries.

109. Martha Roscoe, "Memories of Cecile Clarke," Clarke Museum Newsletter, vol. 1, no. 1 (Spring 1982). This interview is in the Martha Roscoe Collection, Humboldt County Historical Society, Eureka, California.

110. Cecile Clarke, "Island History," two-page handwritten memo (c. 1935), CCP.

111. "Indian Relics of County to Be Preserved," *Humboldt Standard*, 10 September 1930.

112. Cecile Clarke diaries, 1932–1933, CCP.

113. Clarke, "Island History," CCP.

114. Diary entries for 24 February 1934; 10 February 1935; 13 December 1967, CCP.

115. This permit, presumably issued in 1930, was revoked in a letter from H. W. Cole to Cecile Clarke (9 February 1931), CCP.

116. "Search for Indian Relics," *Arcata Union*, 17 May 1928.

117. Accession cards, 1926; and diary entries for 10 January 1931; 29 August 1935; 2 July 1967; 12 October 1967, CCP.

118. Letters from Clarke to Gifford (c. January 1941 and 7 August 1942); and from Gifford to Clarke (10 January 1941 and 13 August 1942), UCB Anthropology Archives, CU-23, Box 107.

119. Clarke, "Island History" and "To Ralph Vicenus" (1934), CCP.

120. Albert Elsasser and James Bennyhoff, "11 Pages of Notes on Collection in Eureka Senior High School Museum. Mostly Eureka from Gunther Island (both sites) and Big Lagoon. Collected by Miss Cecile Clarke, Curator," 30 October 1953, Ms007, MD-PAHMA.

121. Clarke, diary entries, 18 and 19 July 1961; memorandum from Tom Hannah to Albert James, 14 August 1991, CCP.

122. Tom Hannah, personal communication to author, 16 April 2008 and 29 September 2009.

123. Hannah's report on his Indian Island excavation and the official report on radiocarbon testing of HUM-67 (28 September 1966) are in CCP. For a typically sensational report on a "lost tribe" of "very remarkable and intelligent people," see Lavine, "Weird Objects."

124. Floyd Rinehart, "Ancient Indians Far Surpass 'Moderns' in Craftsmanship," *Times-Standard*, 7 November 1965.

125. Heizer found no evidence of "an earlier and different culture (or cultures)...nor any indication that there is anything of the sort." Robert F. Heizer, "Report on the Excavation of the Shellmound at Patrick's Point State Park," 1948, 3.

126. "Group to Hear of Probings into Past Here," *Times-Standard*, 20 November 1966.

127. Rinehart, "Ancient Indians."

128. Letter from Tom Hannah to Albert James, Table Bluff Reservation (30 March 1994), CCP; personal communication to author, 5 November 2008.

129. Letters from Albert E. James to Claudia Israel, Director, Clarke Historical Museum (10 March 1994); and from Tom Hannah to Albert James (30 March 1994), CCP.

130. Tom Hannah, "Gunther Island...A Window in Time to Our Past," *Times-Standard*, 5 May 1967.

131. According to an editorial in a local paper in 2008, Hannah was "reported to have amassed a collection of Indian Island burial relics." "Do the Right Thing with Indian Relics," *Times-Standard*, 1 May 2008, 4. Hannah (personal communication to author, 22 February 2010) said that he sold some of his own personal collection, which he got from Doc Stuart and, therefore, indirectly from graves.

132. Personal communication to author, 16 April 2008 and 22 February 2010.

133. Tom Hannah, "The World of Sam and Lizzie Smith," unpublished memoir (c. 2008).

134. Letter from Kroeber to W. F. Chamlee (2 December 1932), UCB Anthropology Archives, CU-23, Box 41.

135. Personal communication to author, 23 April 2008.

136. Robert F. Heizer, "A Question of Ethics in Archaeology—One Archaeologist's View," *Journal of California Anthropology* 1 and 2 (1974), 146.

137. Letters from Cecile Clarke to B. H. Hathaway (24 February 1932) and from Hathaway to Clarke (4 March 1932), CCP.

138. Personal communication to author, 16 April 2008.

139. Mel Lavine, "Ancient Tombs Found on Humboldt Bay!" *Humboldt Times*, 1 November 1953; Stuart, "Zoomorphs," 7.

140. See, for example, several photographs of skulls and mug shots of living Indians in Edward Gifford's *Californian Anthropometry* (1926).

Six: Unwelcome Attention

1. Told by Robert Spott to Harry Roberts, in Harry K. Roberts, "Walking in Beauty: Reflections of a Yurok Education," ed. Thomas Buckley.

2. Thomas R. Hester, "Robert Fleming Heizer, 1915–1979," National Academy of Sciences, accessed 27 April 2011, http://www.nap.edu/openbook.php?record_id=5406&page=157.

3. Mel Lavine, "Weird Objects Throw Light on Mystery Tribe of Long Ago," *Humboldt Times*, 10 February 1952.

4. These examples come from correspondence that can be found in Accession 655 files, MD-PAHMA.

5. Thanks to Michael Moratto for providing a copy of this letter.

6. Emphasis added. Robert F. Heizer, "The California Archaeological Survey: Establishment, Aims and Methods," *Reports of the California Archaeological Survey* no. 1, University of California, Berkeley (1948).

7. Franklin Fenega, "Methods for Archaeological Site Survey in California," *Reports of the University of California Archaeological Survey* no. 5 (1949), 2.

8. Undated, handwritten letter from Jack (Mills) to Bob (Heizer), c. August 1949, Archaeological Archives Ms315, MD-PAHMA.

9. Robert Heizer, untitled memo re Charles Miles (c. 1954), Archaeological Archives, Ms315, MD-PAHMA.

10. Letter from Edward Gifford to Cecile Clarke, 12 November 1953, CCP.

11. See, for example, letters from George E. Phebus Jr. to Thomas Hannah (31 December 1966 and 28 February 1967). Thanks to Tom Hannah for providing copies of this correspondence.

12. Michael J. Moratto, "Tsahpekw: An Archaeological Record of Nineteenth Century Acculturation among the Yurok," paper presented at joint meeting of the Southwestern Anthropological Association and the Society for California Archaeology, Asilomar State Beach, California (25–28 March 1970).

13. A. L. Kroeber, *Handbook of the Indians of California*, ix.

14. Handwritten memo by Robert F. Heizer (c. 1954), Archaeological Archives Ms315, MD-PAHMA.

15. Charles Miles, *Indian and Eskimo Artifacts of North America*; Miles, "The Gunther Island Sites," *The Masterkey* 39, no. 3 (1965), 92–103.

16. Robert Heizer, untitled memo (c. 1954), Archaeological Archives Ms315, MD-PAHMA.

17. Letters from Gifford to Charles Miles (4 May 1935); Miles to Gifford (26 November 1945); Miles to Gifford (8 December 1945); Gifford to Miles (16 October 1946); and Miles to Gifford (7 November 1948), UCB Anthropology Archives, CU-23, Box 103.

18. Handwritten draft of Heizer and Elsasser's 1964 essay "Archaeology of HUM-67, the Gunther Island Site in Humboldt Bay," Archaeological Archives Ms090–B, MD-PAHMA. In the published version of the essay (in *Reports of the University of California Archaeological Survey* no. 62, 15 May 1964), this sentence is omitted.

19. Stuart had a case for his grievance. On 30 November 1948, Heizer had written him a letter promising to "submit the manuscript for your inspection and approval" before publication. Thanks to Michael Moratto for providing me with a copy of this letter and of Stuart's defaced copy of the title page.

20. Albert B. Elsasser, "The Site on Gunther Island (CA-HUM 67) in Humboldt Bay," paper presented at the Annual Meeting of the Society for California Archaeology, San Diego (23–26 March 1983).

21. Letter from Heizer to George Beshore (2 June 1949); and Heizer memorandum (c. 1954) re events of July 1949, Archaeological Archives, Ms97–B, and Ms315, MD-PAHMA.

22. Heizer, undated memorandum (c. 1954) re Charles Miles; letter from Heizer to Charles Miles (7 January 1954), Archaeological Archives, Ms315, MD-PAHMA.

23. Letter from Miles to Gifford (7 November 1948), UCB Anthropology Archives, CU-23, Box 103.

24. Elmer Hodgkinson, "Dr. Stuart Rediscovered a Lost People," *Times Standard*, 8 March 1970.

25. Letter from Tom Hannah to Albert James (14 August 1991), CCP.

26. Steven Conn, *Museums and American Intellectual Life, 1876–1926*, 19.

27. Heizer's proposal (25 October 1947) can be found in Archaeological Archives Ms097–A, MD-PAHMA.

28. Letter from Robert Heizer to A. E. Henning, chief of California's Division of Beaches and Parks (16 December 1947) Archaeological Archives Ms097–A, MD-PAHMA.

29. Letter from A. E. Henning to Heizer (27 January 1948), Archaeological Archives Ms097–A, MD-PAHMA.

30. Heizer and Elsasser, "Archaeology of HUM-67" (15 May 1964), 2.

31. Kroeber field notes (23 July 1918), Kroeber Papers.

32. Site Records, 1/72103–72153, MD-PAHMA.

33. Site Records, 1/72186–72192, MD-PAHMA.

34. Site Records, 1/90395–90406, 90350–90387, MD-PAHMA.

35. Letter from Heizer to A. E. Henning (26 February 1948); and from Henning to Heizer (27 February 1948), Archaeological Archives Ms097–A, MD-PAHMA.

36. Some 2,275 items were significant enough to be recorded and accessioned. Despite

searching the area where human remains were found, the team did not locate a cemetery. See Robert F. Heizer, "Report on the Excavation of the Shellmound at Patrick's Point State Park," 17, 21–88.

37. Department of Anthropology Clip Sheet, 17 August 1948; Science Service press release, 13 August 1948, Archaeological Archives, Ms097–A, MD-PAHMA.

38. "Sea Lions Took Poor Indians for Joy Ride," *Berkeley Daily Gazette*, 17 August 1948. Newspaper reporting failed to note that sea lions were important to the Yurok diet and consequently were incorporated into their ceremonies.

39. "U of C Field Class Gathers Data on Prehistoric Humboldt Indians," *Ferndale Enterprise*, 27 August 1948.

40. Henry Palm, "U. C. Unearths Relics of Odd Indian Tribe," *San Francisco Examiner*, 12 September 1948.

41. Ibid.

42. Mel Lavine, "Ancient Tombs Found on Humboldt Bay!" *Humboldt Times*, 1 November 1953.

43. George Beshore, "Relics of Early Indian Days Unearthed in Humboldt," *Humboldt Times*, 12 June 1949."

44. Letter from Mrs. Glyndon (Ruth) Smith to Robert Heizer (31 October 1948), UCB Anthropology Archives, CU-23, Box 74. Ruth Smith was president of the Eureka Women's Club and a former fellow teacher of Cecile Clarke at Eureka High School. See "Ruth E. Smith," *The Humboldt Historian* 39, no. 4 (July–August 1991), 31.

45. "Federation Holds 40th Annual Convention Here," *Humboldt Times*, 14 October 1948, 5.

46. Letter from Heizer to Mrs. Glyndon Smith (3 November 1948), UCB Anthropology Archives, CU-23, Box 74.

47. Letters from James Tryner, Patrick's Point State Park, to Robert Heizer (13 February 1949); and from Heizer to Tryner (4 November 1949). Both letters are on file at the State Park Archaeology Lab, Sacramento, California, R_106_16.pdf. The items retained by Heizer are identified by the National Park Service, National NAGPRA, "Notice of Inventory Completion," *Federal Register* 63, no. 86 (5 May 1998), 24824–24825.

48. Robert F. Heizer and John E. Mills, eds., *The Four Ages of Tsurai*. 14.

49. Letter from Heizer to James P. Tryner, Division of Beaches and Parks (13 May 1949), Archaeological Archives, Ms097–A, MD-PAHMA.

50. Letter from Heizer to Earl Hallmark, then owner of the land on which the Tsurai site is located (1 June 1949), Archaeological Archives, Ms315, MD-PAHMA.

51. "Indians Object to Digging by Party of Archaeologists," *Humboldt Standard*, 13 August 1949, 1.

52. James Bennyhoff, untitled memo re 5 August 1949 and 14 August 1949 (23 February 1954), Archaeological Archives, Ms315, MD-PAHMA.

53. Letter from Robert Heizer to George Waldner (21 September 1949), UCB Anthropology Archives, CU-23, Box 176. Waldner was a state park commissioner with whom Heizer had a friendly relationship. It is unclear if this handwritten letter was typed and sent to Waldner, but it certainly expresses Heizer's point of view.

54. "Excavation of Ancient Indian City Approved," *Arcata Union*, 19 August 1949, 1; "Pipe of Peace Smoked; Excavation Continues," *Humboldt Times*, 18 August 1949, 1–2.

55. Ibid.

56. Kroeber, *Handbook*, 46.

57. Letter from J. M. Stewart to Robert Heizer (8 September 1949), Archaeological Archives, Ms315, MD-PAHMA. Heizer noted by hand on the letter from Stewart that he had called the Bureau of Indian Affairs official to tell him that Doc Stuart and Charles Miles were responsible for desecrating Yurok cemeteries.

58. Letter from E. P. French to Robert Heizer (29 September 1949), Archaeological Archives, Ms97–B, MD-PAHMA.

59. Letter from J. R. Knowland to Heizer (25 November 1949), Archaeological Archives, Ms97–B MD-PAHMA.

60. Letter, Heizer to Waldner (21 September 1949).

61. Letter, Gifford to Clarke (12 November 1953).

62. This account relies on confidential memoranda and letters written by Berkeley archaeologists and therefore reflects their points of view. I have not been able to find Stuart's and Miles's views about what happened. Bennyhoff, untitled memo (23 February 1954); handwritten letter, Mills to Heizer (c. August 1949).

63. Robert Heizer, untitled memorandum (c. 1954); Bennyhoff, untitled memo (23 February 1954), Archaeological Archives, 315, MD-PAHMA.

64. Ibid.

65. Axel R. Lindgren, Introduction to Heizer and Mills, *The Four Ages of Tsurai.*

66. Llewellyn L. Loud, *Ethnogeography and Archaeology of the Wiyot Territory*, UCPAAE 14, no. 3, 270.

67. A. B. Elsasser, "Archaeological Site Survey Record, Hum 112," 29 October 1953, MD-PAHMA.

68. Letter from Heizer to Tryner (27 May 1950). This letter is on file at the State Park Archaeology Lab, Sacramento, California, R_106_16.pdf.

69. Letter from Robert Heizer to Arlean Towne (24 February 1975), reproduced in Arlean Towne, "History of Central Californian Archaeology, 1880–1940," Appendix E.

70. E. F. Benedict, "The Yuroks: Their Origin, Legends and Culture," *Del Norte Triplicate*, 8 April 1949, 9.

Seven: Vigorous Complaint

1. Governor Peter H. Burnett, "Governor's Annual Message to the Legislature," 14.

2. "Museums and the American Indian," in American Indian Historical Society, *The Native American Today: The Second Convocation of American Indian Scholars*, 190–212.

3. Quoted in Peter Nabokov, *Native American Testimony: A Chronicle of Indian-White Relations, from Prophecy to the Present, 1492–1992*, 424.

4. Livingston Stone, US Commissioner of Fish and Fisheries, *Report of Operation During 1874 at the U.S. Salmon Hatching Establishment on the McCloud River, California* (April 1875). Washington, D.C.: 43rd Congress, 2nd Session, Senate Miscellaneous Document No. 108.

5. Robert Spott, "Address," *Transactions of the Commonwealth Club of California* 21, no. 3 (1926), 133–135.

6. Memorandum of Lease-Agreement, 1 May 1929, between Little River Redwood Company and County of Humboldt. And the prohibition was retained in a lease agreement between Hammond Lumber Company and Humboldt County, 1 May 1949. Thanks to Don Tuttle for providing me with copies of the lease.

7. Letter from H. W. Cole to Cecile Clarke (9 February 1931), CCP.

8. Axel R. Lindgren, Introduction to *The Four Ages of Tsurai: A Documentary History of the Indian Village on Trinidad Bay*, ed. Robert F. Heizer and John E. Mills.

9. H. H. Stuart, "Field Notes," Accession no. 655, MD-PAHMA.

10. Janet Eidsness, "Initial Cultural Resources Study for Proposed Hazard Tree Removal and Water Tank Replacement Project, Big Lagoon Park Company," 58.

11. Robert F. Heizer and Albert B. Elsasser, "Archaeology of HUM-67, the Gunther Island Site in Humboldt Bay, Northwestern California," *Reports of the University of California Archaeological Survey* 62 (1964) 15, fn 3.

12. Vine Deloria Jr., "This Country Was a Lot Better Off When the Indians Were Running It," in *Red Power: The American Indians' Fight for Freedom*, ed. Alvin M. Josephy Jr., Joane Nagel, and Troy Johnson, 34.

13. Russell Means, "The Activist Legacy of Red Power," in *Red Power*, ed. Josephy et al., 62.

14. Margaret Mead, "The American Indian as a Significant Determinant of Anthropological Style," in *Anthropology and the American Indian*, ed. James E. Officer and Francis McKinley, 72.

15. See, generally, Josephy, *Red Power,* and Kathleen S. Fine-Dare, *Grave Injustice: The American Indian Repatriation Movement and NAGPRA.*

16. Rupert Costo, "Moment of Truth for the American Indian," in American Indian Historical Society, *Indian Voices: The First Convocation of American Indian Scholars,* 3.

17. Vine Deloria Jr., *Custer Died for Your Sins: An Indian Manifesto,* 100.

18. Westerman's 1970 album *Custer Died for Your Sins* was based on Deloria's book.

19. "11 in Museum Indian Protest Fined, Jailed," *Los Angeles Times,* 30 April 1971.

20. Indians of All Tribes, "Proclamation" (November 1969), in Josephy, *Red Power,* 42–43.

21. American Indian Historical Society, *The Native American Today,* 202, 209, 212.

22. Deloria, *Custer Died,* 273.

23. Fine-Dare, *Grave Injustice,* 70–71.

24. Josephy, *Red Power,* 36.

25. According to its website (www.narf.org), "founded in 1970, the Native American Rights Fund (NARF) is the oldest and largest nonprofit law firm dedicated to asserting and defending the rights of Indian tribes, organizations and individuals nationwide."

26. According to Deloria in Josephy, *Red Power,* 50.

27. This history of NICPA is based on the author's interviews with and information provided by Jentri Anders, Jim Benson, Sandra Burton, Dave Fredrickson, Victor Golla, Walt Lara Sr., Tom Parsons, Chris Peters, and Joy Sundberg; and on research in NICPA files, 1970–1983, c/o Janet Eidsness, Consultant in Heritage Resources Management, Tribal Historic Preservation Officer (THPO), Blue Lake Rancheria, hereafter cited as NICPA Papers. Thanks to Janet Eidsness for making these documents available to me.

28. *Lyng v. Northwest Indian Cemetery Protection Association* was decided by the US Supreme Court on April 19, 1988. For discussions of this important case, see Josephy, *Red Power,* 218–227; and JeDon Emenhiser, "The G-O Road (Northern California)," in *Encyclopedia of Religion and Nature,* ed. Bron Raymond Taylor, 701–702.

29. Michael J. Moratto, "Tsahpekw: An Archaeological Record of Nineteenth Century Acculturation among the Yurok," 1. Paper presented at joint meeting of the Southwestern Anthropological Association and the Society for California Archaeology, Asilomar State Beach, California (25–28 March 1970).

30. Michael J. Moratto, "Archaeology and Cross-Cultural Ethics in Coastal Northwest California," Society for California Archaeology (April 1971), unpublished manuscript, 2, 15.

31. Ibid., 15–17.

32. NICPA was first recognized in the local press in "Indians of Area Unite on Culture," *Times-Standard,* 5 May 1970.

33. Milton Marks, "NICPA Presentation," undated, typed memo c. 1979, NICPA Files.

34. From a description of the early work of NICPA, in "Catalog of Programs, 1966–1976," Center for Community Development, Humboldt State University, 1976, 15. Thanks to Tom Parsons for providing copies of the Center's annual reports.

35. My thanks especially to Sandra Burton for providing information, documents, and photographs relating to her father and family.

36. Thomas T. Waterman, *Yurok Geography,* UCPAAE 16, no. 5 (31 May, 1920), 246–247.

37. Thanks to Sandra Burton for providing me with a copy of the obituary.

38. Interview by Judith Dides, California Department of Parks and Recreation, with Margaret Lara, Walt Lara, and Joy Sundberg, 8 January 1990.

39. Sandra Burton, personal communication to author, 9 September 2008.

40. Walt Lara Sr., personal communication to author, 8 May 2010. It wasn't until the 1960s that the area became part of Prairie Creek Redwoods State Park.

41. Margaret Marks Lara, obituary, *Times-Standard,* 18 February 1996.

42. Dides interview.

43. Tom Parsons, personal communication to author, 21 April 2008.

44. Sandra Burton, personal communication to author, 19 September 2008.

45. Milton M. Marks, obituary, *Times-Standard*, 21 May 1980.

46. James Benson, personal communication to author, 23 April 2008.

47. David Fredrickson, personal communication to author, 23 April 2008.

48. Polly Quick, personal communication to author, 22 April 2010.

49. Letter from Milton Marks to Pat Dorsey, Humboldt County Board of Supervisors (9 August 1976), NICPA Papers.

50. Walt Lara Sr., "Respect for the Dead," *News from Native California* 9, no. 4 (Summer 2006), 21.

51. David Fredrickson, personal communication to author, 23 April 2008.

52. Joy Sundberg, personal communication to author, 24 February 2010.

53. Walt Lara Sr., personal communication to author, 8 May 2010.

54. Margaret Lara's obituary in the *Times-Standard*, 18 February 1996, identified her as a union and Yurok activist.

55. California State Advisory Commission on Indian Affairs, Progress Report to the Governor and the Legislature on Indians in Rural and Reservation Areas (February 1966). $6,000 in 1965 would be the equivalent of about $40,000 in today's money.

56. For accounts of the protests, which failed, see Richard J. Maloy, "Park Protest Moves to Capital," *Times-Standard*, 23 May 1977; Richard J. Maloy, "Protest Reaches Its High Point," *Times-Standard*, 24 May 1977; "Park Expansion Protest Taken to the Capitol Steps," *The Union*, 26 May 1977; Sally Connell, "Logging Convoy Finally Touches Down," *Times-Standard*, 2 June 1977; Jerry Partain, "Misinformation Clouds Park Issue," *The Union*, 9 June 1977.

57. *The Union*, 2 June 1977.

58. Thelma Hufford, "Orick News," *The Union*, 16 June 1977, 18.

59. Joy Sundberg, personal communication to author, 3 November 2009.

60. Elmer Hodgkinson, "Dr. Stuart Rediscovered a Lost People," *Times Standard*, 8 March 1970.

61. "Cox Warns on Grave Plundering," *Times-Standard*, 4 April 1970.

62. See, for example, "Vandals, Souvenir Hunters Loot Archaeological Sites," *Sacramento Bee*, 13 April 1970.

63. Tom Parsons, personal communication to author, 21 April 2008.

64. In Humboldt, she quickly became active in Democratic Party politics, serving (1977–1984) as the first woman elected to the Humboldt County Board of Supervisors. Sara Mitchell Parsons, interviewed by Janet Paulk, 5 May 1999, Georgia Women's Movement Oral History Project, Special Collections, Georgia State University Library, accessed 28 April 2011, www.library.gsu.edu/spcoll/women/oralhistory. See also "Former Supervisor to Sign Book," *North Coast Journal*, 2 August 2001; and Sara Mitchell Parsons, *From Southern Wrongs to Civil Rights: The Memoir of a White Civil Rights Activist*.

65. Center for Community Development, Humboldt State University, "Catalog of Programs, 1966–1976," 1.

66. Andrew Garrett, director of Yurok Language Project, University of California, Berkeley, personal communication to author, 1 December 2008. See also www.linguistics.berkeley.edu/~yurok.

67. Michael Moratto, personal communication to author, 29 April 2008.

68. Moratto, "Archaeology," 18–19.

69. Ibid., 19; Moratto, personal communication to author, 29 April 2008.

70. Moratto, personal communication to author, 16 July 2008.

71. "Protection Accord for Yurok Village," *Times-Standard*, 22 June 1970; "Archaeological Remains Concern of Area Indians," *Del Norte Triplicate*, 24 June 1970.

72. Articles of Incorporation of the Northwest Indian Cemetery Protective Association, 7 August 1970, NICPA Papers.

73. Polly Quick, personal communication to author, 22 April 2010.

74. County of Humboldt, Board of Supervisors, Resolution no. 71–14, "Establishing County Policy Regarding Protection of Indian Graves, Burial Grounds, Cemeteries and Ceremonial Sites within Humboldt County," 16 March 1971.

75. Center for Community Development, Humboldt State University, "Annual Reports for 1975–1979," 6.

76. Center for Community Development, "Catalog of Programs, 1966–1976," 1.

77. Chris Peters, Seventh Generation Fund, personal communication to author, 17 July 2008; Walt Lara Sr., personal communication to author, 21 November 2008.

78. Andrew Genzoli, "Indian Culture Revival," *Times-Standard*, 12 March 1974, 5.

79. This summary of NICPA activities draws upon files in the NICPA Papers.

80. "Area Indians Won't Tolerate Inundation of Burial Sites from behind Proposed Dam," *Times-Standard*, 9 January 1973, 1.

81. Bonnie Coyne, "Trinidad City Council Approves Protection of Indian Burial Site," *Times-Standard*, 13 February 1975.

82. "Indians End Land Seizure," *San Jose News*, 21 March 1975, 3.

83. UPI, "Indian Tribe Regains Ancestral Burial Site," undated news story, NICPA Papers.

84. Frederic Golden, "Some Bones of Contention," *Time* (21 December 1981).

85. Jim Benson, personal communication to author, 23 April 2008 and 4 May 2010.

86. Polly McW. Bickel (Quick), *A Study of Cultural Resources in Redwood National Park*.

87. The staff reports and lobbying efforts regarding this legislation—including letter from Milton Marks and James Benson, representing NICPA, to Governor Edmund G. Brown Jr. (24 August 1976)—are available in Messages received by Governor re Assembly Bill 4239 (1976), Legislative Papers, California State Archives, Office of the Secretary of State, Sacramento, California.

88. Margaret Dubin, "Preserving California's Indian Heritage: The Native American Heritage Commission," *News from Native California* 21, no. 3 (Spring 2008), 23–30; Tsim D. Schneider, "Laws That Affect the Commission's Work," *News from Native California* 21, no. 3 (Spring 2008), 27–30; "Native American Heritage Commission History," accessed 11 February 2011, www.nahc.ca.gov/nahc_history.html.

89. "Native American Heritage Commission History."

90. Polly Bickel (Quick), "Changing Roles for the Anthropologist: Current Work among Native Americans in North America," paper presented at the annual meeting of American Anthropological Association, Washington, D.C., 1982.

91. Frank A. Norick, "The Reburial Controversy in California," *Museum Anthropology* 6, no. 3 (July 1982), 2–6.

92. Letter from A. D. Philbrook to John H. Knight (25 October 1973), in Jim Woodward, "A Preliminary Report on Plans to Reconstruct a Yurok Indian Village as Part of the Dry Lagoon State Park General Plan," 48.

93. Dave Fredrickson," The Consciousness-Raising of a California Archaeologist," unpublished lecture, Marin Museum of the American Indian, 4 March 2001.

94. Ralph Beals, "Traffic in Antiquities," *American Antiquity* 36, no. 3 (July 1971), 374.

95. Janet Eidsness, "Places and People: California's Native American Heritage Resources," paper delivered at annual meeting of Society for California Archaeology in Riverside, 2004; William R. Hildebrandt and Michael J. Darcangelo, *Life on the River: The Archaeology of an Ancient Native American Culture.*

96. Deloria, *Custer Died*, 275.

97. His album *Songs of the West* (1961) is still available from Smithsonian Folkways.

98. Letter from Dave Fredrickson to Polly Quick (8 September 1984). Thanks to Polly Quick for making this available to me.

99. David Fredrickson, personal communication to author, 23 April 2008; Fredrickson, "Consciousness-Raising."

100. Jim Benson, personal communication to author, 3 March 2010.

101. David Fredrickson, personal communication to author, 23 April 2008.

102. After the death of Milton Marks in 1980, this became a contentious issue and, following passage of NAGPRA, subject to a repatriation claim. See National NAGPRA, *Federal Register* 64, No. 185 (24 September 1999).

103. See letter from Marks to Pat Dorsey (9 August 1976), NICPA Papers.

104. John W. Milburn et al., "A Preliminary Report on the Archaeology of CA-Hum-129," California Department of Parks and Recreation (January 1979), 11–14.

105. Fredrickson, "Consciousness-Raising."

106. David Fredrickson, personal communication to author, 23 April 2008.

107. Native American Conference on Cultural Resources in Redwood National Park, "Resolution," Eureka, California, 23 May 1978, published in Bickel, *A Study of Cultural Resources in Redwood National Park*, 193–194.

108. Woodward, "Preliminary Report," 28, 30–31, 42, 45. A study of the feasibility of reconstructing a Yurok village was authorized by the California legislature in 1963 (House Resolution No. 327). Funds were appropriated to build the village in 1968–1969. After many delays, the Patrick's Point village was opened in 1990.

109. Schneider, "Laws That Affect the Commission's Work." 27–30.

110. There was an effort by NICPA's supporters to continue its work through the California Indian Culture and Cemetery Protective Association (CICCPA), incorporated in 1987 to provide "archaeological and cultural technical assistance to those involved in the mitigation of the effects on California Indian burial sites and culturally sensitive or significant land." But due to lack of funding, CICCPA quickly dissolved. Thanks to Janet Eidsness for providing a copy of CICCPA's articles of incorporation and the minutes of its first meeting, 25 April 1987.

111. Personal communication to author from Jentri Anders, 4 August 2008; Jim Benson, 21 June 2008; and Chris Peters, 17 July 2008.

Eight: An Argument about the Past

1. "A Symbolic Apology to Indians," *New York Times*, 7 October 2009; Rob Capriccioso, "Obama Ushers in a New Era for Indian Country," *Indian Country Today*, 5 November 2009.

2. Jan Hammil, director of AIAD, quoted in Kathleen S. Fine-Dare, *Grave Injustice: The American Indian Repatriation Movement and NAGPRA*, 78.

3. Rosemary Cambra, "Restoring Life to the Dead," in Peter Nabokov, *Native American Testimony: A Chronicle of Indian-White Relations, from Prophecy to the Present, 1492–1992*, 426.

4. Ron Russell, "The Little Tribe That Could," *San Francisco Weekly*, 28 March 2007, accessed 4 January 2010, www.sfweekly.com.

5. Robert L. Cooper, "Constitutional Law: Preserving Native American Cultural and Archaeological Artifacts," *American Indian Law Review* 4, no. 1 (1976), 99–103; Fine-Dare, *Grave Injustice*, 62–63.

6. Randall H. McGuire, "Why Have Archaeologists Thought the Real Indians Were Dead and What Can We Do about It?" in *Indians and Anthropologists: Vine Deloria Jr., and the Critique of Anthropology*, ed. Thomas Biolsi and Larry J. Zimmerman, 65.

7. Jack F. Trope and Walter R. Echo-Hawk, "The Native American Graves Protection and Repatriation Act: Background and Legislative History," in *Repatriation Reader: Who Owns American Indian Remains?*, ed. Devon A. Mihesuah, 129–130.

8. Ibid., 209–213.

9. For a summary of the case and its significance, see Alvin M. Josephy Jr., Joane Nagel, and Troy Johnson, eds., *Red Power: The American Indians' Fight for Freedom*, 2d ed., 218–227.

10. JeDon Emenhiser, "The G-O Road (Northern California)," in *Encyclopedia of Religion and Nature*, ed. Bron Raymond Taylor, 701–702.

11. Josephy, *Red Power*, 228.

12. Trope and Echo-Hawk, "NAGPRA," 136.

13. National Museum of the American Indian Act, Public Law 101–185, 101st Congress, 28 November 1989.

14. An Act to Amend the National Museum of the American Indian Act, Public Law 104–278, 104th Congress, 9 October 1996.

15. For a discussion of the "Report of the Panel for a National Dialogue on Museum-Native American Relations," 28 February 1990, see Trope and Echo-Hawk, "NAGPRA," 138–139.

16. Ibid., 139.

17. McGuire, "Why Have Archaeologists Thought," 78, 81.

18. Makah Indian Tribe and the National Association of Tribal Historic Preservation Officers, *Federal Agency Implementation of the Native American Graves Protection and Repatriation Act*.

19. Trope and Echo-Hawk, "NAGPRA,"151.

20. Cara Buckley, "Journey Home: Museum Returns the Remains of a Tribe's Forebears," *New York Times*, 10 June 2008.

21. McGuire, "Why Have Archaeologists Thought," 80.

22. Larry J. Zimmerman, "Anthropology and Responses to the Reburial Issue," in Biolsi and Zimmerman, *Indians and Anthropologists*, 108.

23. James E. Officer and Francis McKinley, eds., *Anthropology and the American Indian*, 15, 109, 110.

24. Mead, "The American Indian," in *Anthropology and the American Indian*, ed. Officer and McKinley, 68–74.

25. Vine Deloria Jr., "Some Criticisms and a Number of Suggestions," in *Anthropology and the American Indian*, ed. Officer and McKinley, 93–99.

26. Officer and McKinley, *Anthropology and the American Indian*, 73–74, 97–99, 109.

27. American Anthropological Association, "Statement on Ethics" (May 1971, as amended through Nov. 1986), http://www.aaanet.org/cmtes/ethics/AAA-Statements-on-Ethics.cfm.

28. International Council of Museums, "Code of Ethics for Museums" (2004), www.icom. museum/ethics.html.

29. World Archaeological Congress, "The Vermillion Accord on Human Remains" (1989), www.worldarchaeologicalcongress.org/site/about_ethi.php.

30. Society for American Archaeology, "Principles of Archaeological Ethics" (1996), www.saa. org/AbouttheSociety/PrinciplesofArchaeologicalEthics/tabid/203/Default.aspx.

31. The United Nations' convention and its implementation are fully discussed by Ben Kiernan, *Blood and Soil: A World History of Genocide and Extermination from Sparta to Darfur*, 9–20.

32. John Walton Caughey, *California*, 381, 391.

33. Sherburne F. Cook, *The Conflict between the California Indian and White Civilization*, 255–263.

34. Carey McWilliams, *Brothers under the Skin*, 50, 67. See also his *California: The Great Exception*.

35. Vine Deloria, *Custer Died for Your Sins*, 51.

36. Theodora Kroeber and Robert F. Heizer, *Almost Ancestors: The First Californians*, 19.

37. For typical accounts of the past in tourist guides, see Bureau of Land Management, Medford District Office, Oregon, "Rand: National Historic Site" (August 2004); Bureau of Land Management, Oregon, "Rogue River Float Guide" (2004); Virginia M. Fields and Peter E. Palmquist, *100 Years of Humboldt County Culture and Artistry: 1850 to 1950*, 25.

38. A. L. Kroeber, *Handbook of the Indians of California*, 887.

39. Maidee Thomas Nelson, *California, Land of Promise*, 96.

40. Durlynn C. Anema et al., *California Yesterday and Today*, 167.

41. Hubert Howe Bancroft, *California Inter Pocula*, 253. This misperception of the antagonists as "an underclass" drawn from "the margins of the new Anglo society" is perpetuated by Tomás Almaguer, *Racial Fault Lines: The Historical Origins of White Supremacy in California*, 118.

42. T. Kroeber and Heizer, *Almost Ancestors*, 18–20.

43. Byron Nelson Jr., *Our Home Forever: The Hupa Indians of Northern California*, 45, 90.

44. Jack Norton, *Genocide in Northwestern California: When Our Worlds Cried*.

45. Thomas Buckley, *Standing Ground: Yurok Indian Spirituality, 1850–1990*, 71.

46. W. H. Hutchinson, *California: Two Centuries of Man, Land, and Growth in the Golden State*, 124.

47. T. H. Watkins, *California: An Illustrated History*, 130.

48. Kiernan, *Blood and Soil*, 349–354.

49. Laurence M. Hauptman, *Tribes and Tribulations: Misconceptions about American Indians and Their Histories*, 3–14.

50. Buckley, *Standing Ground*, 9.

51. James J. Rawls, *Indians of California: The Changing Image*, 201.

52. Almaguer, *Racial Fault Lines*, 108.

53. Karl Kroeber, Foreword to Theodora Kroeber, *Ishi in Two Worlds: A Biography of the Last Wild Indian in North America*, xii.

54. Ray Raphael and Freeman House, *Two Peoples, One Place*, 156.

55. Larry McMurtry, *Oh What a Slaughter: Massacres in the American West, 1846–1890*, 56.

56. K. Kroeber, Foreword to *Ishi in Two Worlds*, xi.

57. Thomas Bender, *A Nation among Nations: America's Place in World History*, 248.

58. Ibid., 132.

59. Albert L. Hurtado, *Indian Survival on the California Frontier*, 218.

60. Robert F. Heizer, "A Question of Ethics in Archaeology—One Archaeologist's View," *Journal of California Anthropology* 1 and 2 (1974), 145–151.

61. Quoted by Albert L. Hurtado in his introduction to *The Destruction of California Indians: A Collection of Documents from the Period 1847 to 1865 in Which Are Described Some of the Things That Happened to Some of the Indians of California*, ed. Robert F. Heizer, viii–ix.

62. Robert F. Heizer, ed., *They Were Only Diggers: A Collection of Articles from California Newspapers, 1851–1886, on Indian and White Relations*, ix–x.

63. Robert F. Heizer, ed., *Federal Concern about Conditions of California Indians, 1853–1913: Eight Documents*, ii.

64. Heizer, *They Were Only Diggers*, vii.

65. Ibid., 148.

66. Nancy Scheper-Hughes, "Ishi's Brain, Ishi's Ashes: Anthropology and Genocide," *Anthropology Today* 17 (2001), 12–19.

67. For information about current policies and laws, see the website of the Native American Heritage Commission at www.nahc.ca.gov.

68. "In 1981," according to the National Park Service, "the human remains and associated funerary objects were turned over to local Yurok people for reburial." "Notice of Inventory Completion," *Federal Register* 63, no. 86, 5 May 1998, 24824.

69. National Park Service, National NAGPRA, "Notice of Inventory Completion," *Federal Register* 65, no. 10, 14 January 2000, 2425. Other human remains, excavated by Dave Fredrickson from Tsahpekw (Stone Lagoon) in 1976, were repatriated prior to NAGPRA.

70. National Park Service, National NAGPRA, "Notice of Inventory Completion," *Federal Register* 67, no. 8, 11 January 2002, 1506–1507.

71. Plus two additional human remains: one sent to the Hearst Museum in 1905 by the owner

of Indian Island; and one excavated by Berkeley anthropologists James Bennyhoff and Albert Elsasser in 1953 during a dig at a Wiyot site on the south spit of Humboldt Bay. National Park Service, National NAGPRA, "Notice of Inventory Completion," *Federal Register* 69, no. 196, 12 October 2004, 60662–60663.

72. Jeff Barnard, "Tribe Welcomes Home Relics Kept in Museum," *Oakland Tribune*, 22 May 2004. See also Yurok Tribe, "NAGPRA Collections," http://www.yuroktribe.org.

73. Quoted in Peter Fimrite, "Indians Exult at Return of Artifacts," *San Francisco Chronicle*, 13 August 2010, 1. See also John Driscoll, "Back Home Where They Belong," *Times-Standard*, 14 August 2010, 1.

74. Personal communication from Pam Service, Director, Clarke Historical Museum, 12 April 2008, 22 May 2009.

75. Yurok Tribe, "History and Culture," 2006, www.yuroktribe.org; Arnold R. Pilling, "Yurok," in *Handbook of North American Indians*, vol. 8, "California," ed. Robert F. Heizer, 148.

76. Buckley, *Standing Ground*, 48; Patrick's Point State Park, "Sumeg Village," pamphlet, 2005.

77. Wiyot Tribe, "History and Culture," accessed 2 April 2008, www.wiyot.com/history (discontinued).

78. Donna Tam, "Restoring History," *Times-Standard*, 13 September 2008, 1.

79. The phrase was coined by German historian Jörg Wollenberg, quoted in Wolfram Wette, *The Wehrmacht: History, Myth, Reality*, 223.

80. L. Mounday et al., "Archaeological Site Survey Record, CA-HUM 124."

81. Donald C. Tuttle, "Environmental Information" and "Environmental Impact Statement, Big Lagoon County Park Improvement Project," County of Humboldt, 1973. Thanks to Don Tuttle for providing me with copies of these reports.

82. Jim Woodward, "Archaeological Site Survey Record, CA-HUM-124."

83. The land was sold for $4,315,000 and transferred to the state on 23 December 1981. A condition of the sale was naming the new park after the president of the board of the lumber company. Details on the sale can be found in Kenneth L. Gray, "Harry A. Merlo Project: Inventory of Features."

84. Ibid., 5, 8.

85. Jim Woodward and George R. Stammerjohan, "A Cultural Resource Inventory of Harry A. Merlo State Recreation Area," 5.

86. George R. Stammerjohan and James Woodward, "Cultural Resources: Harry A. Merlo Project." Waterman (*Yurok Geography*, 266) identifies this place as Ke'ixkem.

87. When Woodward and Stammerjohan visited the site in 1987, they found a "disturbed midden. Most of the recent disturbances were confined to shallow irregular pits and holes around the bases of trees." They also reported that "the looters were caught and cited by park rangers this past [1987] summer."

88. Jim Woodward, "A Preliminary Report on Plans to Reconstruct a Yurok Indian Village as Part of the Dry Lagoon State Park General Plan," 22, 24.

89. Yurok Tribal Council, resolution no. 07–84, 29 November 2007; Janet Eidsness, "Initial Cultural Resources Study for Proposed Hazard Tree Removal and Water Tank Replacement Project, Big Lagoon Park Company"; Greg Collins, "Archaeological Site Condition Assessment Record, CA-HUM 124."

90. Donna Tam, "Saving the Big Lagoon: Enhancement Project Combats Looting and Abuse by Park Visitors," *Times-Standard*, 4 December 2010.

91. National Park Service, "Provenience of Native American Human Remains in Published Notices of Inventory Completion" (19 July 2006); and "National NAGPRA Online Databases," accessed 4 February 2010, www.nps.gov/history/nagpra/ONLINEDB/index.htm.

92. On this very contentious issue, see Richard C. Paddock, "UC Berkeley's Bones of Contention," *Los Angeles Times*, 13 January 2008; and www.nagpra-ucb-faq.blogspot.com.

93. Vine Deloria Jr., "Anthros, Indians, and Planetary Reality," in Biolsi and Zimmerman, *Indians and Anthropologists*, 212.

94. Anthony Garcia, personal communication to author, 29 March 2010.

95. The following analysis is based on interviews with Bambi Kraus, president of the National Association of Tribal Historic Preservation Officers, 26 March 2010; Buffy McQuillen, Repatriation and Cultural Collections Manager, Yurok Tribe, 12 May 2010; Patricia Nietfeld, Supervisory Collections Manager, Terry Snowball, Cultural Protocols Coordinator, and Carrie Feldman and Cara Fama, Research Specialists, Cultural Resources Center, National Museum of the American Indian, 24 March 2010; Felicia Pickering, Museum Specialist, Department of Anthropology, National Museum of Natural History, 24 March 2010; and Anthony Garcia, Repatriation Coordinator, University of California, Berkeley, 29 March 2010.

96. "NAGPRA Suffers Surprising Proposed Budget Cuts," *Indian Country Today*, 7 February 2010.

97. Bambi Kraus, personal communication to author, 26 March 2010.

98. Ira Jacknis, personal communication to author, 1 April 2010.

99. Regina Woods, "Poisoned Indian Religious Artifacts a Relic of the Clash of Cultures," *Human Rights Reporting*, Journalism School, Columbia University, 2004.

100. Quoted in James C. McKinley Jr., "Geronimo's Heirs Sue Secret Yale Society over His Skull," *New York Times*, 20 February 2009.

101. Yurok Tribal Council, *Yurok Tribe* (2007), 17.

102. Buffy McQuillen, personal communication to author, 12 May 2010.

103. Carla Marinucci, "California Gaming Tribes Top Campaign Donors," *San Francisco Chronicle*, 24 November 2009; David D. Kirkpatrick, "Senecas See Comeback over Sale of Cigarettes," *New York Times*, 6 March 2010; Andy Newman, "Raising the Ante," *New York Times*, 18 April 2008.

104. Ed Lion, "Ancient Yurok Village Plundered by Vandals," *Times-Standard*, 30 December 1989.

105. Elaine Weinreb, "Conflict over Ancient Yurok Village in Trinidad," *McKinleyville Press*, 1 April 2009. An extensive proposal for a "Tsurai Management Plan," prepared by Kathleen Sloan and Megan Rocha of the Yurok Tribe, was completed in April 2007 and awaits funding and action.

106. In 2000 a collector was convicted of digging up graves at Tsahpekw; and in 2007 a looter was convicted of excavating human remains and artifacts from a burial site at Tsurai. See Janet P. Eidsness, "It Takes a Tribe: Looter Convicted in Humboldt County and New Legislation Proposed," California Archaeological Site Stewardship Program Newsletter (April 2002); and Sarah Hobart, "Grave Robber Sentenced," *McKinleyville Press*, 6 March 2007.

107. Jessie Faulkner, "YouTube Video Leads to Graverobber's Arrest," *Times-Standard*, 20 December 2008.

108. Allison White, "YouTube Grave Robber Sentenced to Jail Time, Community Service," *Times-Standard*, 24 October 2009.

109. "A Grave Is a Grave," *Times-Standard*, 18 September 2009, 4.

110. Shannon Tushingham and Suntayea Steinruck, "Recent Looting Cases on the North Coast of California," *California Archaeology* 2, no. 1 (2010), 136.

111. Jamie Roscoe, personal communication to author, 12 October 2009.

112. Nick Grube, "Tolowa Cemetery Raided," *Daily Triplicate*, 17 April 2010. See also Tushingham and Steinruck, "Recent Looting Cases," 136–139.

113. Mike Stark, "Felony Charges Rare for Relic Looters," Tuscaloosanews.com, 12 October 2009.

114. Associated Press, "Lenient Sentences Given for Plundering of Artifacts," *New York Times*, 17 September 2009.

115. Kirk Johnson, "Suicide Raises Legal Issues in Indian Artifact Cases," *New York Times*, 9 March 2010.

116. See, for example, "Discover Humboldt County," www.humboldtsearch.com.

117. Humboldt County Convention and Visitors Bureau, "Welcome to Humboldt County" (Eureka 2008); www.redwoods.info; "101 Things to Do: Humboldt County, California" 23, no. 7 (2009), www.101things.com; Fodor's, *Northern California*; "North Coast 101," *Times-Standard* (June 2006), www.times-standard.com.

118. John Doerper, *Coastal California*, 154–157.

119. For a critique of the NMAI, see Steven Conn, *Do Museums Still Need Objects?*

Nine: Never Too Late

1. Anne Whitehead, *Memory*.

2. Joan Didion, *Slouching Towards Bethlehem*, 20.

3. Thomas Bender, *A Nation among Nations: America's Place in World History*, 299–300.

4. For information about the memorial, see the website of the Chinese Reconciliation Project Foundation at www.crpftacoma.org.

5. Andreas Nachama (director), *Topography of Terror: Gestapo, SS and Reich Security Main Office on Wilhelm-and-Prinz-Albrecht-Strasse, A Documentation*.

6. Drew Gilpin Faust, *This Republic of Suffering: Death and the American Civil War*, xiv.

7. Ann Fabian, *The Skull Collectors: Race, Science, and America's Unburied Dead*, 171–184.

8. Ibid., 271.

9. Elisabeth Bumiller, "Teams Seeking Remains Dig Back to World War II," *New York Times*, 6 September 2009, 1.

10. John Banville, "A Century of Looking the Other Way," *New York Times*, 23 May 2009.

11. The following analysis is based on my field notes and Edward Rothstein, "A Burial Ground and Its Dead Are Given Life, " *New York Times*, 26 February 2010; and a press packet provided by Cherie Butler, Chief of Interpretation, African Burial Ground National Monument, New York.

SOURCES AND BIBLIOGRAPHY

This book is based on more than fifty interviews, archival research in several collections and museums, and two years of participant observation.

Interviews

The following interviews were conducted in person and by phone 2008–2010. The interviewees are grouped by topic.

Anthropology and Archaeology: Janet Eidsness, Larry Felton, Dave Fredrickson, Victor Golla, Bill Hildebrandt, Ira Jacknis, Tom King, Michael Moratto, Jamie Roscoe, Nancy Scheper-Hughes, Don Verwayen, Jim Woodward.

Museums and Repatriation: Thomas Blackburn, Cara Fama, Carrie Feldman, Larri Fredericks, Anthony Garcia, Bambi Kraus, Kent Lightfoot, Coleen Kelley Marks, Buffy McQuillen, Larry Myers, Pat Nietfeld, Felicia Pickering, Hélène Rouvier, Pam Service, Terry Snowball.

Northwest Indian Cemetery Protection Association: Jentri Anders, Jim Benson, Sandra Burton, Chris Peters, Polly Quick, Joy Sundberg, Walt Lara Sr., Tom Parsons.

Humboldt County and California History: Joan Berman, Edie Butler, Tom Hannah, Ben Madley, Jerry Rohde, Hank Seemann, Ned Simmons, Don Tuttle, Susie Van Kirk, Don Verwayen.

Yurok History: Gene Brundin, Mariana Ferreira, Andrew Garrett, Tom Gates, Bob McConnell, Shaunna McCovey, Virgil Moorehead.

Archives and Collections

A. L. Kroeber Papers, 1869–1972, Bancroft Library, University of California, Berkeley.

Archaeological Archives, Phoebe A. Hearst Museum of Anthropology, University of California, Berkeley.

Archives of UC Berkeley Department of Anthropology, Bancroft Library, University of California, Berkeley.

California Collection, Huntington Library, San Marino, California.

California State Archaeology Collections, Sacramento, California.

Cecile Clarke Papers, Clarke Historical Museum, Eureka, California.

Humboldt County Archaeological Collections, National Museum of the American Indian, Washington, D.C.

Humboldt County Archives, Humboldt County Historical Society, Eureka, California.

Humboldt County Archives, Trinidad Museum Society, Trinidad, California.

Humboldt County Collection and Pamphlet Collection, Humboldt Room, Humboldt State University Library, Arcata, California.

Inventory of Records, Favell Museum, Klamath Falls, Oregon.

Inventory of Vancouver Expedition Collection, British Museum, London.

Northwest Indian Cemetery Protective Association (NICPA) Papers, 1970–1983, c/o Janet Eidsness, Consultant in Heritage Resources Management, Tribal Historic Preservation Officer (THPO), Blue Lake Rancheria.

Robert E. Schenk Archives of California Archaeology, Phoebe A. Hearst Museum of Anthropology, University of California, Berkeley.

Susie Baker Fountain Papers, Humboldt Room, Humboldt State University Library, Arcata, California.

William Boyle, A. W. Ericson, and Ruth Kellet Roberts Photograph Collections, Humboldt

Room, Humboldt State University Library, Arcata, California.

Yurok Collection and Yurok Collections Accession Histories, Department of Anthropology, National Museum of Natural History, Washington, D.C.

Books

Adams, David Wallace. *Education for Extinction: American Indians and the Boarding School Experience, 1875–1928*. Lawrence: University of Kansas Press, 1995.

Almaguer, Tomás. *Racial Fault Lines: The Historical Origins of White Supremacy in California*. Berkeley: University of California Press, 1994.

American Indian Historical Society. *Indian Voices: The First Convocation of American Indian Scholars*. San Francisco: The Indian Historian Press, 1970.

————. *The Native American Today: The Second Convocation of American Indian Scholars*. San Francisco: American Indian Educational Publishers, 1974.

Anema, Durlynn C. et al. *California Yesterday and Today*. Morristown, N.J.: Silver Burdett, 1984.

Ariès, Philippe. *Western Attitudes toward Death from the Middle Ages to the Present*. Baltimore: Johns Hopkins Univ. Press, 1974.

Atherton, Gertrude. *California: An Intimate History*. New York: Harper & Brothers, 1914.

Bancroft, Hubert Howe. *The Native Races*. San Francisco: A. L. Bancroft & Co., 1883.

————. *California Inter Pocula*. San Francisco: The History Company, 1888.

————. *History of California, 1860–1890*. San Francisco: The History Company, 1890.

Bandini, Helen Elliott. *History of California*. New York: American Book Co., 1908.

Beckham, Stephen Dow. *Requiem for a People: The Rogue Indians and the Frontiersmen*. Norman: Univ. of Oklahoma Press, 1971.

Beebe, Lucious, and Charles Clegg. *The American West: The Pictorial Epic of a Continent*. New York: E. P. Dutton, 1955.

Bender, Thomas. *A Nation among Nations: America's Place in World History*. New York: Hill and Wang, 2006.

Benjamin, Walter. *Berlin Childhood around 1900*. Cambridge: The Belknap Press of Harvard Univ., 2006.

Bernardin, Susan et al., eds. *Trading Gazes: Euro-American Women Photographers and Native North Americans, 1880–1940*. New Brunswick: Rutgers Univ. Press, 2003.

Bieder, Robert E. *Science Encounters the Indian: The Early Years of American Ethnology*. Norman: Univ. of Oklahoma Press, 1989.

————. *A Brief Historical Survey of the Expropriation of American Indian Remains*. Washington, D.C.: Native American Rights Fund, 1990.

Biolsi, Thomas, and Larry J. Zimmerman, eds. *Indians and Anthropologists: Vine Deloria, Jr., and the Critique of Anthropology*. Tucson: Univ. of Arizona Press, 1997.

Blackburn, Thomas C., and Travis Hudson. *Time's Flotsam: Overseas Collections of California Material Culture*. Menlo Park: Ballena Press, 1990.

Bledsoe, A. J. *History of Del Norte County, California, with a Business Directory and Traveler's Guide*. Eureka: Wyman & Co., 1881.

Bolton, Herbert E., and Ephraim D. Adams. *California's Story*. Boston: Allyn & Bacon, 1922.

Bolz, Peter, and Hans-Ulrich Sanner, eds. *Native American Art: The Collections of the Ethnological Museum Berlin*. Seattle: Univ. of Washington Press, 1999.

Buckley, Thomas. *Standing Ground: Yurok Indian Spirituality, 1850–1990*. Berkeley: Univ. of California Press, 2002.

Carr, John. *Pioneer Days in California*. Eureka: Times Publishing Co., 1891.

Carranco, Lynwood, and John T. Labbe. *Logging the Redwoods*. Caldwell, Idaho: The Caxton Printers, 1989.

Caughey, John Walton. *California*. New York: Prentice-Hall, 1940.

Center for Community Development. *Yurok Language, Literature and Culture*. Arcata: Humboldt State Univ., 1974.

Chase-Dunn, Christopher, and Helly M. Mann. *The Wintu and Their Neighbors: A Very Small-World System in Northern California*. Tucson: Univ. of Arizona Press, 1998.

Cleland, Robert Glass. *A History of California: The American Period*. New York: Macmillan Co., 1930.

———. *From Wilderness to Empire: A History of California, 1542–1900*. New York: Alfred A. Knopf, 1944.

———. *California Pageant: The Story of Four Centuries*. New York: Alfred A. Knopf, 1946.

Cole, Douglas. *Captured Heritage: The Scramble for Northwest Artifacts*. Norman: Univ. of Oklahoma Press, 1995.

Conn, Steven. *Museums and American Intellectual Life, 1876–1926*. Chicago: Univ. of Chicago Press, 1998.

———. *Do Museums Still Need Objects?* Philadelphia: Univ. of Philadelphia Press, 2010.

Cook, Sherburne F. *The Conflict between the California Indian and White Civilization*. Berkeley: Univ. of California Press, 1943.

———. *The Population of the California Indians, 1769–1970*. Berkeley: Univ. of California Press, 1976.

Cornford, Daniel, ed. *Working People of California*. Berkeley: Univ. of California Press, 1995.

Crow, John A. *California as a Place to Live*. New York: Charles Scribner's, 1953.

Davis, Barbara A. *Edward S. Curtis: The Life and Times of a Shadow Catcher*. San Francisco: Chronicle Books, 1985.

Dawson, Grace S. *California: The Story of Our Southwest Corner*. New York: Macmillan, 1939.

de Massey, Ernest. *A Frenchman in the Gold Rush: The Journal of Ernest de Massey, Argonaut of 1849*. Trans. Marguerite Eyer Wilbur. Cleveland: Arthur H. Clark Co., 1927.

Deloria, Vine Jr. *Custer Died for Your Sins: An Indian Manifesto*. New York: Macmillan, 1969.

Deverell, William. *Whitewashed Adobe: The Rise of Los Angeles and the Remaking of Its Mexican Past*. Berkeley: Univ. of California Press, 2004.

Didion, Joan. *Slouching Towards Bethlehem*. New York: Farrar, Straus & Giroux, 1961.

Doerper, John. *Coastal California*. New York: Compass American Guides, 2005.

Dunn, Arthur W. *Civics: The Community and the Citizen*. Sacramento: State Board of Education, 1910.

Eddy, J. M. *In the Redwood's Realm: By-Ways of Wild Nature and Highways of Industry, as Found under the Forest Shades and amidst Clover Blossoms in Humboldt County*. San Francisco: D. S. Stanley & Co., 1893.

Erikson, Erik Homburger. *Observations on the Yurok: Childhood and World Image*. University of California Publications in American Archaeology and Ethnology 35, no. 10, 257–302. Berkeley: Univ. of California Press, 1943.

Fabian, Ann. *The Skull Collectors: Race, Science, and America's Unburied Dead*. Chicago: Univ. of Chicago Press, 2010.

Faust, Drew Gilpin. *This Republic of Suffering: Death and the American Civil War*. New York: Vintage Books, 2008.

Fields, Virginia M., and Peter E. Palmquist. *100 Years of Humboldt County Culture and Artistry: 1850 to 1950*. Eureka: Humboldt Cultural Center, 1986.

Fine-Dare, Kathleen S. *Grave Injustice: The American Indian Repatriation Movement and NAGPRA*. Lincoln: Univ. of Nebraska Press, 2002.

Flower, Enola. *A Child's History of California*. Caldwell, Idaho: The Caxton Printers, 1941.

Gifford, Edward Winslow. *Californian Anthropometry*. University of California Publications in

American Archaeology and Ethnology 22, no. 2, 217–390. Berkeley: Univ. of California Press, 1926.

Glassberg, David. *Sense of History: The Place of the Past in American Life*. Amherst: Univ. of Massachusetts Press, 2001.

Goddard, Pliny Earle. *Hupa Texts*. University of California Publications in American Archaeology and Ethnology 1, no. 2, 96–368. Berkeley: Univ. of California Press, 1904.

Gray, A. A. *History of California from 1542*. Boston: D.C. Heath, 1934.

Gunther, Erna. *Indian Life on the Northwest Coast of North America: As Seen by the Early Explorers and Fur Traders during the Last Decades of the Eighteenth Century*. Chicago: Univ. of Chicago Press, 1972.

Gutiérrez, Ramón A., and Richard Orsi, eds. *Contested Eden: California before the Gold Rush*. Berkeley: Univ. of California Press, 1998.

Handler, Richard, ed. *Central Sites, Peripheral Visions: Cultural and Institutional Crossings in the History of Anthropology*. Madison: Univ. of Wisconsin Press, 2006.

Hanna, Phil. *California through Four Centuries: A Handbook of Memorable Historical Dates*. New York: Farrar and Rinehart, 1935.

Hauptman, Laurence M. *Tribes and Tribulations: Misconceptions about American Indians and Their Histories*. Albuquerque: Univ. of New Mexico Press, 1995.

Heaven, Louise (AKA Norman, Lucia). *A Youth's History of California*. San Francisco: A. Roman, 1867.

Heizer, Robert F., ed. *An Anthropological Expedition, or Get It through Your Head, or Yours for the Revolution*. Berkeley: Univ. of California Dept. of Anthropology, 1970.

———. *They Were Only Diggers: A Collection of Articles from California Newspapers, 1851–1886, on Indian and White Relations*. Ramona, Calif.: Ballena Press, 1974.

———. *Handbook of North American Indians*, vol. 8. Washington, D.C.: Smithsonian Institution, 1978.

———. *Federal Concern about Conditions of California Indians, 1853–1913: Eight Documents*. Socorro, N.M.: Ballena Press, 1979.

———. *The Destruction of California Indians: A Collection of Documents from the Period 1847 to 1865 in Which Are Described Some of the Things That Happened to Some of the Indians of California*. Lincoln: Univ. of Nebraska Press, 1993.

Heizer, Robert F., and John E. Mills, eds. *The Four Ages of Tsurai: A Documentary History of the Indian Village on Trinidad Bay*. 1952. Reprint, Trinidad, Calif.: Trinidad Museum Society, 1991.

Heizer, Robert F., and M. A. Whipple, eds. *The California Indians: A Source Book*. Berkeley: Univ. of California Press, 1971.

Hildebrandt, William R., and Michael J. Darcangelo. *Life on the River: The Archaeology of an Ancient Native American Culture*. Berkeley: Heyday Books, 2008.

Hittell, John S. *A History of San Francisco and Incidentally of the State of California*. San Francisco: A. L. Bancroft, 1878.

———. *Hittell's Hand-Book of Pacific Coast Travel*. San Francisco: A. L. Bancroft & Co., 1885.

Hittell, Theodore H. *History of California*. San Francisco: N. J. Stone, 1898.

Hrdlička, Aleš. *Directions for Collecting Information and Specimens for Physical Anthropology*. Washington, D.C.: Smithsonian Institution, 1904.

Hunt, Rockwell D. *California and Californians*. San Francisco: The Lewis Publishing Co., 1926.

———. *New California the Golden*. Sacramento: California State Department of Education, 1937.

Hunt, Rockwell D., and Nellie Van de Grift Sánchez. *A Short History of California*. New York: Thomas Y. Crowell Company, 1929.

Hurtado, Albert L. *Indian Survival on the California Frontier*. New Haven: Yale Univ. Press, 1988.

Hutchinson, W. H. *California: Two Centuries of Man, Land, and Growth in the Golden State*. Palo Alto, Calif.: American West Publishing Co., 1969.

Jackson, Helen Hunt. *A Century of Dishonor: A Sketch of the United States Government's Dealings with Some of the Indian Tribes.* 1885. Reprint, Norman: Univ. of Oklahoma Press, 1995.

Jefferson, Thomas. *Writings.* New York: The Library of America, 1984.

Josephy, Alvin M. Jr., Joane Nagel, and Troy Johnson, eds. *Red Power: The American Indians' Fight for Freedom.* 2d. ed. Lincoln: Univ. of Nebraska Press, 1999.

Kiernan, Ben. *Blood and Soil: A World History of Genocide and Extermination from Sparta to Darfur.* New Haven: Yale Univ. Press, 2007.

Kroeber, Alfred L. *The Languages of the Coast of California North of San Francisco.* University of California Publications in American Archaeology and Ethnology 9, no. 3, 273–345. Berkeley: Univ. of California Press, 1911.

———. *Anthropology.* New York: Harcourt, Brace & Co., 1923.

———. *Handbook of the Indians of California.* 1925. Reprint, New York: Dover Publications, 1976.

———. *Yurok Myths.* Berkeley: Univ. of California Press, 1976.

Kroeber, Theodora. *The Inland Whale.* Berkeley: Univ. of California Press, 1959.

———. *Alfred Kroeber: A Personal Configuration.* Berkeley: Univ. of California Press, 1979.

———. *Ishi in Two Worlds: A Biography of the Last Wild Indian in North America.* Berkeley: Univ. of California Press, 1989.

Kroeber, Theodora, and Robert F. Heizer. *Almost Ancestors: The First Californians.* San Francisco: Sierra Club, 1968.

Lamb, W. Kaye, ed. *A Voyage of Discovery to the North Pacific Ocean and Round the World, 1791–1795.* London: The Hakluyt, 1984.

Lorentzen, Bob. *The Hiker's Hip Pocket Guide to the Humboldt Coast.* Mendocino: Bored Feet Press, 2001.

Loud, Llewellyn L. *Ethnogeography and Archaeology of the Wiyot Territory.* University of California Publications in American Archaeology and Ethnology 14, no. 3, 221–436. Berkeley: Univ. of California Press, 1918.

Lowenthal, David. *The Past Is a Foreign Country.* Cambridge: Cambridge Univ. Press, 1985.

Makah Indian Tribe and the National Association of Tribal Historic Preservation Officers. *Federal Agency Implementation of the Native American Graves Protection and Repatriation Act.* Washington, D.C.: National Association of Tribal Historic Preservation Officers, 2008.

McCovey, Mavis, and John F. Salter. *Medicine Trails: A Life in Many Worlds.* Berkeley: Heyday Books, 2009.

McCovey, Shaunna Oteka. *The Smokehouse Boys.* Berkeley: Heyday Books, 2005.

McEvoy, Arthur F. *The Fisherman's Problem: Ecology and Law in the California Fisheries, 1850–1980.* Cambridge: Cambridge Univ. Press, 1990.

McGroarty, John. *California: Its History and Romance.* Los Angeles: Grafton, 1911.

McMurtry, Larry. *Oh What a Slaughter: Massacres in the American West, 1846–1890.* New York: Simon and Schuster, 2005.

McWilliams, Carey. *Brothers under the Skin.* Boston: Little, Brown, and Co., 1944.

———. *Southern California: An Island on the Land.* Santa Barbara: Peregrine Smith, 1973.

———. *California: The Great Expectation.* Berkeley: Univ. of California Press, 1998.

Meyer, Carl. *Bound for Sacramento: Travel Pictures of a Returned Wanderer.* Trans. Ruth Frey Axe. Claremont: Saunders Studio Press, 1938.

Mihesuah, Devon A., ed. *Repatriation Reader: Who Owns American Indian Remains?* Lincoln: Univ. of Nebraska Press, 2000.

Miles, Charles. *Indian and Eskimo Artifacts of North America.* New York: Random House, 1986.

Milner, Clyde A. II, Carol A. O'Connor, and Martha A. Sandweiss, eds. *The Oxford History of the American West.* New York: Oxford Univ. Press, 1994.

Moore, Marijo, ed. *Eating Fire, Tasting Blood: An Anthology of the American Indian Holocaust.* Philadelphia: Running Press, 2006.

Nabokov, Peter, ed. *Native American Testimony: A Chronicle of Indian-White Relations from Prophecy to the Present, 1492–1992.* New York: Penguin Books, 1991.

Nachama, Andreas, director. *Topography of Terror: Gestapo, SS and Reich Security Main Office on Wilhelm-and-Prinz-Albrecht-Strasse, A Documentation.* Berlin: Stiftung Topographie des Terrors, 2010.

Nelson, Byron Jr. *Our Home Forever: The Hupa Indians of Northern California.* Salt Lake City: Howe Brothers, 1978.

Nelson, Maidee Thomas. *California, Land of Promise.* Caldwell, Idaho: Caxton Printers, 1962.

Niezen, Ronald. *Spirit Wars: Native North American Religions in the Age of Nation Building.* Berkeley: Univ. of California Press, 2000.

Norton, Henry K. *The Story of California: From the Earliest Days to the Present.* Chicago: A. C. McClurg, 1913.

Norton, Jack. *Genocide in Northwestern California: When Our Worlds Cried.* San Francisco: The Indian Historian Press, 1979.

Noss, Reed F., ed. *The Redwood Forest: History, Ecology, and Conservation of the Coast Redwoods.* Washington, D.C.: Island Press, 2000.

Officer, James E., and Francis McKinley, eds. *Anthropology and the American Indian.* San Francisco: The Indian Historian Press, 1973.

Paddison, Joshua, ed. *A World Transformed: Firsthand Accounts of California before the Gold Rush.* Berkeley: Heyday Books, 1999.

Palmquist, Peter. *Fine California Views: The Photographs of A. W. Ericson.* Eureka: Interface California, 1975.

Parsons, Sara Mitchell. *From Southern Wrongs to Civil Rights: The Memoir of a White Civil Rights Activist.* Tuscaloosa: Univ. of Alabama Press, 2000.

Pearsall, Clarence E. et al., eds. *The Quest for Qual-A-Waloo.* Oakland: The Holmes Book Co., 1966.

Pfaelzer, Jean. *Driven Out: The Forgotten War against Chinese Americans.* New York: Random House, 2007.

Potts, Richard, and Christopher Sloan. *What Does It Mean to Be Human?* Washington, D.C.: National Geographic Society, 2010.

Powers, Stephen. *Tribes of California.* Berkeley: Univ. of California Press, 1976.

Raphael, Ray, and Freeman House. *Two Peoples, One Place.* Eureka: Humboldt County Historical Society, 2007.

Rawls, James R. *Indians of California: The Changing Image.* Norman: Univ. of Oklahoma Press, 1984.

Read, Georgia Willis, and Ruth Gaines, eds. *Gold Rush: The Journals, Drawings, and Other Papers of J. Goldsborough Bruff.* New York: Columbia Univ. Press, 1944.

Rensch, Hero Eugene, and Ethel Grace Rensch. *Historical Spots in California.* Palo Alto, Calif.: Stanford Univ. Press, 1932, 1933.

Royce, Josiah. *California from the Conquest in 1846 to the Second Vigilance Committee in San Francisco: A Study of American Character.* Boston: Houghton Mifflin, 1886.

Sackman, Douglas Cazaux. *Wild Men: Ishi and Kroeber in the Wilderness of Modern America.* New York: Oxford Univ. Press, 2010.

Samuel, Raphael. *Theatres of Memory: Past and Present in Contemporary Culture.* London: Verso, 1994.

Service, Pamela F., and Raymond W. Hillman. *Eureka and Humboldt County.* Eureka: Clarke Historical Museum, 2001.

Solnit, Rebecca. *Savage Dreams: A Journey into the Landscape Wars of the American West.* New York: Vintage Books, 1995.

Spott, Robert, and A. L. Kroeber. *Yurok Narratives.* Berkeley: Univ. of California Press, 1942.

Spruce, Duane Blue, ed. *Spirit of a Native Place: Building the National Museum of the American Indian.* Washington, D.C.: National Geographic Society and National Museum of the American Indian, 2004.

Starn, Orin. *Ishi's Brain: In Search of America's Last "Wild" Indian.* New York: W. W. Norton & Co., 2005.

Stern, Alexandra Minna. *Eugenic Nation: Faults and Frontiers of Better Breeding in Modern America.* Berkeley: Univ. of California Press, 2005.

Tayac, Gabrielle, ed. *IndiVisible: African-Native American Lives in the Americas.* Washington, D.C.: National Museum of the American Indian, 2009.

Taylor, Bron Raymond, ed. *Encyclopedia of Religion and Nature.* Vol. 2. London: Continuum, 2005.

Tharp, Twyla. *The Creative Habit: Learn It and Use It for Life.* New York: Simon & Schuster, 2003.

Thompson, Lucy. *To the American Indian: Reminiscences of a Yurok Woman.* 1916. Reprint, Berkeley: Heyday Books, 1991.

Thornbury, D. L. *California's Redwood Wonderland: Humboldt County.* San Francisco: Sunset Press, 1923.

Till, Karen E. *The New Berlin: Memory, Politics, Place.* Minneapolis: Univ. of Minnesota Press, 2005.

Trigger, Bruce G. *A History of Archaeological Thought.* Cambridge: Cambridge Univ. Press, 1989.

Vancouver, George. *A Voyage of Discovery to the North Pacific Ocean and Round the World.* London: G. G. and J. Robinson, 1798.

Wagner, Harr, and Mark Keppel. *California History.* San Francisco: Harr Wagner Publishing Co., 1922.

Warburton, Austen D., and Joseph F. Endert. *Indian Lore of the North California Coast.* Santa Clara, Calif.: Pacific Pueblo Press, 1966.

Washington, Harriet A. *Medical Apartheid: The Dark History of Medical Experimentation on Black Americans from Colonial Times to the Present.* New York: Harlem Moon, 2006.

Waterman, Thomas T. *Yurok Geography.* University of California Publications in American Archaeology and Ethnology 16, no. 5, 177–314. Berkeley: Univ. of California Press, 1920.

———. *Yurok Geography.* 1920. Reprint, Trinidad, Calif.: Trinidad Museum Society, 1993.

Waterman, T. T., and A. L. Kroeber. *Yurok Marriages.* University of California Publications in American Archaeology and Ethnology 35, no. 1, 1–14. Berkeley: Univ. of California Press, 1934.

Watkins, T. H. *California: An Illustrated History.* New York: American Legacy Press, 1983.

Weigle, Marta, and Barbara A. Babcock, eds. *The Great Southwest of the Fred Harvey Company and the Santa Fe Railway.* Phoenix: The Heard Museum, 1996.

Wette, Wolfram. *The Wehrmacht: History, Myth, Reality.* Cambridge, Mass.: Harvard Univ. Press, 2006.

White, Richard. *The Middle Ground: Indians, Empires, and Republics in the Great Lakes Region, 1650–1815,* Cambridge: Cambridge Univ. Press, 1991.

———. *"It's Your Misfortune and None of My Own": A New History of the American West.* Norman: Univ. of Oklahoma Press, 1991.

Whitehead, Anne. *Memory.* London: Routledge, 2009.

Wrobel, David M., and Michael C. Steiner, eds. *Many Wests: Place, Culture, and Regional Identity.* Lawrence: Univ. of Kansas Press, 1997.

Journals, Magazines, Government Documents

Beals, Ralph. "Traffic in Antiquities." *American Antiquity* 36, no. 3 (July 1971), 374–375.

Bourne, Joel K., Jr., "Redwoods: Super Trees." *National Geographic* 216, no. 4 (Oct. 2009), 28–59.

Brook, Harry Ellington. "Olden Times in Southern California." *Land of Sunshine*, July 1894.

Burnett, Governor Peter H. "Governor's Annual Message to the Legislature," 7 Jan. 1851. *Journals of the Senate and Assembly of the State of California*. San Francisco: G. K. Fitch and V. E. Geiger, 1852.

Cooper, Robert L. "Constitutional Law: Preserving Native American Cultural and Archaeological Artifacts." *American Indian Law Review* 4, no. 1 (1976), 99–103.

Davis, Lee. Review of *Time's Flotsam*. *Journal of California and Great Basin Anthropology* 17, no. 1 (1995), 141.

Dixon, Maynard. "The Singing of the West." *Sunset* 18, no. 2, December 1906.

Dornback, Mary Gist. "Anthropologist, Educator—UC's Alfred Kroeber Dies." Council of California Indians Newsletter, 15 Dec. 1960.

Dubin, Margaret. "Preserving California's Indian Heritage: The Native American Heritage Commission." *News from Native California* 21, no. 3 (Spring 2008), 23–30.

Eidsness, Janet P. "It Takes a Tribe: Looter Convicted in Humboldt County and New Legislation Proposed." California Archaeological Site Stewardship Program Newsletter, April 2002.

Fay, J. Michael. "The Redwoods Point the Way." *National Geographic* 216, no. 4 (Oct. 2009), 60–63.

Fenega, Franklin. "Methods for Archaeological Site Survey in California." *Reports of the California Archaeological Survey* no. 5 (1949), 1–16.

Gannett, Henry. "The Redwood Forest of the Pacific Coast." *National Geographic* 10, no. 5 (May 1898), 154–159.

Gieseke, E.W. "Discovery of Humboldt Bay, California, in 1806 from the Ship *O'Cain*, Jonathan Winship, Commander." *Terrae Incognitae* 29 (1997), 1–24.

———. "Unlikely Partners: Bostonians, Russians, and Kodiaks Sail the Pacific Coast Together, 1800–1810." *Mains'l Haul* 43 (Summer-Fall 2007), 34–69.

Gihon, Thomas. "An Incident of the Gold Bluff Excitement." *Overland Monthly* 18, no. 108 (Dec. 1891), 646–661.

Golden, Frederic. "Some Bones of Contention." *Time*, 21 December 1981.

Hannah, Shirley M. "Country School Teacher Reminisces." *The Humboldt Historian* (July–Aug. 1969), 1, 8.

Hannah, Thomas S. "Gone Hunting." *The Humboldt Historian* (May-June 1976), 16.

Heizer, Robert F. "The California Archaeological Survey: Establishment, Aims and Methods." *Reports of the California Archaeological Survey* no. 1 (1948).

———. "A Question of Ethics in Archaeology—One Archaeologist's View." *Journal of California Anthropology* 1 & 2 (1974), 145–151.

Heizer, Robert F., and Albert B. Elsasser. "Archaeology of HUM-67, The Gunther Island Site in Humboldt Bay," *Reports of the University of California Archaeological Survey* 62 (1964), 5–122.

Hittell, John S. "The Story of an Unfortunate City." *Overland Monthly* 1 (1868), 140–145.

Indian Country Today. "NAGPRA Suffers Surprising Proposed Budget Cuts." *Indian Country Today*, 7 February 2010.

Jacknis, Ira. "Alfred Kroeber as Museum Anthropologist." *Museum Anthropology* 17, no. 2 (1993), 27–33.

———. "A Museum Prehistory: Phoebe Hearst and the Founding of the Museum of Anthropology, 1891–1901." *Chronicle of the University of California* 4 (2000), 47–77.

———. "The First Boasian: Alfred Kroeber and Franz Boas, 1896–1905." *American Anthropologist* 104, no. 2 (2002), 520–532.

Keeling, Richard. "Kroeber's *Yurok Myths*: A Comparative Re-evaluation." *American Indian Culture and Research Journal* 6, no. 3 (1982).

King, J. C. H. "Vancouver's Ethnography." *Journal of the History of Collections* 6, no. 1 (1994), 35–58.

Kroeber, A. L. "The Indians of California." *Transactions of the Commonwealth Club of California* 4 (Dec. 1909), 430–437.

———. "At the Bedrock of History." *Sunset* 25, no. 3, September 1910.

———. "Thomas Talbot Waterman." *American Anthropologist* 39, no. 3 (July-Sept. 1937), 527–529.

———. "Two Papers on the Aboriginal Ethnography of California," *Reports of the University of California Archaeological Survey* 56 (1 March 1962).

Kroeber, A. L., and E. W. Gifford, "World Renewal: A Cult System of Native Northwest California." *Anthropological Records* 13, no. 1 (1949).

Lara, Walt Sr. "Respect for the Dead." *News from Native California* 9, no. 4 (Summer 1996).

Lassila, Kathrin Day, and Mark Alden Branch. "Whose Skull and Bones?" *Yale Alumni Magazine,* May–June 2006.

Miles, Charles. "The Gunther Island Sites." *The Masterkey* 39, no. 3 (1965), 92–103.

Mills, John E. "Recent Developments in the Study of Northwestern California Archaeology." *Reports of the California Archaeological Survey* no. 1 (1950), 21–25.

Nash, Gerald D. "California and Its Historians: An Appraisal of Histories of the State." *Pacific Historical Review* 50, no. 4 (Nov. 1981), 387–413.

Pratt, R. H. "The Advantages of Mingling Indians with Whites." *Proceedings of the National Conference of Charities and Correction* (1892), 45–49.

Preston, Douglas J. "Skeletons in Our Museums' Closets." *Harper's* (Feb. 1989), 66–75.

Read, Charles H. "An Account of a Collection of Ethnographical Specimens Formed during Vancouver's Voyage in the Pacific Ocean, 1790–1795." *Journal of the Anthropological Institute of Great Britain and Ireland* 21 (1892), 99–108.

Rohde, Jerry. "Genocide and Extortion." *North Coast Journal,* 25 Feb. 2010, 10–17.

Scheper-Hughes, Nancy. "Ishi's Brain, Ishi's Ashes: Anthropology and Genocide." *Anthropology Today* 17 (2001), 12–19.

Schneider, Tsim D. "Laws That Affect the Commission's Work." *News from Native California* 21, no. 3 (Spring 2008), 27–30.

Spott, Robert. "Address." *Transactions of the Commonwealth Club of California* 21, no. 3 (1926), 133–135.

Steward, Julian H. "Alfred Kroeber, 1876–1960: A Biographical Memoir." *American Anthropologist* 63, no. 5 (Oct. 1961), 1038–1060.

Stone, Livingston. *Report of Operation During 1874 at the U.S. Salmon Hatching Establishment on the McCloud River, California,* April 1875. Washington, D.C.: 43rd Congress, 2nd Session, Senate Miscellaneous Document 108.

Sunset. "California: 36 Best Campgrounds." *Sunset,* May 2009.

Tee, Garry J. "The Elusive C. D. Voy." *Journal of the Historical Studies Group* 39 (Sept. 2010), 17–50.

Tourtellot, Jonathan B. "Destination Scorecard: 115 Places Rated." *National Geographic* (March 2004), 60–67.

Tushingham, Shannon, and Suntayea Steinruck. "Recent Looting Cases on the North Coast of California." *California Archaeology* 2, no. 1 (2010), 136–139.

University of California, "History of the California Area." University of California Botanical Garden Newsletter 28, nos. 2 &3, Spring–Summer 2003.

U.S. Department of Interior. "Native American Graves Protection and Repatriation Act Regulations." *Federal Register* 60, no. 232, 4 December 1995, 62134–62169.

Van Dyke, Walter. "Early Days on the Klamath." *Overland Monthly* 18, no. 104 (Aug. 1891), 174–181.

Ward, Albert E. "Navajo Graves: An Archaeological Reflection of Ethnographic Reality." *Ethnohistorical Report Series* 2 (1980), 1–54.

Willard, C. D. "The Padres and the Indians." *Land of Sunshine*, September 1894.

Manuscripts

Bickel (Quick), Polly McW. "A Study of Cultural Resources in Redwood National Park." Denver: National Park Service, U.S. Department of Interior, 1979.

———. "Changing Roles for the Anthropologist: Current Work among Native Americans in North America." Paper presented at annual meeting of the American Anthropological Association, Washington, D.C., 1982.

Collins, Greg. "Archaeological Site Condition Assessment Record." California Department of Parks and Recreation, 15 April 2008. This report is on file at the State Park Archaeology Lab, Sacramento, Calif.

Curtis, Greenleaf. "Journal," c. 1860s. Crescent City: Del Norte Historical Society.

Dides, Judith. Transcript of interview with Margaret Lara, Walt Lara, and Joy Sundberg, 8 January 1990. Sacramento: California Dept. of Parks and Recreation.

Eidsness, Janet. "Places and People: California's Native American Heritage Resources." Paper presented at meeting of Society for California Archaeology, 2004.

———. "Initial Cultural Resources Study for Proposed Hazard Tree Removal and Water Tank Replacement Project, Big Lagoon Park Company," 5 November 2007. This report is on file at the North Coastal Information Center, Klamath, California.

Elsasser, Albert B. "The Site on Gunther Island (CA-HUM 67) in Humboldt Bay." Paper presented at the Annual Meeting of the Society for California Archaeology, San Diego, March 1983.

Elsasser, Albert, and James Bennyhoff. "11 Pages of Notes on Collections in Eureka Senior High School Museum," 30 October 1953. Archaeological Archives, Phoebe A. Hearst Museum of Anthropology, Berkeley.

Ferreira, Mariana. "Sweet Tears and Bitter Pills: The Politics of Health among Yuroks of Northern California." Ph.D. dissertation, Univ. of California, Berkeley, 1996.

Fredrickson, Dave. "The Consciousness-Raising of a California Archaeologist," 4 March 2001, Marin Museum of the American Indian.

Gates, Thomas M. "Along the Ridgelines: A History of the Yurok Trail System." Ph.D. dissertation, Univ. of North Carolina at Chapel Hill, 1995.

Gray, Kenneth L. "Harry A. Merlo Project: Inventory of Features." California Dept. of Parks and Recreation, June 1982. This report is on file at the State Park Archaeology Lab, Sacramento, Calif.

Heizer, Robert F. "Report on the Excavation of the Shellmound at Patrick's Point State Park," 1948. State Park Archaeology Lab, Sacramento, Calif.

Heizer, Robert F., and Albert B. Elsasser. "Archaeology of HUM-67, the Gunther Island Site in Humboldt Bay, Northwestern California." Archaeological Archives, Phoebe A. Hearst Museum of Anthropology, Berkeley, 15 May 1964.

Milburn, John W. et al. "A Preliminary Report on the Archaeology of HUM-129." California Dept. of Parks and Recreation, Jan. 1979. This report is on file at the State Park Archaeology Lab, Sacramento, Calif.

Moratto, Michael J. "Tsahpekw: An Archaeological Record of Nineteenth Century Acculturation among the Yurok." Paper presented at meeting of Southwestern Anthropological Association and the Society for California Archaeology, Asilomar State Beach, Calif., March 1970. This paper is available in the Robert E. Schenk Archives of California Archaeology.

———. "Archaeology and Cross-Cultural Ethics in Coastal Northwest California." Society for California Archaeology, April 1971.

Mounday, L., E. Ritter, J. Carroll, and M. De Shields. "Archaeological Site Survey Record, CA-HUM 124." California Dept. of Parks and Recreation, 23 June 1969. This report is on file at the State Park Archaeology Lab, Sacramento, Calif.

Roberts, Harry K. "Walking in Beauty: Reflections of a Yurok Education," ed. Thomas Buckley. Trinidad, Calif.: Trinidad Museum Society, August 1980.

Rohde, Jerry. "Big Lagoon Rancheria Cultural Assessment: Ethnogeographical and Historical Review." Arcata: Center for Indian Community Development, Humboldt State University, September 2008.

Roscoe, Martha. "Memories of Cecile Clarke," 1982. Humboldt County Historical Society, Eureka, Calif.

Schulz, Peter D. "Background Report on NAGPRA-Related Issues Involving Archaeological Collections from Site HUM-19." Calif. Dept. of Parks and Recreation, 11 Aug. 2003.

Towne, Arlean. "History of Central Californian Archaeology, 1880–1940." M.A. thesis, California State University, Sacramento, 1976.

Tuttle, Donald C. "Environmental Information" and "Environmental Impact Statement, Big Lagoon County Park Improvement Project." Humboldt County, 1973.

Waterman, Thomas T. "Yurok Marriages," field notes, c. 1909–1928. Trinidad: Trinidad Historical Museum.

Woodward, Jim. "A Preliminary Report on Plans to Reconstruct a Yurok Indian Village as Part of the Dry Lagoon State Park General Plan." California Department of Parks and Recreation, July 1982. This report is on file at the State Park Archaeology Lab, Sacramento, Calif.

———. "Archaeological Site Survey Record, CA-HUM 124." California Dept. of Parks and Recreation, Nov. 1987. This report is on file at the State Park Archaeology Lab, Sacramento, Calif.

Woodward, Jim, and George R. Stammerjohan. "Cultural Resources: Harry A. Merlo Project." California Department of Parks and Recreation, Aug. 1982. This report is on file at the State Park Archaeology Lab, Sacramento, Calif.

———. "A Cultural Resource Inventory of Harry A. Merlo State Recreation Area." California Dept. of Parks and Recreation, Dec. 1987. This report is on file at the State Park Archaeology Lab, Sacramento, Calif.

INDEX

INDEX

Janis Lewin

About the Author

Tony Platt is the author of more than ten books and 150 essays and articles on race, inequality, and social justice in American history, among them *Beyond These Walls: Rethinking Crime and Punishment in the United States*, *Bloodlines: Recovering Hitler's Nuremberg Laws, from Patton's Trophy to Public Memorial*, and *The Child Savers: The Invention of Delinquency*. His work has been translated into German, Spanish, Italian, and Japanese. In addition to scholarly books and publications, Platt has written for the *Los Angeles Times*, the *San Francisco Chronicle*, *Truthdig*, *History News Network*, *Z Magazine*, *Monthly Review*, and the *Guardian*, and his commentaries have aired on NPR.

Now an emeritus professor, Platt taught at the University of Chicago, the University of California, Berkeley, and California State University, Sacramento, where he received awards for teaching and scholarship. He has also been a visiting professor at Chuo University, Tokyo, and Queen's University, Belfast, and a visiting researcher at the Huntington Library and National Museum of American History. He lives in Berkeley and Big Lagoon, California.